THE NEW TESTAMENT MADE HARDER

THE NEW TESTAMENT MADE HARDER

SCRIPTURE STUDY QUESTIONS

JAMES E. FAULCONER

NEAL A. MAXWELL INSTITUTE *for* RELIGIOUS SCHOLARSHIP

Brigham Young University
Provo, Utah

THE NEW TESTAMENT MADE HARDER
Scripture Study Questions

Cover and book design: Jenny Webb

Cover image: © Depositphotos.com. Used by permission.

The paper used in this publication meets the minimum requirements of the American National Standard for Information Sciences—Permanence of Paperfor Printed Library Materials. ANSI Z39.48-1984.

ISBN 978-0-8425-2871-9

Printed in the United States of America

maxwellinstitute.byu.edu

CONTENTS

Wherever you look about you, in literature and life, you see the celebrated names and figures, the precious and much heralded men who are coming into prominence and are much talked about, the many benefactors of the age who know how to benefit mankind by making life easier and easier, some by railways, others by omnibuses and steamboats, others by the telegraph, others by easily apprehended compendiums and short recitals of everything worth knowing, and finally the true benefactors of the age who make spiritual existence in virtue of thought easier and easier. . . . You must do something, but inasmuch as with your limited capacities it will be impossible to make anything easier than it has become, you must, with the same humanitarian enthusiasm as the others, undertake to make something harder.

JOHANNES CLIMACUS
Concluding Unscientific Postscript

Introduction

THIS IS MOSTLY A BOOK of questions, questions about the material assigned for the Sunday School lessons of the LDS Church's Gospel Doctrine New Testament curriculum. There is so much material in the New Testament that it would require several volumes to write study questions for everything in it. So I have shortened my task by focusing on the texts assigned for Sunday School reading.

Some readers may already be familiar with the other books in this series: *The Doctrine and Covenants Made Harder, The Book of Mormon Made Harder,* and *The Old Testament Made Harder.* They should feel free to skip this introduction since there is not likely to be anything new in it for them.

But those who are coming to this book and its companions for the first time might reasonably wonder about the title. It is only partly a joke, and it is the result of an experience I had long ago when I was a graduate student. For various reasons I was fortunate enough to do a tutorial with a philosophy of science professor who was also a part-time rabbi. For our first session he asked me to come with a list of questions on Genesis 1. Genesis was the book we were going to work on. I brought my questions. They were about such things as how to correlate the biblical and scientific accounts of creation. But when he saw them he was openly dismayed.

"If you are a religious person, why would you be interested in questions like these?" he asked. "They have nothing to do with what is important about this reading."

Needless to say I was surprised, but I was also dumbfounded. I didn't have anything to say in response. So we went to his questions. They were about the details of the account, about words and relationships between words, about the order in which things were presented, about differences between what was said in one verse and what was said in another. We spent hours talking and thinking about his questions, and much to my surprise I realized that I was learning a tremendous amount about the plan of salvation as well as about Genesis! I hadn't expected a rabbi to be teaching me things of the gospel, but he was. He was sometimes surprised by things that I explained in a way that, as far as he knew, Christians were unaware of but that had come from a latter-day prophet. We were learning from each other, but I was learning a great deal by looking at the text itself closely and thinking about what that meant for me and my family.

That experience was life changing. It showed me a way of reading scripture I'd not been aware of previously. I'd read each of the scriptures cover to cover more than once. I'd read them topically, with a question in mind looking for answers to my question. Both of those ways of reading were and continue to be important to me as part of scripture study. But I'd never read with the attention to detail that the rabbi was showing, and I'd never read asking questions of the text that generated additional questions for me. But this way of reading wasn't a way of making the scriptures easy to understand. It was a way of making me stop and think about them, a way of forcing me to reconsider what I thought I already knew. It is not too much to say that it was a way of making the scriptures harder. It didn't make their content any more difficult to understand, but it did force me to work harder as I read.

Of course, this book doesn't ask every question that one could ask about the assigned readings. Some lessons contain so much material that I've had to select only part of the reading for questions. So lots of questions remain to be asked. In fact, the more questions you ask of scripture, the more questions there will be to ask. My hope is that as you read my questions you will have additional questions of your own and that, as you begin to think in terms of questions, you will develop a habit of looking at the details of scripture and asking about their significance. My testimony is that doing so will be profitable to you, not only intellectually, but spiritually.

The aim of these materials is to help us prepare for Sunday School lessons. We often talk about the need for class members in our Gospel Doctrine classes to prepare, but few read the lesson ahead of time, and even fewer spend time doing more than that. These questions are to help those who would like to study the readings but aren't sure how to go about doing so.

But, of course, Sunday School teachers will also be reading and preparing for the lesson. Though these materials aren't directed specifically at them, I hope they can be helpful. If you don't have questions of your own around which you can organize your lesson, perhaps these will help you. If you are preparing a lesson, perhaps you will find a question or two among them that you can use as foci for your lesson. Perhaps reading these questions will help you think of your own questions.

In my experience, one or two good questions in the hands of a prepared teacher are sufficient for an excellent lesson. Of course, that presumes that the teacher has learned to control the discussion in a class so that it does not get away from the scriptures into personal flights of fancy or onto the gospel hobbyhorses we sometimes take such pleasure in riding. Mostly that takes practice, enough practice to give you confidence.

There are a variety of methods that can help a teacher organize her class time. Here is one that I have used and can recommend: Class begins with a brief review of the lesson from the week before (about five minutes or less), followed by an overview of the reading for this week (another five or ten minutes, at most). That leaves about twenty-five or thirty minutes that the class can spend discussing one or two salient questions that are specifically about the scriptures assigned for the week. They may come from the lesson manual provided by the Church. They may come from this book. In the best eventuality, they come from your personal study of the material. The lesson manual will tell you what the focus of your teaching should be, and it gives suggestions for how to teach that, but ultimately the teacher must decide how she can best teach that lesson to her class using the scriptures assigned.

If you are using my way of organizing, then after the review and overview, choose one of the passages of scripture about which you want to lead a discussion and, as is often done in LDS Sunday School classes, have someone read that passage aloud. Then ask the question you want to talk about. Presumably this is the question you are most interested in pursuing, or a question that will lead to that question. Ask the person who read if he or she has an answer to your question. If the reader does, ask for other possible answers. If the reader doesn't, ask if others can help. Don't be intimidated by silence; patiently wait for someone to have time to think about the question and to respond.

Many are accustomed to teachers asking questions to which everyone in class already knows the answer: the teacher asks a question and we in the class repeat the answer as if in a kind of catechism. There is a place for that, but it ought not to be the dominant experience of those in Gospel Doctrine class. If instead your questions are open-ended (as I hope most of the questions in this book are), without a specific, supposedly right answer, members of the class are likely to be somewhat intimidated. They won't be able to answer immediately because you are asking them to do something they are not yet used to. Wait for them to speak, and be pleased with whatever the first attempt at a response is. Use it to continue to talk about and think about the question.

As discussion begins, you may well need to guide it. Ask related questions to help keep discussion on track—not toward the answer you are looking for (presumably you haven't already decided what the answer is), but toward thinking about the question with which you began. Don't let class drift off into unrelated matters. Sometimes a teacher must say something like "That's an interesting question, but it doesn't seem directly related to what we are discussing right now. Perhaps we could take it up after class," or something like that. In particular, keep the discussion flowing along lines that are more likely to result in an increase in faith and repentance, and in enduring to the end. The introduction to the lesson manual says, "As a Gospel Doctrine teacher, you can show your love for the Lord by feeding his sheep, ensuring that each member of your class is 'remembered and nourished by the good word of God'" (Moroni 6:4). Keep that in mind as you lead the discussion.

Class discussion will almost never cover everything in the assigned material or in the lesson manual. There is always more in the material suggested for any lesson than can be covered in one lesson. Our curriculum writers know that. They have given us a large chunk of material for study and suggestions for how we can lead the discussion of that material, more material than can be used for any particular lesson. They expect teachers to use their knowledge of class members, their inspired insight, and, especially, their prayerful study to prepare them to teach effectively. Approaching the class session as I've described is one way to cover something sufficiently well to help class members appreciate the reading and be prepared to do more individual study. When it goes well, as it usually does in the hands of a teacher who has prepared well, both by study and also by the prayer of faith (see D&C 88:118 and 109:7, 14), a lesson of this sort not only is a good experience in itself, it also encourages those in the class to learn from the scriptures after the class is over.

A good question or two about a passage of scripture can also be the basis for an excellent talk for sacrament meeting: If the passage on which you are focusing is sufficiently brief, read it at the beginning of the talk, restating the parts most important to your talk in your own words. Make a point of raising your question in the context of the scriptures that brought it to your attention. Then discuss your thinking about the question. Explain the ideas that came to you in thinking about it. Talk about the implications of what you have learned. Show how what you have learned is relevant to your life and to the lives of those to whom you are speaking. To conclude, summarize what you have said, if your talk has been long enough to need a summary, and bear your testimony.

In this study material, I usually quote from the King James Version, but when I depart from it, I am using my own translation unless otherwise noted.

I owe many people thanks for their contributions to my work and my life, especially my wife and family. Patricia and Larry Wimmer were very much a part of the learning experiences behind this set of questions, as were others, including many years of students. Jenny Webb and Don Brugger have been marvelous editors, and I must thank Adam Miller and Joe Spencer for first encouraging me to publish these. To all, thanks.

Jewish History between the Old and New Testaments

WE HAVE LITTLE EVIDENCE on which to build the kind of history of Israel after the Babylonian captivity that we moderns expect. One reason is because the ancient idea of history was different from our own. We think the historian's job is to create an objective account of past events. But ancient Israelite historians saw their task as showing how God's purposes and meanings are made apparent in human history. That means that they and we would disagree about what an accurate historical account is, so they might not have recorded the information that we believe would be important. Adding to the problem is that perhaps beginning during the Babylonian exile and at least with the return to Judea, there appears to have been a program of rewriting the ancient documents to make them conform to a new self-understanding of what it meant to be Jewish, a self-understanding that seems to have been heavily influenced by Persian ideas. And, of course, over the course of 2,600 years many documents and records have been lost or destroyed. These kinds of things mean that our view of Israel prior to the New Testament period is fuzzy, to say the least.

Nevertheless, we have a reasonably good chronology of major events:

1

606	The fall of Nineveh, capital of Assyria. Babylon (in modern-day Iraq) becomes the major power. Daniel and others are taken to Babylon from Israel.
604	Nebuchadnezzar is king of Babylon.
598	Judah's king, Jehoiachin, and the prophet Ezekiel (with many others, though not most of the population) are carried captive into Babylon. Lehi leaves Jerusalem.
587	The fall of Jerusalem; the leaders of Judah are taken captive into Babylon. Some, including Jeremiah (who is a hostage), escape to Egypt. Mulek leaves Jerusalem.
562	The death of Nebuchadnezzar and the beginning of the decline of Babylon.
538	Babylon falls to Cyrus, king of Persia (in modern-day Iran).
535	Zerubbabel (the Persian governor) and Jeshua lead approximately 50,000 Jews back to Jerusalem to rebuild the temple.
533	The cornerstone of the Jerusalem temple is laid.
522	The Samaritans have been opposed to the temple construction because they have not been allowed to help rebuild it. Jews, on the other hand, have largely been indifferent to its reconstruction. As a result, work on it has stopped. Haggai and Zechariah encourage the Jews to finish the temple. King Darius of Persia commands the Samaritan opposition to cease.

516	Zerubbabel's temple, the rebuilt Jerusalem temple, is completed. It is called the second temple.
486	Esther, wife of King Xerxes in Persia (460 is an alternative date), saves her people.
458	Ezra leads a second group of 1,496 back to Jerusalem.
445	Nehemiah (Artaxerxes's cupbearer) arrives in Jerusalem.
433	Nehemiah returns to Persia to serve Artaxerxes.
431	Nehemiah's second mission to Jerusalem
323	Alexander the Great's kingdom breaks up at his death. One of his generals, Ptolemy, takes over Egypt; another, Seleucus, rules Babylonia. The Ptolemies control Palestine.
198	Ptolemaic domination of Palestine ends with the defeat of the Ptolemies by the Seleucids at Caesarea Philippi.
c. 175	Jason purchases the high priesthood from the Seleucid king Antiochus III and replaces his brother Onias III, who was the rightful high priest of the Jerusalem temple. Jason is a "Hellenizer," one who wishes to make Greek culture the culture of Israel. The ruling classes adopt Greek as their language, and they adopt Greek education, including building a gymnasium. In Greek gymnasia young men exercised and practiced military sports in the nude, which was a scandal to Jews.

171   Antiochus replaces Jason with Menelaus (who has bought the office for a higher price than Jason paid). Menelaus is not a descendent of the priestly family of Zadok.

168   Jason joins with anti-Hellenist Jews to dethrone Menelaus. He wants to get his office back; they want to make sure that a descendent of Zadok is the high priest. Antiochus interprets this as an attempt to overthrow his rule. He tears down the walls of Jerusalem and loots the temple. Jason and his followers flee to Leontopilis, in Egypt, where they establish an alternate temple.

167   Antiochus assumes that the Jews, like people in other places, will be willing to recognize Yahweh as the same as Zeus. He orders the worship of Zeus in the temple and sacrifices a pig on the altar.

167–64   The temple becomes a temple to Zeus. The reaction of the Jews is full-scale revolt, led by a priestly family, the Hasmoneans.

164   The Jews win the right to practice Judaism and to resume temple worship.

152   Since no Zadokite priest is available to assume the office of high priest, the Hasmonean family takes the office "until there should arise a faithful prophet" (1 Maccabees 14:41).

142   The Jews win full autonomy, the right to rule themselves within the Seleucid kingdom.

19   Herod begins his complete reconstruction of the second temple, with priests as masons and carpenters. Though mostly complete by about 13 BC, it is not finished until AD 64 and is destroyed by the Romans in AD 70.

The first stage of what we now understand as Orthodox Judaism began in this period between the Babylonian destruction of the first temple in 587 BC and the Roman destruction of Herod's temple in AD 70. (The next major and perhaps most important period of Orthodox Judaism's development occurred after the destruction of the second temple.) We know little about what Judaism was like prior to the Babylonian captivity. As already mentioned, it appears that the religious books were edited and perhaps rewritten afterward to make them conform better to the new ways in which the Jews understood themselves after their experiences in Babylon and Persia. Most scholars believe that in pre-Babylonian Judaism God had a consort, and at least one scholar (Margaret Barker) has argued that in early Judaism God had a Son. But such claims belong to scholarly speculation.

Adding to the confusion is that archaeological evidence suggests that the Babylonians carried off only a relatively small portion of the population, mostly political and religious leaders. In fact, the depiction of the Samaritans in Ezra and Nehemiah may portray the reaction of the majority who had been left behind and who became angry at or resentful of the minority (and now foreign) leaders who returned and sought to impose themselves and new ideas onto the community that had escaped deportation.

Issues such as these meant that the question of identity—"Who is a Jew, and what does it mean to be one?"—was important to those living during the intertestamental period and into New Testament times. Also important were questions of ritual and temple purity. As we have seen in the Old Testament, the Jerusalem temple had not always been the only temple. Since about the time of Josiah, however, there has been only one temple, and there is a desire to keep it ritually pure. Given the temple's status as what identifies Judaism, and given the things that have happened to it under the Seleucid rulers, and especially given that the temple physically symbolized the relation of God to Israel, this emphasis on purity is quite understandable. Out of these sorts of question about identity and purity arose the two primary political groups in Jerusalem during Jesus's life, the Pharisees and the Sadducees.

The Pharisees were a fundamentalist, anti-Hellenist (i.e., anti-Greek) group trying to preserve Judaism in the face of what they perceived to be the encroachment of Greek and Roman culture. The word *pharisee* may mean "separatist," signifying those who want to remain separate from the dominant Greco-Roman culture. The Pharisees were a sociopolitical movement that had considerable political influence in Jerusalem, though more before the time of Christ than during. They believed that the temple had become corrupt. Their response to that corruption and to the hellenization of Israel was a focus on reading and interpreting the Torah (the Law) and on careful obedience to it, which they understood to be more important than temple worship and sacrifice. Worship was centered on the home and synagogue rather than on the temple. As Richard Draper says, the Pharisees sought to make the ritual purity that was required of priests serving in the temple the standard for ordinary believers in order to create a holy community.[1] Probably few priests who offered temple sacrifices were Pharisees, but probably most scribes (sometimes referred to as lawyers) were. Scribes not only copied religious texts to preserve them, but they were called on to interpret the Law and to settle disputes over its interpretation.

Though there was only one temple, the Jerusalem temple, most communities seem to have had a synagogue. Sacrifices were done in the temple but not in the synagogues, which were devoted to worship and the study of the Law. If we can infer backward from later Judaism, we can assume that men and women sat separately in these synagogues and listened to a leader read and interpret passages from the Law (Torah) and the rest of the books that we now refer to as the Old Testament. The synagogue was not only a place of worship, it was also the seat of local government: the elders of the synagogue were also the civic authorities of the community.

The term *Sadducee* may be another pronunciation of the word *Zadokite*. (And *Zadok* may be a form of the word *zadik*, meaning "righteous.") The Sadducees were a political party with the rulers of the temple at its center, the extended family of the high priest. In theory the descendants of the Hasmoneans were ruling until they could be replaced by a descendant of Zadok. For Sadducees, temple worship was the heart of Judaism, which explains the animosity between them and the Pharisees. The Sadducees were Hellenists, meaning that they cooperated with the Seleucids and then the Romans, both Greek speaking, and they were willing to adopt Greek culture. This made them an aristocratic minority.

There were also other groups, such as the people of Qumran, the Essenes. They were a monastic sect who, like the Pharisees, were opposed to the corruption of the temple. They appear to have awaited the coming of the Messiah (who would destroy the "sons of darkness") by studying scripture. But we know even less about the Essenes than we know about the Pharisees and Sadducees—and we know about the latter mostly through reports in the New Testament, where they are not treated in a particularly objective manner.

It cannot be emphasized enough that our knowledge of what happened during the intertestamental period is sketchy. Knowing something about that history, even something sketchy, can help us understand the events we are reading about. For example, knowing the animosity between the Pharisees and Sadducees makes the cooperation of their leaders in Jesus's trial and condemnation all the more striking.

But *it is important to remember that our job as students of the New Testament is not that of the historian.* We are doing textual exegesis and thinking about what the results of that exegesis mean for our own lives, which is very different from writing history. It is closer to the job of the ancient historian than it is to that of the modern: our job is to see the hand of God in human history, including our own lives, not to give a reportorial, "photographically" accurate account of the events. As a result, even when we delve into what we can know and understand of the history of the time period, we should do so in support of our exegesis. History is relevant to the degree that it helps us understand the meaning of what we read.

What Is the New Testament?

THE NEW TESTAMENT is a collection of twenty-seven books and letters with different styles of writing, written at different times by different authors. It covers a period of approximately 100 years or less, compared to the Old Testament, which covers over 2,000 years. There are two foci for these books and letters. In the Gospels it is the testimony of Jesus. In the letters it is teaching what the gospel means to members of the Church.

The New Testament begins with four Gospels, four announcements of the good news that Jesus was born, taught, died for us, and was resurrected to sit at the right hand of the Father. Each is a testimony of Jesus's mission and divinity written by a different author for a different audience and different purpose. There are "harmonies" of the Gospels, documents that show how to harmonize the events of Jesus's ministry as each of the Gospels reports them. There is one in the LDS edition of the Bible. But I don't refer to such harmonies because they treat the Gospels as histories and may encourage us to forget that they are fundamentally testimonies.

Following the four Gospels is the Acts of the Apostles, the second part of Luke's story and the closest thing to a modern history that we will find in the New Testament, though it too is not a modern history. It is an account of the Church after the death of Jesus, but unlike a modern history it has a purpose: to show the ways that the Spirit has revealed itself through the Church as it has grown and spread throughout the world. Acts is not a testimony of Christ, at least not directly, but it is a testimony of the Spirit.

The largest part of the New Testament is made up of thirteen letters, most of which bear Paul's name, though perhaps not all were written by him. Some may have been written by a secretary acting in his name. Some may have been written by a disciple who understood Paul's teaching and wrote in his name. Most of these letters were written to churches in which some question had arisen about what it means to be a Christian or about how to deal with problems within the Church.

The last book in the collection that is the New Testament is the book of Revelation. This is an apocalyptic vision attributed to the Apostle John. In it we see a vision of the final triumph of God over evil on this earth. Some believe that at least part of the first part of the vision is the same as the revelation that Jesus received during his forty-day fast at the begisnning of his ministry.

But the order of the collection is not the order of composition. That wasn't true of the Old Testament, though its books are at least roughly in chronological order. But it isn't at all true of the New Testament. Here is one reconstruction of the chronological order of the New Testament books and letters, with the approximate date of composition following in parentheses:

> 1, 2 Thessalonians (50–51)
> 1, 2 Corinthians (54–56)
> Matthew (55–60) and Luke/Acts (55–60)
> Galatians (56)

Romans (56–60)
James (before 60–62)
Mark (60–65) and Colossians (60–65)
Philemon (61–62)
Philippians (62)
1 Peter (64–65)
1, 2 Timothy/Titus (65)
Hebrews (69)
Ephesians (after 70)
John (70–80)
1–3 John (80–90)
Jude (85–95)
Revelation (90–95)
2 Peter (100–110)

Note, however, that most (but not all) contemporary biblical scholars assume that the Gospel of Mark was written before the other Gospels, though not before other New Testament texts.

As mentioned, there are questions about the authorship of some of the letters. There are also questions about the authorship of the Gospels. Perhaps a majority of biblical scholars are skeptical that the Gospels were written by the people they are ascribed to. Everyone agrees that there was probably a period after Jesus's ministry in which stories of his life and work were told and transmitted orally and that eventually those stories were put into writing. The question is when and by whom. One can ask whether they were put into writing by the apostles Matthew, Mark, and John and their acquaintance Luke, and contemporary scholars are

11

often skeptical that they were. Likewise, many are skeptical that John the Beloved was the author of Revelation.

Because Mark has very few unique verses and most of it can be seen repeated in Matthew and Luke, early Christians assumed that Mark was a synopsis of either Matthew or perhaps Luke. Today most scholars believe instead that Mark was the first document and that Matthew and Luke were written using Mark as a source.

Of the letters, there are varying degrees of doubt concerning the authorship of Ephesians, Philippians, Colossians, 2 Thessalonians, 1 Timothy, 2 Timothy, Titus, and Hebrews. From very early in the Christian tradition there have been doubts about Paul's authorship of Hebrews. For example, Origen (185–254) was skeptical about it being written by Paul, and nothing internal to the letter says it was written by him. Nevertheless, Christians have long recognized that Hebrews and the other disputed epistles were written by the inspiration of God.

The questions in this book won't be concerned with authorship. They will assume that the Christian tradition is correct in assuming that the Gospels, Acts, the letters, and Revelation were inspired by the Holy Ghost and authentically testify of Jesus Christ. In that case, questions of authorship are less important. As we study, our question will be "What do these materials say to believers and, in particular, what do they say to me?" As a matter of convenience, I will refer to the authors of the letters by the names traditionally ascribed to them. I assume that those traditional ascriptions are generally sound, but whether they are is irrelevant to the questions we will use for study.

Lesson 1

Isaiah 61:1–3; Luke 3:4–11 (JST); John 1:1–14;
John 20:31

Isaiah 61:1–3

Verse 1: In the clause "The Spirit of the Lord God is upon me," what does the preposition *upon* suggest that is different from the more familiar *with*?

Why does the next clause begin with *because*? What does this clause explain? Does it explain the first clause of the verse? If so, how?

What does it mean to be *anointed* to preach the gospel ("good tidings")? In ancient Israel, who was anointed? Today, who receives that anointing? Is the word *anointing* being used metaphorically or literally here? In other words, is this an anointing with oil, or is the writer speaking of receiving the Spirit as an anointing? If the latter, how is the metaphor appropriate to the writer's message?

Why are the good tidings to be preached to the meek? The Hebrew word translated *meek* literally means "poor people." It can mean people in distress: the humble, the afflicted. *Broken-hearted* is often used in parallel with *poor* in the Psalms. Does that parallel help make sense of the meaning here? For what distress or broken-heartedness is the preaching of the Lord's word good tidings?

13

"An opening of the prison" is an interpretive translation of a Hebrew phrase that is literally just "an opening." What other openings could be meant by such a term? The opening of eyes or ears, for example? Given the context, why did the translators choose to translate the phrase as they did?

Another translation of "the acceptable year of the Lord" is "the year of the Lord's favor." To what might this refer? To whom will this favor be given?

"The day of vengeance of our God" and "the acceptable year of the Lord" are parallel. What does "God's day of vengeance" mean? Why and when would God take vengeance? On whom?

Luke 3:4–11 (JST)

Compare the Joseph Smith Translation version of Luke 3:4–11 (pp. 805–6 of the LDS edition of the Bible) with Luke 3:4–5 in the King James Version. Then compare them both to Isaiah 40:3–5. What differences do you see? What do you make of those differences? What do you make of the fact that Joseph Smith made no changes to Isaiah in chapter 40 but added quite a bit here where John is quoting Isaiah 40?

The JST version gives us considerable insight into Jesus's mission. How do you think people who heard John's message would have understood what he was saying? What would they have expected Jesus to be like? Why? Look at each of the things that John says of him and identify how Jesus accomplished each thing. Which things still remain to be accomplished?

John 1:1–18

The assigned verses are part of a larger section that appears to be based on an early Christian hymn. For study purposes we will look at that hymn, verses 1–18.

Perhaps this hymn was written by John; perhaps John is quoting a hymn already familiar to the Christians for whom he is writing. Verses 1 and 2 form the first verse (strophe) of the hymn, verses 3 through 5 form the second strophe, verses 10 through 12 form the third strophe, verse 14 forms the fourth strophe, and verse 16 forms the final strophe. Verses 6 through 9, the end of 12 and all of 13, 15, 17, and 18 are probably commentary on the hymn.

Here is my translation of the hymn itself. The numbers to the left are the verse numbers in chapter 18.

I

1   In the beginning was the Word,

    and the Word was in the presence of God,

    and the Word was God—

2   The same was in God's presence in the beginning.

II

3   Through him all things came into being,

    and without him nothing came into being that came into being.

4   In him was life, and this life was people's light.

5   And the light shines in darkness,

      and the darkness did not overcome it.

III

10   He was in the world,

      and the world was brought into being by him,

      but the world did not know him;

11   he came to his own,

      but his own did not receive him.

12   But to as many as did receive him, he gave authority to become the children of God.

IV

14   And the Word came into being as flesh

      and dwelt among us.

      And we have seen his glory,

      a glory like that of a singular Son coming from beside the Father,

      filled with grace and truth.

V

16   And we have all received

      from his fullness,

      grace for grace.

We will begin our discussion of these verses with the hymn itself (verses 1–5, 10–12, 14, and 16). Then we will discuss John's commentary on the hymn.

Verse 1: Why does John begin his testimony of Christ's ministry with the same words we find at the beginning of Genesis (Genesis 1:1), "In the beginning . . ."? Why does John begin his book by referring to *the* beginning rather than to the birth of Christ? Is he concerned with the creation itself or with something else? If the latter, what?

The Greek word translated *beginning* has a variety of meanings. For example, it can mean "first in time," "ultimate principle," "ruler," or "norm." Thus, a person who spoke Greek would hear not only the meaning we get in the translation ("In the beginning was the word"), but also the connotations created by these other meanings. Those connotations would have influenced how a person reading John when it was first written would understand the passage. The implication of those connotations would be that Christ is the ultimate principle, standard, or ruler, a ruler who has existed, in the presence of God, from the beginning. How does considering those additional meanings of *beginning* change your understanding of this verse?

Why is Christ called "the Word"? The Greek word translated *Word* is *logos*. It has two broad meanings: (1) the explanation or revelation of something (including meanings like "account," "speech," "proportion," "relation," "measure," and "mind"), and (2) the most essential element of things, the thing that makes every other thing intelligible. (The latter broad meaning gives rise to specific meanings like "revelation," "law," "truth," "knowledge," "virtue," "nature," and "spirit.") In what ways does the first of these meanings apply to Christ? In what way does the second apply?

The word *logos* comes from the verb *legein*, which means "to gather." Does that provide any additional insight as to why this hymn might call Jesus the Word?

Though John writes in Greek and seems to be addressing a primarily Greek audience, he is probably also depending on the Old Testament use of the word *word*. For us, given the way English works, a word is a sign of a thing, a concept. But in the Old Testament, God's word refers more to an event or a deed than it does to a concept. A word is what does something. As a result, in the Old Testament, *word* usually refers to prophetic revelation and, often, specifically to the Mosaic law. It refers specifically to the giving of the revelation rather than to its content. In line with this, *word* also can refer to the word spoken to create something, as in Genesis 1:1. (We can see this use of *word* in Ezekiel 37:4 and Jacob 4:9, and, by implication, in Isaiah 40:26.)

How is Christ the word of the Old Testament? What does it mean to say that he is?

Notice that the verse uses the word *was* three times and that each use is slightly different: "the Word was in the beginning" tells us that he existed, "the Word was in God's presence" tells us of his relation to God, and "the Word was God" tells us of his attributes. If this verse is a statement of the thesis of the book of John, then the book of John will testify that Christ exists and that he comes from the presence of the Father, and it will testify of his attributes. As you read John's testimony, watch for those testimonies.

The phrase "the Word was with God" can literally be translated "the Word was before ["in front of," "in the presence of," or even "toward"] God." What does it mean to say that Christ was with the Father in the beginning? What does it mean to be in the presence of God? In what sense might Christ have been "toward" the Father? (Moses 4:1–2 seems relevant here.)

What is the hymn telling us when it tells us that "the Word was God"? Why is that important for us to know and recognize?

Verse 2: This verse repeats the content of verse 1: "The same [i.e., the God mentioned in the third part of verse 1] was in the beginning [compare the first part of verse 1] with [or "in the presence of"] God [repeating the second part of verse 1]." Why do you think the hymn repeats that content of verse 1 so specifically? Refer back to the translation of the hymn that I've made and notice that this is the end of the first strophe (verse) of the hymn. Does that explain the repetition?

What is this hymn about? How is it particularly appropriate that it introduce the book of John?

Perhaps this verse acts as a transition to the discussion of verse 3, taking us back to the mention of "the beginning."

Verse 3: Verse 3 begins the second strophe of the hymn. What is this strophe (verses 3–5) about?

When the hymn says that "all things" were made by Christ, to what is it referring? Is it referring only to the world and the objects in the world?

19

Literally, verse 3 says, "Through him all things came into being and without him nothing came into being that had come into being." Does that differ from saying that he made all things? How or how not? How do you understand the phrase "come into being"? How might someone else? Why do you think John speaks of coming into being rather than being made?

Why does the hymn repeat the first half of the verse in the second half of the verse, only putting it in the negative? Is this just for poetic effect, or is there a point to the repetition?

Verse 4: What does it mean to say that life was in the Word? Physical life? Spiritual life?

When did the physical creation occur? When did the spiritual creation, the spiritual life, with which John is concerned occur? What is the connection of this verse to the previous verse? In other words, what does the meaning of this verse have to do with that of verse 3?

A more literal translation of the second half of the verse might be "and this life was the light of human beings." To what does "this life" refer? What does the last half of the verse mean?

In the Old Testament, the word *light* usually refers to experienced brightness; it refers to experience rather than to a thing or a state. Therefore, in the Old Testament the word *light* also refers to salvation: our experience of being in the right relation with God or our experience of our relation with God made right. God is our light (Psalm 27:1): he enlightens us by making our salvation possible (Psalm 97:11). The contrast of light and dark is not as important to the Old

Testament (or to the BC part of the Book of Mormon) as it is to John, so in making that contrast John seems to introduce an essentially new element. What new teaching is he giving?

Notice that in the Gospel of John light stands at least for revelation (see John 12:36) and, therefore, also for the Revealer (John 1:5; 8:12; 9:5; and 12:46).

As you think about what this verse means, it may be helpful to remember that this strophe of the hymn is about the creation. Does verse 4 continue that theme in some way? In what way?

Verse 5: Like verse 3, this acts as a transition from the second strophe to the third (in verses 10 through 12). Notice that the verbs in verse 4 were in the past tense, but in this verse the first is in the present tense: verse 4—"In him *was* life; and the life *was* the light of men"; verse 5—"the light *shines* in darkness." Why does the hymn shift from the past to the present and then back to the past?

What does it mean to say that the light shines in darkness? What does it mean to say that the darkness did not comprehend the light? To us, the word *comprehend* means, most often, "understand." But that is misleading; it didn't mean that to the King James translators, and the Greek word used here doesn't mean "understand." Instead, it means "to seize," "to make one's own," "to overcome." Perhaps a more understandable translation of the verse would be "And the light shines in darkness, and the darkness did not overcome it." How does that fact about the meaning of *comprehend* change your understanding of this verse? Does it change your understanding of John's teaching?

This strophe began as a discussion of creation (verse 3). What does verse 5 have to do with that topic?

Verse 10: Notice how this verse is related to the first two strophes: (1) verse 10 tells us that he was in the world, a contrast with strophe 1, where he was described as being in the presence of God; (2) it says that the world was made by him, repeating the topic of strophe 2. Verse 10 also introduces the subject of this strophe—"the world knew him not"—a topic suggested by the closing part of verse 5.

Verse 11: It might not be surprising that the world did not recognize him when he came to them, but even his own people did not recognize him. Are verses 10 and 11 parallel in meaning as well as grammar, or are they only grammatically parallel?

As you read this hymn, it may be helpful to remember that the word *him* refers to "the Word." We know that "the Word" stands for Christ, but the direct reference is to the particular name mentioned in verse 1 and, therefore, to the things that name suggests. What does "the Word" and its meanings have to do with this verse and the previous verse?

Verse 12: The Greek word translated *receive* could also be translated *accept.* Though most did not receive him, he gave the power to be the children of God to those who did. If we are already the children of God, how can he give us the power to become his children? (See Mosiah 5, especially verse 7.) Is it significant that he gives them the power to become children rather than making them children?

The last part of the verse indicates that we receive him by believing on his name. What is entailed in believing on his name? (See Mosiah 4.)

Verse 14: How do you think that those of a Greek culture, including educated Jews, would have responded to this announcement: God was made flesh and dwelt among human beings? How would Greek and Roman intellectuals have responded?

What does it mean to say that Jesus is full of grace? That he is full of truth?

Notice that, structurally, this verse repeats verse 1. Like verse 1 it testifies of Christ's existence, of his relation to the Father, and of his attributes: "the Word was made flesh, and dwelt among us"—he exists; "we beheld his glory, the glory of the unique Son of the Father"—his relation to the Father; full of grace and truth—his attributes. What effect does the meaning of this verse have on the interpretation of verse 1?

Though "only begotten" is an accurate translation, I think that translation changes the emphasis of the original. The Greek emphasizes the uniqueness of the Son. Literally, this says "the glory of a singular Son coming from the Father."

What does it mean for a person to have grace? What are the possibilities, and how might they apply to saying that God has grace? What does it mean to say that a person is "full of truth"? Can you think of any circumstances in which we might say that (or something much like that) of a human being? What does it mean to say it of God?

The word translated *grace* could also be translated *mercy*. The phrase "grace and truth" seems to imitate a pair of characteristics used to describe God in the Old Testament: his loving-kindness (*ḥesed*) and his faithfulness in keeping his covenants (*'emet*). Exodus 34:6 is representative of many Old Testament scriptures that mention these attributes of God, probably the most important of the divine attributes discussed in the Old Testament: "And the Lord passed by before him, and proclaimed, The Lord, The Lord God, merciful and gracious, longsuffering, and abundant in goodness and truth." (See also Psalms 25:10; 61:7; 86:15; and Proverbs 20:28.) This early hymn explicitly identifies Christ with the God of the Old Testament. So what? Why is that important to John's message?

The word translated *truth* means "truth," but it originally meant "what is unconcealed" or "what is revealed" (though by the time of Christ that origin had probably long been forgotten). Nevertheless, does thinking about the word *truth* in that way add any meaning to your understanding of the phrase "grace and truth"?

Verse 16: The Savior gives us of the fullness that he receives, grace for grace—literally "grace in place of grace." What does "grace for grace" mean? Does it mean "one kind of grace replacing another," perhaps the expression of divine mercy (*ḥesed*, loving-kindness) in the Mosaic covenant replaced by its expression in the new covenant? Does it mean that "grace is piled upon grace," indicting an abundance of fullness? Or does it mean "grace in return for grace"? Look at the other places where this phrase occurs in scripture and see whether those help you understand better the meaning of the phrase

(Helaman 12:24; D&C 93:12, 20). Does Doctrine and Covenants 84:38 teach the same thing that is taught here?

Having looked at the hymn that John is quoting, let's look now at what he says about that hymn:

Verses 6–9: Why does John think that it is important to respond to verses 1 through 5 by talking about John the Baptist? Can you explain what in the first five verses might have prompted him to interject this discussion of John the Baptist? Why was/is the testimony of verses 8–9 important?

Verse 13: What does this verse tell us about how we come to have the power to become the children of God?

What does it mean to say that those who believe on God are not born of blood? That they are not born of the will of the flesh? That they are not born of the will of man? What does it mean to be born of God?

In the Old Testament *flesh* often refers to human weakness, as in Isaiah 40:6. *Blood* in the Old Testament is usually associated with death. Might John have those associations in mind? If so, how does that help us understand this verse? Some have suggested that *blood* means "natural generation," that the word *flesh* means "natural desires, such as the desire to have children," and that "the will of man" means "the human ability to choose." Does that add insight into a possible meaning of this verse?

Verse 15: Just as John began his commentary on this hymn by talking about John the Baptist, he ends by talking about John the Baptist. Why? Why was John the Baptist so important to explaining the mission of Jesus? (Compare Mark 1:7 and Matthew 3:11.)

Verse 17: What is the contrast between the law, on the one hand, and grace and truth, on the other? How have we received the fullness, and what is the fullness mentioned in verse 16?

How does this verse suggest that we should understand "grace for grace" in verse 16?

Verse 18: How did Joseph Smith clarify the meaning of this verse? How does it help us understand the meaning of the hymn as a whole? Specifically, how does it help us understand verse 16?

John 20:31

In context, the word *these* in the first phrase refers to the seven miracles that John has just told about. How do those miracles testify of Jesus? Does this verse help us understand John's purpose?

What does he mean when he says that he has written these things "that ye might believe"? How can stories about miracles help our belief? Whose belief will it help? In other words, was John writing for other Christians or to convert those who were not yet Christians?

How does a book whose purpose is to bring us to believe that Jesus is the Anointed One (the meaning of the word *Christ*), the Son of God who can give us life, differ from a standard history? In other words, how does testimony differ from history? Does that tell us anything about how we should read the Gospels? Does it say anything about how we should *not* read them?

Lesson 2

Luke 1; Matthew 1:18–25; 2 Nephi 33:1;
John 1:6–9; Alma 7:10

We are all familiar with the chapters from Matthew and Luke, so familiar that I suspect we often read them or hear them read without paying a lot of attention to them. It is as if we go on autopilot when we read them. However, there is a great deal in these two chapters. I hope these questions will help you see some things in them that you've not noticed before.

Luke 1

Verses 1–4: Luke is the only writer who begins his Gospel by telling us why he is writing it. Why does he do that? We don't know who Theophilus was, but in Greek the phrase "most excellent" is a title, comparable to "your honor" in our culture, so he was probably a civil official of some kind.

Verses 5–25: Why does Luke begin with John the Baptist's birth rather than with Jesus's birth?

Notice the parallels between his description of the two births: the parents are introduced (verses 5–7 and 26–27), an angel appears to announce the birth (verses 8–23 and 28–30), a sign is given (verses 18–20 and 34–38), and a woman who has had no children becomes pregnant miraculously (verses 24–25 and 42). Why has Luke taken so much care to make these two stories parallel?

Zacharias was chosen to burn incense on the incense altar, the holiest place in the temple, just outside the holy of holies. Since the priests making the offering were chosen by lot and there were only two times a year when any particular group ("course") of priests was eligible, the chances of this happening at all were slim; the chances of it happening to the same person twice were null. Why do you think the Lord chose that occasion to make the announcement of John the Baptist's birth?

What did the burning incense represent? Is that relevant to understanding this event?

Do you think that John was a Nazirite (verse 15)? (Read about the Nazirites in your Bible Dictionary.) If so, why do you think he was?

How does Gabriel describe John the Baptist's mission in verse 17? How does his mortal mission relate to his post-mortal mission?

Joseph Smith tells us that Gabriel, the angel who made these announcements, is Noah (*History of the Church* 3:386). Why is it significant that Noah/Gabriel make these announcements? Does 1 Peter 3:20–22 suggest any reasons for Gabriel being the one to make the announcements?

How does this story compare to the story of Abraham and Sarah and the birth of Isaac? What is the significance of that comparison?

Verses 26–38: What do you make of Gabriel's address to Mary in verse 28? How ought we to think of her?

Compare Mary's response to the angel to Zacharias's. What does that tell you about each?

Gabriel describes Jesus's mission in verses 32–33. Do those verses describe both his mortal ministry and the ministry that will begin with his second coming? How so, or not so, for each case?

Verses 39–56: Why might Elisabeth's reaction (verses 42–45) have been reassuring to Mary?

How does Elisabeth know that Mary will be the mother of the Lord? What is Elisabeth saying in verse 45?

Given your reading of the Old Testament, can you explain the importance of the themes of Mary's hymn in verses 50–54? What do those themes have to do with the birth that she is expecting?

Verses 57–66: Zacharias's name means "whom Jehovah remembers" and John's name means "favored by Jehovah." Does the meaning of those names tell us anything about why the angel told Zacharias to name the child John and why the family and friends wanted to name him after his father?

How would the family have understood the name Zacharias to be meaningful for this birth? How is the name John meaningful?

Verses 67–80: What does Zacharias tell us about Jesus in his blessing of John? How does what he says about Jesus reflect what we saw the prophets of the Old Testament saying?

Zacharias specifically says that Jesus has come to make it possible for Israel to perform the mercy that was promised and to remember the covenant. Reread Exodus 19:5–6 to recall the promise of the covenant. Given that promise, what does Zacharias foresee Jesus restoring?

The Greek word translated *serve* in verse 74 specifically refers to temple service. What do you make of the fact that the priest who has been serving in the temple is prophesying that Jesus will come and make temple service possible?

What does Zacharias tell us about John in this blessing? Why does Zacharias call Jesus "the dayspring," in other words, the dawn? Be sure to consider the connection between verses 78 and 79.

Does Herod's decree (Matthew 2:16) perhaps explain why John was raised in the desert? Some have speculated that he was raised by Essenes or a similar group. If John were raised by such a group, what might that suggest about his family's relation to the temple and its priesthood? Why would it be appropriate that the forerunner of the Savior be raised among those who felt that way?

Matthew 1

To help illuminate the context better, I will provide study questions for all of Matthew 1 rather than just for the reading assignment.

Verses 1–16: It is clear that Matthew is not giving an exact genealogy. For example, he tells us that there were fourteen generations between each of the three important events in Israel's history—from Abraham, to David, to the Babylonian captivity, to the coming of Christ: three groups of fourteen generations each, culminating in the birth of Christ. But if we compare this genealogy to the other genealogies in the Old Testament we can see that this is incorrect. Why would Matthew knowingly give us a genealogy that isn't accurate? (Notice that Ezra does something similar: he omits six generations of priests from his genealogy. Compare Ezra 7:1–5 to 1 Chronicles 6:3–15.)

Notice that Matthew says that there are fourteen generations in each of the three groups (verses 17–18), but he puts only thirteen in the last group. It is unlikely that Matthew didn't know that he had only thirteen in that group, so how do you explain that oddity?

Genealogies in the Bible rarely mention women, but this one mentions three: Tamar (spelled "Thamar" here, verse 3), Rachab (verse 5), Ruth (verse 5), and Bathsheba, the wife of Uriah (spelled "Urias" here—verse 6). Why would Matthew mention these women? What are the stories about these women? Do those stories have anything to do with the story of Mary and Joseph? If Matthew's audience is the Jews, why might he include these particular women in the genealogy?

Verse 1: By using the phrase "book of the genealogy," Matthew deliberately imitates passages such as Genesis 2:4 and 5:1. Why? What is he trying to tell us about what follows?

In Jewish thinking at the time of Christ, the "number" of David's name is fourteen. (Jewish numerologists added up the number values of the consonants in names and believed that those numbers were significant. The Hebrew letter that we transliterate as *d* is the fourth letter in the

Hebrew alphabet, and the letter that we transliterate as *v* is the sixth letter, so the number of David's name is 4+6+4, fourteen.) Does that tell us anything about why Matthew has constructed his genealogy as he has?

Verses 18–25: What does *espoused* (verse 18) mean? What does *privily* (verse 19) mean? Jewish divorce law, unlike the laws and customs of other people at the time, required that divorce be formal: a man wishing to divorce his wife (to do so, he had to find "some uncleanness in her" or "something indecent about her"—Deuteronomy 24:1) had to give her a document contradicting their marriage contract. She was then free to remarry. What does this story tell us about Joseph's character? Why do you think that Matthew focuses on Joseph but Luke says very little about him?

Is it significant that Joseph is a dreamer, like Joseph of old? Is the meaning of Joseph's name significant, "to take away my reproach"?

The angel says that Mary's child's name should be "Jesus: for he shall save his people from their sins" (verse 21). How does the fact that he will save us explain his name? If the child is to be named "Jesus," then why does verse 23 say his name will be "Emmanuel"?

Why does Matthew end this part of his story with a quotation from Isaiah?

Lesson 3

Luke 2; Matthew 2; Matthew 3:24–26 (JST); 1 Nephi
11:1–23; Helaman 14:1–8; 3 Nephi 1:4–21; 27:13–16;
Doctrine and Covenants 93:11–20

Luke 2

As in chapter 1, Luke goes out of his way to tell the story of
Jesus's birth as a parallel to the story of John the Baptist's
birth: the joy at the birth of the child, the circumcision and
naming, prophecies of expectation by someone closely associated with the temple, and a concluding remark about
the growth and development of the child. Why do you
think he tells the stories with these parallels?

Verse 6: The Greek word translated *accomplished* could also
have been translated *fulfilled*. Luke uses that Greek word for
fulfilled, eight times in chapters 1 and 2. Why?

Verse 7: Some historical and linguistic notes: Newborn ba-
bies appear to have been washed and then rubbed down
with salt in the belief that the salt would harden their skin.
Swaddling clothes are strips of cloth four or five inches wide
and about six yards long. They were used to bind children
when they were born. The belief was that if the baby's arms
were bound tightly to its sides, they would grow straight
and firm. The word translated *inn* means "guest room" or
"dining room."

Verses 8–20: Though Matthew shows us Christ's birth (or at least his infancy—the wise men may have come some time after he was born) as it relates to the rich and powerful, Luke shows us the birth in relation to the poor. Why do you think Luke tells the story this way?

Why is it significant that, from among the many poor people living around Bethlehem, the angel appears to the shepherds? What symbolic significance could that have? What was David the king's occupation? How is Jesus sometimes described?

Verse 11: The angels announce the good news, the gospel: the Savior, the Messiah (which means "the Anointed One"), the Lord has been born. How does each of these titles differ in meaning? Luke is the only one of the four Gospel writers who uses the title *Savior*, and he uses the verb *save* more than Matthew and Mark put together. Why might that be? What does it tell us about his Gospel?

Verses 21–28: Notice that Luke shows us here that Jesus was raised according to the Mosaic law. He is circumcised and named, and his parents follow the law regarding the sacrifices to be made. Why would that have been important to Luke's audience? Oddly, however, Luke seems to be confused about the rituals required by the law. According to Leviticus 12:2–8, forty days after the birth of a male child, a woman was to be purified by offering a lamb at the temple, or a pair of doves if she was poor. Exodus 13:2, 12–13 says that the firstborn male belongs to God and could be redeemed by an offering by the father. Luke has conflated the two offerings. Do you think that is a confusion on Luke's part or a conflation of the ceremonies that has occurred for the post-Babylonian Jews?

Verses 22–24, 25–27: In the first set of verses, Luke refers to the law three times. In the second set, he refers to the Spirit three times. Do you think that is intentional? If so, what do you make of that parallel?

Verse 25: Some have speculated that Simeon is a member of the priestly class who, having seen the corruption of the temple priesthood, is waiting for its restoration. This speculation is based on the fact that he calls himself a servant in verse 29 and that word is generally reserved for those with the priesthood.

Simeon has been "waiting for the consolation of Israel." What does that mean? A rabbinic tradition has it that the phrase refers to the last words spoken between Elijah and Elisha, words that will be revealed when Elijah returns. Could that rabbinic tradition have significance for Latter-day Saints?

The word translated *consolation* is *paraklēsis*. It is closely related to the word translated *comforter* in places like John 14:16, 26 and 15:26. Literally the Greek word means "one who calls out" or "one who calls to," so it means "an exhorter" or "one who beseeches." Luke uses the word in Luke 3:18 to describe John the Baptist's preaching. How does this word describe Jesus? How is it possible that a word that means "exhorter" can also mean "comforter"?

Verse 28: In Judaism of the second century and later, it was customary for a rabbi to take a child in his arms to give him a blessing. We assume that many of the customs of later Judaism were also customs during the time of Christ.

Verse 32: Simeon recognizes that Jesus is the Savior of all people, Gentile and Jew. Why is that theme important to Luke? How did Matthew include that theme in his story?

Verses 34–35: When Simeon speaks of the fall and rise of many in Israel, he may have Isaiah 8:14 in mind. Note also that the only other times that Luke uses the Greek word that is here translated *rise*, he is referring to resurrection, so that is probably also what he means here. How is the word *resurrection* appropriate here?

With what does Simeon bless Mary? When Simeon says that Jesus will minister so "that the thoughts of many hearts may be revealed," what does he mean?

Verses 36–38: Anna confirms Simeon's testimony. Four women in the Old Testament are called prophetesses: Miriam (Exodus 15:20), Deborah (Judges 4:4), Huldah (2 Kings 22:14), and Isaiah's wife (Isaiah 8:3). The rabbis also recognized Sarah, Hannah (1 Samuel 2:1), Abigail (1 Samuel 25:32), and Esther as prophetesses. By calling Anna a prophetess, Luke explicitly compares her to these women. In what ways is she comparable to them? If we think of Simeon and Anna as types, whom might they represent?

Phanuel means "face of God," and *Asar* (Asher) means "good luck." Is Luke mentioning these names because he believes they add an additional layer of symbolism to his story?

Verses 41–51: Notice how important the temple is to Luke's story. It begins in the temple, with Gabriel's appearance to Zacharias. The infant Jesus's divinity and calling are confirmed by witnesses in the temple. And the only incident we know from his childhood is one in the temple. Later, in verse 49, the phrase translated "about my Father's business" is probably better translated "in my Father's house," and is, therefore, another instance where Luke is emphasizing the importance of the temple. When we get to the end of Luke's Gospel (Luke 24:53), we will see that his story ends with the disciples in the temple. Why do you think the temple was so important to Luke's understanding of the gospel? He is, after all, not himself a Jew.

Luke shows us a young boy who knows the scriptures, who is at home in the temple, who understands that God is his father, and who obeys his parents. The person we see here is anything but a rebel. Why might Luke have thought it important to show his audience that?

Verse 49: This verse could summarize Jesus's life. Did Luke write it with that in mind?

Matthew 2

Verse 1: Who were the wise men? The phrase "wise men" is a translation of the Greek word *magoi.* It is because of this word that sometimes we refer to the wise men as "magi." We get the word *magician* from *magoi.* "The east" may refer to Mesopotamia, the center of astronomical studies at the time. Compare Numbers 24:17, Psalm 72:10–11, and Isaiah 60:1–7. What do such verses suggest to us about the wise men?

Why does Matthew tell us about the homage paid to Jesus by the wise men, but Luke tells us about the homage paid to him by shepherds? Why does each story emphasize what it does?

Why might Matthew have thought it was important to tell the Jewish community about the visit of the Gentile wise

37

men? We see that the Gentile visitors have come to adore the Messiah. What is the reaction of the Jews to the news of his birth? What might that foreshadow? Given that foreshadowing, how might this chapter be an excellent introduction to Matthew as a whole?

Early Christians celebrated Epiphany, the holiday commemorating the coming of the wise men, before it began to celebrate Christmas. Why do you think that might have been?

Verse 2: What do the wise men mean when they say that they have seen his star? Notice that, in spite of our traditions, they do not say that they have followed his star. Note also that they literally say, "We have seen his star at its rising" rather than "we have seen his star in the east." So what?

Verses 3–4: Why is Herod troubled? What would Herod's wise men know that the magi wouldn't know? In other words, why did the wise men consult with Herod and his court? (Note that Herod died in 4 BC.)

Verse 6: Matthew quotes Micah 5:1–3. Since his quotation doesn't correspond to either the Greek version of the Old Testament that was commonly used in Jesus's day (the Septuagint) or the established Hebrew version, he is either quoting somewhat loosely or he may be quoting a version of Micah that we no longer have. Does this discrepancy between Matthew's quotation and the texts for Micah that we have suggest anything interesting?

Verse 11: Why does Matthew mention the gifts the wise men gave? What is frankincense? What is myrrh? (Look in your Bible Dictionary.) How might Jesus's family have been able to use these gifts?

Verses 13–15: Why does Matthew quote scripture so often when he tells what happened to Jesus?

Verses 13–23: The parallels between the story of Moses and that of Jesus are striking, as are the parallels between the pharaoh and Herod: the pharaoh tried to kill all male children (Exodus 1:22); Moses had to flee because his life was in danger (Exodus 2:15); when the pharaoh died, Moses returned (Exodus 4:19–20). In addition, as *Word Biblical Commentary* points out,[1] the language of Matthew 2:19 is almost identical to that of Exodus 2:23 (of the Septuagint, of course, since it is a Greek version of the Old Testament). What are we to make of such parallels? What is Matthew doing by drawing our attention to them?

Verse 16: How large a city or village do you think Bethlehem was at the time? How many children would you think were living there?

Verse 17: Notice that "Jeremy the prophet" means "Jeremiah the prophet." Matthew is quoting Jeremiah 31:15. As with Micah 5, he is not quoting exactly.

Verse 23: No scripture in the Old Testament mentions Nazareth, so what prophets can Matthew be thinking of? Some have suggested that Matthew has Isaiah 11:1 in mind: "And there shall come forth a rod out of the stem of Jesse, and a Branch (*nsr*) shall grow out of his roots." How do you explain what Matthew says here?

Matthew 3:24–26 (JST)

Read JST Matthew 3:24–26, found in the appendix of the LDS edition of the Bible. What new information does

Joseph Smith's expansion of the text following KJV Matthew 2:23 offer?

1 Nephi 11

The following study materials can also be found in *The Book of Mormon Made Harder*, lesson 3.

Verse 1: Compare the personage who responds to Nephi's desire with the one who responded to Lehi (1 Nephi 1:5–6). Are they the same being?

How does Nephi's desire to know what his father had seen (see 1 Nephi 10:17), presumably a desire expressed in prayer, differ from his prayer in 1 Nephi 2:16?

Three things seem to precipitate Nephi's vision: he wants to know what his father has seen, he believes that God can reveal that to him, and he is pondering in his heart. The word *ponder* originally meant "to weigh," and based on that meaning it came to mean "to weigh something mentally." What meanings does the word *heart* have in the scriptures? What does it mean to weigh something in your heart? What might Nephi have been weighing in his heart?

Why does this vision occur on a high mountain? How is Nephi's experience like that of others? Is there any significance to that parallel?

Verses 2–7: The Spirit already knows the answers to the questions that he asks Nephi in verses 2–4, so why does he ask?

Having asked Nephi what he wants and what he believes, the Spirit then praises God before proceeding with the revelation (verse 6). Why?

The word *hosanna* means "save, please" or "save now." Why does the Spirit's address to Nephi, a praise of God, begin with *hosanna*? Does the fact that the second clause begins with *for*, meaning "because," help us understand the cry of hosanna?

According to the Spirit, what will explain why Nephi will see the vision he wants to see?

Verse 7: The Spirit tells Nephi that he will see the tree that his father saw. Then he will see and bear record of the Son of God descending from heaven. And he begins the verse by telling Nephi that this combination of things will be a sign. A sign of what?

The Spirit uses the word *witness* to mean "see" in this verse rather than to mean "testify" or "bear record." Why does he use the word *witness* rather than the word *see*?

Verses 8–10: Before Lehi saw the tree, he went through a dark and dreary space and a large and spacious field (1 Nephi 8:7–9). Why do you think those things are omitted from Nephi's experience?

Is it significant that Nephi says the tree he saw was *like* the tree his father saw (verse 8)? What tree does Nephi see? What justifies your answer?

Why is beauty a representation of good and godliness? Is there a connection between truth, goodness, and beauty?

How does Nephi know that the tree is precious (verse 9)?

Verse 10: Here the Spirit asks the same question that he asked in verse 2. Why? Is there some sense in which this is the beginning of a second vision? If so, can you explain the connection of the two visions?

Verse 11: What has Nephi seen so far? When he asks for "the interpretation thereof," what does he want to have explained for him? As you read the interpretation, compare it to what Lehi says about the tree (1 Nephi 8:11–12).

Nephi identifies the Spirit as the Spirit of the Lord. Does that phrase refer to the Holy Ghost or to the Son?

Why does Nephi tell us that he spoke with the Spirit as one person speaks with another? How is that relevant to this particular story?

How does the vision that follows correlate with Lehi's vision, and if what follows is an interpretation of the beautiful tree, what does that tell us about Lehi's vision?

Verses 12–15: Do you see any significance in the repetition of *look* in verses 8 and 12?

As you read these verses and those that follow, keep in mind that they are the answer to the question, "What does the tree mean?" Ask yourself how this vision answers that question. How does this interpretation fit into Lehi's vision? Why doesn't Lehi's vision include this interpretation?

What do you make of the fact that verses 13 and 15 describe the virgin in the same language used in verses 8–9 to describe the tree?

In the Old Testament, the prophets frequently have to deal with people who worship the goddess Asherah, whose symbol is a pole or tree. In Canaanite religion, Asherah was the queen of heaven, the consort of El, and the mother of the gods. Does Nephi's vision help us understand better why the Israelites might have found Canaanite religion so easy to adopt? One LDS author has argued that the Asherah was legitimately part of preexilic Hebrew worship and that Nephi's vision reflects that fact (Daniel C. Peterson, "Nephi and His Asherah," http://maxwellinstitute.byu.edu/publications/jbms/?vol=9&num=2&id=223).

An angel appears before Nephi (verse 14) and continues the pattern of asking Nephi questions about his beliefs and, now, what he has seen. What is the point of that pattern?

Verses 16–18: As used here, the word *condescension* means "a voluntary stoop or descent from one's rightful position." Why does the angel ask Nephi about the condescension of God rather than about something else? It is relatively easy to see what condescension has to do with the part of the vision that is about to come, but does it have anything to do with what Nephi has already seen?

How is Nephi's answer, "I know that he loveth his children," an answer to the angel's question (verse 17)?

Why does Nephi add, "I do not know the meaning of all things"? Since no human being does, that is a strange thing to say.

How is verse 18 related to the question of verse 16?

Verses 19–23: There is a kind of empty spot in the vision here: the virgin is carried away and then, after a while, reappears, and as far as we know Nephi sees nothing in the interim (verse 19). Why do you think the vision might have been given in that way? Why not proceed directly to the part of the vision that we see in verse 20?

Having shown Nephi the birth of Jesus, the angel asks (verse 21) whether Nephi now understands the meaning of the tree. How is the birth of Christ the interpretation or explanation of the tree?

Having seen the birth, Nephi says that the tree is the love of God (verse 22). How does he get that from what he has seen? What does it mean that the love of God "sheddeth itself abroad in the hearts of the children of men"? (Compare Romans 5:5.)

In verse 8 Nephi saw that the tree was the most beautiful thing and the most white, in other words, the brightest thing. In verse 9 he saw that it was most precious. Now Nephi sees that it is most desirable (verse 22), and the angel says that it is the most joyous thing to the soul (verse 23). How are these things connected to each other? What does "joyous to the soul" mean? Does it mean the same as "joyous *for* the soul"?

Helaman 14:1–8

These questions are from *The Book of Mormon Made Harder*, lesson 35.

Verse 1: What might prevent these things from being written?

Verse 2: Why does the prophet give them a sign?

Verse 8: Does this mean that those who believe after having seen the sign will be saved? If so, isn't that unfair to those who haven't seen such signs?

3 Nephi 1:4–21

Verses 4–8: How do you understand the mixture of sorrow ("lest by any means those things which had been spoken might not come to pass") and hope ("they did watch steadfastly for that day and that night and that day which should be as one day as if there were no night")?

Verses 10–11: These verses both refer to "his people," in other words the people of Nephi. But does that phrase mean the same thing in each verse? Why do you answer as you do?

Verses 12–13: "Be of good cheer" occurs with regularity in the New Testament and the Doctrine and Covenants. Given the way we use the word *cheer* today, it seems to mean "Be happy." But in the King James Version of the Bible, the phrase was used to translate the Greek imperative verb *tharseo*, meaning "Take courage." "Courage" is one of the older meanings of *cheer*. The word itself descends from a Middle English word that means "face." It probably came to mean courage as well as to have its contemporary meaning, good feeling, because to have courage requires facing one's foes or problems with a lifted up head and a face that no longer droops. Given that older meaning of *cheer*, what is the Lord admonishing Helaman? Why that particular admonition in these circumstances? Is that admonition a guarantee that all will be well?

45

Verse 14: What does the Lord mean when he says, "I come unto my own"? Why does he say that to Helaman? In other words, what is he telling him?

Can you explain what "all things which I have made known unto the children of men from the foundation of the world" means?

The Lord says that he came to do the will of both the Father and the Son. Then he explains that by saying "of the Father because of me, and of the Son because of my flesh." What does the first half of that explanation mean? What does the second half mean?

3 Nephi 27:13–16

These questions can be found in *The Book of Mormon Made Harder*, lesson 42.

Verse 13ff.: Is the Savior giving a definition of the gospel in these verses? Though at first glance it might appear so, perhaps not. Of course, we don't know what the Nephite word translated *gospel* was, so we don't know any more about its meaning than we can deduce from the English word, but we do know about the English word and about the Greek word used by those who wrote the New Testament.

The English and Greek words both originally meant "to preach the good news." For example, in Matthew 2:10 the phrase translated "I bring you good tidings" could also have been translated "I bring you the gospel." (It is a verb rather than a noun in that verse, but the meaning is the same.) The word *gospel* wasn't used to denote a set of doctrines in New

Testament times or in its first uses in English. Only later (perhaps about 1200) did the word come to be identified with the accounts of Christ's ministry (the four Gospels), and only later than that did it come to refer to the doctrinal content of Christian preaching. It seems most likely, therefore, that in the Book of Mormon the word *gospel* has the older meaning: preaching glad tidings. If that's true, we could paraphrase the first part of this verse like this:

> *Behold I have preached my glad tidings to you, and these are the glad tidings I have preached to you. . . .*

Notice the first element of the good news: Christ came into the world to do the will of his Father, and he did so because his Father sent him. How is that good news?

We might expect Jesus to say something like "I came into the world to do the will of my Father in order to make salvation available to all." What is important about the reason he gives for his mission?

Verse 14: The phrase "lifted up" has an obvious literal meaning in reference to the crucifixion. But what else might it say to us? For example, is any analogy intended between Christ being lifted up on the cross and the way in which the Father will lift us up? (Does this verse have anything to do with verses that tell us we must take up our cross (e.g., Matthew 16:24; Mark 8:34; 10:21; Luke 9:23; Galatians 6:12; Jacob 1:8; Alma 39:9; 3 Nephi 12:30; and D&C 23:6; 56:2; and 112:14)?

What does the phrase "that I might draw all men unto me" imply? Why use the word *draw*?

Verse 15: What does this verse tell us about what Jesus means when he says he will "draw all men" unto him?

Verse 16: What does it mean to say that those who repent and are baptized will be filled? Does it have to do with having our hunger satisfied? Or are we missing something that is given with repentance and baptism?

Doctrine and Covenants 93:11–20

Verse 11: When did John behold the glory of the Only Begotten? Is he referring to a specific experience? What does it mean to say that glory was "*as* the glory of the Only Begotten of the Father" (italics added)?

In the readings for lesson 3 we saw John speak of Jesus as full of grace and truth. Does the phrase mean the same thing here that it meant in John 1? If so, what is that? If not, what does it mean here?

Does "even the Spirit of truth" repeat the meaning of "full of grace and truth"? Both modify "the Only Begotten of the Father." What does this phrase tell us about him?

Why is it important to know that God himself came and "dwelt in the flesh"?

Why is it important to John that he add "and dwelt among us"?

Does the word *dwelt* in the last two phrases carry meaning that we should consider when thinking about what John is teaching? Is there a difference between dwelling somewhere and merely being there?

Verses 12–13: What does "of the fulness" mean? Fullness of what? What does "grace for grace" mean? Is it the same as "from grace to grace"?

How did John see that Jesus didn't receive "of the fulness" at first?

Verse 14: Does this verse suggest that the Father *did* receive "of the fulness at the first?" To what does "the first" refer in that phrase?

Verse 15: Was John present at Jesus's baptism? If he wasn't, how could he give this testimony? If he was, what evidence is there?

Verses 16–17: Does verse 16 tell us that Jesus received the fullness of the glory of the Father at his baptism, or has it moved to a new topic?

These verses tell us that Jesus received a fullness of the Father's glory *and* that he received all power on heaven and earth. Does John want us to understand those to be two ways of saying the same thing, or is he talking about two different things that the Father gave his Son?

What does it mean to say that the Father dwelt in the Son since one embodied being cannot dwell in another?

Verse 18: To whom is this promise made?

Verse 19: How does what John teaches in the preceding verses teach us how to worship? Does that have implications for our Sunday worship? For our temple worship? For our private devotions?

The verse suggests that knowing how to worship and what we worship are necessary for coming to the Father in the name of the Son. How so?

Verse 20: What would it mean for us to have the same fullness and glory as the Son? Why is obedience required for that? What does obedience show? What does it do for us?

Does the way in which we receive grace for grace help us understand how Christ did? Or is it the other way around, understanding how he did can help us understand what it means for us too?

Lesson 4

Matthew 3:1–4:11; John 1:35–51

Matthew 3

Verses 1–2: What function did the herald of a king serve in ancient times? Why did kings need heralds? Is John the herald of a king? Why does this King need a herald?

Compare John the Baptist's message to Jesus's message in Matthew 4:17. Why do you think Matthew uses almost exactly the same words in each case? What is he teaching?

Given Matthew's focus on Jesus's royal birth, how are we to understand "the kingdom of heaven is at hand"? How many ways can you think of understanding that the kingdom of heaven is soon to come or is nearby? Does it help to know that the word *kingdom* might better be translated *reign*?

Verse 3: Matthew (like the other three synoptic Gospel writers) quotes from Isaiah 40:3 to describe John the Baptist's mission. (Matthew quotes from the Greek version rather than the Hebrew, which explains why there are differences between what he says and our version of Isaiah 40:3.) How does that verse from Isaiah explain John's mission? Does it shed any light on what John means when he warns that the kingdom of heaven is at hand?

Verse 4: This verse reminds us of Elijah. (See 2 Kings 1:8; see also Matthew 11:14 and 17:10–12.) Why is that parallel important?

Does Zechariah 13:4 teach us anything about John the Baptist?

Verses 5–6: Notice the contrast that Matthew sets up between "Jerusalem, and all Judaea, and all the region round about Jordan" in verse 5 and the Pharisees and Sadducees in the next verse. He tells us that *everyone* came to be baptized, confessing their sins—and many of the Pharisees and Sadducees also came. It appears that though Jews of this time baptized converts to Judaism, they did not baptize those who were born Jews. When John baptizes Jews, too, he implicitly compares them to the Gentiles. Why would this part of John the Baptist's message have been shocking?

Verses 7–8: The Pharisees and Sadducees seem not to have been political allies or allies otherwise. Why does John the Baptist, and then Jesus, treat them as a group? Why does he single them out? Does his message to them differ from his message in general? How?

Verse 9: Against what mistake does John the Baptist warn the Pharisees and Sadducees? What would it mean for a Sadducee to say, "I have Abraham for my father"? For a Pharisee?

Has God raised up children to Abraham that are not genetic children, children from stones, as it were? If so, who are they? Does this discussion of the seed of Abraham have anything to do with the fact that John baptized Jews (verse 6)?

Verse 10: Does "the axe is laid unto the root of the trees" mean the same thing here that "the kingdom of heaven is at hand" means?

Verses 11–12: Does verse 11 begin a new topic, or is this part of what he said to the Pharisees and Sadducees?

What does John mean when he says that he isn't worthy to carry the Messiah's shoes?

How is *fire* used metaphorically? What does cleansing by water suggest? What does cleansing by fire suggest? Can you think of any incidents of cleansing by fire in the Old Testament? Do they have any bearing on our understanding of these verses? What is the connection between the fire mentioned in verse 11 and that mentioned at the end of verse 12?

Some early Christians, such as Origen, understood these verses to refer to the fires of hell. Do you think that could be right? Why or why not? Might John's audience have understood the purging of the granary floor as something that has already occurred in history, perhaps at the fall of Jerusalem to the sixth-century-BC invaders?

Compare verses 10–12 to Malachi 4:1. What similarities do you see?

Verse 15: What does "to fulfill all righteousness" mean? Read Nephi's explanation of why Jesus needed to be baptized (2 Nephi 31, especially verses 4–7.)

What does Jesus's baptism demonstrate about him? About us?

Verses 16–17: What does the dove symbolize in the story of the flood? Does its meaning in that story help us understand its symbolism here?

In Matthew's Gospel, Jesus is announced as the king at his conception, at his birth, and here at his baptism. What do you make of that? The phrase "in whom I am well pleased" uses a verb that in Greek is in a kind of past tense, the aorist tense. A verb in the aorist tense indicates that the action of the verb is complete or fulfilled. It can be in the past, but isn't necessarily so. What does that tell us about the Father's relation to the Son?

Does Matthew want us to see verses 15–17 as a fulfillment of John the Baptist's prophecy that the kingdom of God is at hand?

Matthew 4

Verses 1–2: Jesus goes into the desert for forty days. What does it mean to say that the Spirit led him so that he could be tempted of ("tried by" or "examined by") the devil ("the seducer," "the slanderer")? What parallels do you see here between Jesus and ancient Israel? What do those parallels teach? Do Hebrews 2:18 and Alma 7:12 help us understand what happens in the desert?

Some Protestant scholars have noted parallels between Satan's temptation of Jesus and his temptation of Eve:

TEMPTATION	GENESIS 3	MATTHEW 4
Appeal to physical appetite	You may eat of any tree (v. 1)	You may eat by changing stones to bread (v. 3)
Appeal to personal gain	You will not die (v. 4)	You will not hurt your foot (v. 6)
Appeal to power	You will be like God (v. 5)	You will have all the world's king-doms (vv. 8–9)

Is there a point to such parallels, or are they simply accidental? If they have a point, what is it?

Verses 3–4: Satan tempts Jesus by challenging him to use his power to satisfy a basic human need. Jesus responds by quoting scripture, Deuteronomy 8:3. What does Jesus's answer tell us about our priorities?

Verses 5–7: Satan tempts Jesus by challenging him to use his power to produce a sign of his divinity, and he quotes scripture (Psalm 91:11–12) to justify his challenge. Jesus responds by again quoting from Deuteronomy (6:16): "Ye shall not tempt ["put to the test"] the Lord your God, as ye tempted him in Massah." How did Israel tempt God in Massah? (See Exodus 17:1–7.) How is that relevant to this temptation?

Verses 8–10: Like the two previous temptations, the third temptation is also about power. What does Satan offer Christ? Jesus's response this time begins with a dismissal: "Get thee hence." Then Jesus quotes Deuteronomy 6:13: "Thou shalt fear the Lord thy God, and serve him, and shalt swear by his name." In context, it is clear that this verse is a reminder that the Israelites are not to worship false gods. How is that relevant to understanding Satan's temptation?

In each of the previous temptations, Satan addressed Jesus as "Son of God." Why? Does it have anything to do with Matthew 3:17? Satan does not address him in that way for the third temptation? Why not?

What is the significance of the fact that Jesus answers Satan each time by quoting from the Law?

How do Jesus's answers define his mission? How do they define for us what it means to be faithful?

Verses 12–16: Why does Jesus go to Galilee? Why does Jesus wait until after John's imprisonment to begin his ministry? How does Matthew understand Jesus's move to Capernaum as a fulfilment of Isaiah's prophecy that the gospel will go the Gentiles (Isaiah 8:23–9:1, using the Greek translation of Isaiah)?

Verse 17: Jesus begins his ministry. What does "at hand" mean? In what senses is the kingdom of heaven at hand?

How does Jesus's message apply to us? How is it the message that we continue to preach?

Verses 18–22: The same Greek word is translated *straightway* in verse 19 and *immediately* in verse 22. By repeating that word, Matthew is emphasizing it. What does his emphasis tell us?

Verses 23–25: Why is so much of Jesus's mission dedicated to healing the sick? Does that healing have symbolic as well as literal significance? Is it related to Jesus's experience in the desert? Does it help us understand scriptures like Mosiah 4:16, Mosiah 18:8–10, and D&C 81:5?

John 1:35–51

Verses 34–39: These verses tell us of the first disciples who followed Jesus. Why was it important for Matthew to tell this story to the people of his day? Why is it important to us today?

What does John's story about the first disciples tell us that Matthew's did not? Why might that be?

Verses 38–39: This conversation between Jesus and the two disciples of John the Baptist is quite prosaic. Why do you think that John included it? Does it have any meaning for us?

How might we understood Jesus's question of them, "What do you want?" What would it mean if he were to ask you that question? How might we understand the disciples' response, "Where do you abide?" How might that be our question? How might we understand his advice, "Come and see," as advice for us?

Verse 42: Why do you think Jesus changes Simon's name? What connotations does the word *stone* have?

Verse 45: What does the story of Nathaniel's call teach us? What does Jesus promise Nathaniel, and how is that significant?

Lesson 5

John 3:1–22; 4:1–42

John 3

Verses 1–2: Why does Nicodemus come by night? That fact is important enough to John to mention. What is John telling us with it?

Why does he call Jesus "Rabbi"?

What does it mean to say that a teacher has "come from God"? How does Nicodemus claim to know that Jesus has come from God? How reliable is the evidence of God that he gives?

Verse 3: How is what Jesus says a response to what Nicodemus has said?

Another translation, more literal and perhaps better: "Unless a person is begotten from above, he cannot see [or "know"] the kingdom [or "reign"] of God." The Greek word translated *from above* in the King James Version is ambiguous. It can mean "above," "from the beginning," "for a long time," and "again" or "anew." Is that ambiguity instructive? How would you decide which meaning to choose?

Why is seeing so often used as the metaphor for knowing? Why not, instead, hearing?

How or when do we see or know the reign of God?

Nicodemus has seen Christ's miracles (verse 2), but he has *not* seen the kingdom of God (verse 3). What does that fact teach us?

Verse 4: The Jews baptized—as is plain from the success of John the Baptist's mission. And we know from other documents that they used the metaphor of rebirth for those who were converted. Why, then, does Nicodemus say such a dumb thing?

Did Nicodemus believe that his first, physical birth had conveyed spiritual advantages on him? Might that assumption help us understand his question? Compare what Jesus says to the multitude in Luke 3:8.

Verse 5: What does it mean to be born of the Spirit?

To think about that question, consider Alma 5:21. How and when do we know that we cannot be saved unless our garments are washed white? Is that knowledge experiential? Conceptual? If it is conceptual or partly conceptual, what conceptual knowledge must we have?

Why is sin portrayed as something that gets our clothing filthy? Is there a sin or set of sins in particular that would do that? Does that contribute to the irony that our garments must be washed in blood in order to become white again?

What does it mean to redeem someone from something or someone? Given that meaning, what does the phrase "redeem people from their sins" mean?

Look also at Alma 5:33–35. How can the Savior say that we can eat and drink of the bread and the waters of life freely if he has a condition on coming to him, namely repentance?

Consider also the verse we will be looking at later, John 3:16. How is its teaching relevant to being born of the Spirit?

Is the covenant of King Benjamin's people (Mosiah 5:5) relevant to understanding this birth by the Spirit?

What does Alma 5:12–14 teach about that covenant?

For now, at least, finish by reading Mosiah 27:24–26 and thinking about how that sheds light on the exchange between Jesus and Nicodemus.

Verse 6: What is Jesus's point here?

Verses 7–8: What is the genealogy of one born of the Spirit?

In Greek (the language of the New Testament) the word translated *spirit* can also mean "breath" or "wind." In fact, that is its first meaning. So the Greek word translated *wind* in this verse is the same as the word translated *Spirit*. Rewrite the verse using *wind* for each and rewrite it using *Spirit* for each. Does either way of rewriting the verse add meaning?

Is there a connection between the gift of the Spirit and the breath of God, given to Adam in Genesis 2:7 (Moses 3:7)?

What does it mean to say that the Spirit/wind/breath goes where it desires or wills? What is Jesus teaching Nicodemus in these verses? How does that teaching compare to what Nicodemus, as a Pharisee, believed? How does that teaching apply to us?

Verses 9–10: Another translation of the word for *master* is *teacher*. If you make that substitution, what is Jesus saying to Nicodemus?

Verses 11–12: Jesus is scolding Nicodemus. Can you put his criticism into plain, contemporary language?

When has Jesus told Nicodemus or others of earthly things that they did not believe? Was it in this exchange? What kinds of things, "heavenly things," is he withholding?

Verse 13: What the Lord says here is odd. Is he talking about his future ascent, after his resurrection? Or about something else? If something else, what?

How is what he teaches in these verses relevant to the discussion with Nicodemus as a whole?

Verses 14–15: The obvious cross-reference for this verse is 2 Nephi 25:20. How many parallels can you find between Moses lifting up the brass serpent and Jesus being crucified?

Verses 16–17: It is difficult to imagine that there are many people who have not heard John 3:16. Evangelists of many denominations quote it frequently when they proselytize. Sometimes, though, when something is very familiar, it is also easily overlooked. Consider this alternative translation of John 3:16, and because verse 17 is an essential part of Jesus's teaching, I have also included it:

> For God so loved the word that he gave the only Son, so that all who trust in him might not be destroyed but might have eternal life. For God did not send the Son into the world to condemn the world, but so that the world might be delivered through him.

Verse 16 begins with *for* because it is explaining something. What is it explaining?

The Greek word *pisteuō* has the basic meaning "to trust," but it can also mean "to believe" and "to have faith in." Does it help make sense of faith in Christ to think about it as trust? What difference(s) can thinking of it that way make?

What is verse 17 explaining?

The word translated *condemn* also means "judge," and most often it means to pass a negative judgment. Its basic meaning is "separation." What belief is Jesus countering when he says that the Father did not send the Son into the world to condemn it?

From what does Jesus save us or deliver us?

Verse 18: How does the meaning of the verse change if we replace "believeth on" with "trusts in"? Why are those who believe on/trust in the Messiah not condemned?

The second half of verse 18 says that if we don't believe, then we have already been judged for not believing. Can you explain what judgment that might be? In what sense does a person's unbelief make him or her *already* judged? Does it help to remember that the basic meaning of the word translated *judged* is "separated"? From what are those who do not believe already separated? What separates (judges) them?

Verse 19: According to this verse, to be condemned is to be someone who loves dark more than light. Notice that Jesus doesn't say, "They are condemned *because* they love darkness more than light." He says that loving darkness is itself condemnation. What do you make of that?

How does what Jesus says here relate to what he says in verse 17?

How does the fact that men's deeds were evil explain that they hate the light? How do evil deeds separate one from light? How would one's evil deeds cause one to hate the light?

Verse 20: How does this verse explain the condemnation or separation of those who hate light?

The word translated *reproved* is *elenchō*. It means "to bring to light or expose," "to bring a person to the point at which he or she recognizes something," "to reprove or correct," and "to punish." Which of those meanings fits the context best? One way to decide that is by putting each into the verse and seeing which gives the best explanation for the hatred of light.

Verses 21–22: We never use the expression "do the truth." What can it mean?

Why do those who do the truth want their deeds made manifest?

What does it mean that one's deeds are "wrought in God"? Is the answer to this question also an answer to the immediately previous question?

John 4

I offer less detailed questions about this chapter.

Verse 10: What is the living water that Jesus offers the Samaritan woman? In the Old Testament, it represents God, as in Jeremiah 17:13. In ancient Israel it sometimes symbolized the Law. Mosiah seems to use it to represent the Holy Ghost when he speaks of the Spirit being poured out on the people (Mosiah 4:20).

Is the gift that Jesus refers to the same as the living water, or is it something else? What is it that she should know if she is to ask for living water?

Verses 19–21: The Samaritan woman asks Jesus the question that burned between the Samaritans and the Jews. Based on the fact that in Deuteronomy 12:1–14 the Lord tells Israel to worship at the place he will show them immediately after he has said that they should place a blessing on Mt. Gerizim (Deuteronomy 11:29), the Samaritans believed that the proper place for the temple was on Mt. Gerizim. While the leaders of Judah were in captivity, those who remained behind (which is who the Samaritans descended from) built a temple on Mt. Gerizim that was later destroyed under the Hasmonean (Jewish) rule. Present-day Samaritans (of which there are less than 1,000) claim that their worship is that of preexilic Israel and that Judaism changed the religion after the exile in Babylon.

Why doesn't Jesus answer the woman's question?

What does his answer in verse 21 mean?

Verses 22–24: What does he mean when he says that she doesn't know what she worships? Did the Jews know whom they worshipped?

What does he mean when he tells her that salvation is of the Jews? The Samaritans claim descent from Ephraim and Manasseh. Aren't they, too, set apart to bring salvation to the world?

What does it mean to say "God is a Spirit"? The Greek could be translated as it is or as "God is Spirit." Either would be correct. Scriptures also say "God is light" (1 John 1:5) and "God is love" (1 John 4:8). How should we understand those kinds of descriptions of God?

Verses 32–38: How is this incident related to the story as a whole? Why has John included it here as part of the story of the Samaritan woman? What has the parable that Jesus tells his disciples to do with his encounter with the woman?

Lesson 6

Luke 4:14–32; 5; 6:12–16; Matthew 10

Before looking at some individual verses from this lesson, consider the overall structure of Luke's narrative and think about how his story of the calling of the Twelve compares to Matthew's. I have put the verses in **bold** that the lesson focuses on, but I have outlined all four chapters so that you can think about how Luke tells the story as a whole. Because of the length of the materials, I have created study questions only for the first part of the lesson, Luke 4:14–32.

Luke's story

John's preaching and message (Luke 3:1–20).

Jesus's baptism (Luke 3:21–22).

His genealogy (Luke 3:23–38).

The forty-day sojourn in the desert and the temptation of Christ (Luke 4:1–13)

Jesus's first sermon, on Isaiah 61:1–2, and its reception in Nazareth (**Luke 4:14–32**).

Jesus casts a devil out of a man in the synagogue (Luke 4:33–37).

He cures Peter's mother-in-law of a fever (Luke 4:38–39).

He cures many others of various diseases, and the evil spirits witness that he is the Christ (Luke 4:40–41).

The people beg him to stay with them, but he says he must preach in other places as well (Luke 4:42–44).

Jesus calls Peter, James, and John (**Luke 5:1–11**).

He heals a leper (**Luke 5:12–15**).

He heals a man of palsy by saying, "Thy sins are forgiven thee" (**Luke 5:16–26**).

He calls Levi (often assumed to be Matthew), a tax collector (**Luke 5:27–28**).

Levi throws a feast for Jesus, and the scribes and Pharisees question why he would eat with the unclean and with sinners (**Luke 5:29–32**).

The scribes and Pharisees question why his disciples do not fast (**Luke 5:33–35**).

He tells them the parables of patching a new garment with old cloth, of putting new wine into old bottles, and of the superiority of old wine (**Luke 5:36–39**).

Some Pharisees question why his disciples prepare food on the Sabbath (Luke 6:1–5).

He heals a man with a withered hand on the Sabbath, with Pharisees observing and looking for something to accuse him of (Luke 6:6–11).

Jesus calls the Twelve (**Luke 6:12–16**).

Notice that, after telling of the first sermon and after telling of the call, Luke recounts various miracles that Jesus performed. Why do you think he does that? How are those miracles related to the events that precede them? What is the symbolic significance of healing the sick and casting out devils? Is there a sense in which the symbolic significance of healing and its literal significance come together in the healing of the palsied man?

After calling Levi as a disciple, Jesus tells us several stories about Jesus's interaction with the scribes (the religious teachers) and the Pharisees. What is the significance of these stories? Why do they come after the story of Levi? What do they show us about Jesus and his teachings?

How do these major stories, beginning with Jesus calling Peter, James and John, and the stories of healing and of confrontation with the scribes and Pharisees, lead us to the story of the calling of the Twelve?

The Twelve

We have four lists of the Twelve, with some variation among them:

MATTHEW 10:2–4	MARK 3:16–19	LUKE 6:14–16	ACTS 1:13
Simon (Peter)	Simon Peter	Simon (Peter)	Peter
Andrew	Andrew	Andrew (Peter's brother)	James

James (of Zebedee)	James (of Zebedee)	James	John
John (brother of James)	John (brother of James)	John	Andrew
Philip	Philip	Philip	Philip
Bartholomew	Bartholomew	Bartholomew	Thomas
Thomas	Thomas	Matthew	Bartholomew
Matthew	Matthew	Thomas	Matthew
James (of Alphaeus)	James (of Alphaeus)	James (of Alphaeus)	James (of Alphaeus)
Lebbaeus Thaddaeus	Thaddaeus	Simon (Zelotes)	Simon Zelotes
Simon (the Canaanite)	Simon (the Canaanite)	Judas (brother of James)	Judas (brother of James)
Judas Iscariot	Judas Iscariot	Judas Iscariot	—

Notice that these occur in three groups of four. For example, in Matthew's list we find these groups: (Peter, Andrew, James, and John), (Philip, Bartholomew, Thomas, Matthew), (James, Thaddaeus, Simon, and Judas). Though the order of the persons in each group of four varies from list to list, each person always appears in the same group. What might explain that?

Here is how the differences between the names on these lists are traditionally resolved:

Peter = Simon Peter = Simon, Bar Jonas (son of Jonas) = Cephas

James = son of Zebedee = Boanerges = son of Thunder

John = son of Zebedee = Boanerges = son of Thunder = John the Beloved = the disciple Jesus loved

Andrew = the brother of Peter

Matthew = Levi

Philip

Nathanael = Bartholomew

Thomas = Didymus (meaning "twin") = Doubting Thomas

James = the son of Alphaeus = James the Less = James the Younger

Thaddaeus = Lebbaeus Thaddaeus = Judas, brother of James

Simon the Zealot = Simon the Canaanite ("Canaanite" doesn't refer to the Canaanite people of the Old Testament; it is a transliteration of an Aramaic word meaning "zealot")

Judas Iscariot
We cannot be sure, but a popular explanation of Judas Iscariot's name, an explanation with scholarly backing, is that *Iscariots* means "man of Kerioth," a town south of

Judah; hence Judas may be the only non-Galilean among the Twelve. Other less popular explanations of the name, though also with scholarly backing: *Iscariot* means that he is a member of the Sicarii, a group of Zealots who assassinated using daggers (*sica* in Latin); *Iscariot* is derived from a Hebrew word meaning "betrayer"; the name is derived from a Greek word meaning "to hand over"—he handed Jesus over to the temple priests; the name refers to his occupation, either a red dyer or a fruit grower; *Iscariot* is an Aramaic word meaning "the man from the city," in other words, "the man from Jerusalem"; like the first and the last explanation, the final proposal assumes that the name refers to his hometown, but instead of Kerioth or Jerusalem, it argues that the name refers to Askaroth or Askar, near Shechem.

Look at the number of relatives among the first Twelve: Peter and Andrew are brothers; James and John are brothers; James, son of Alphaeus, and Thaddaeus seem to be brothers. In addition, some have argued that some of the Twelve were Jesus's cousins. Do you think these relations are significant? If so, what is the significance?

Comparing Luke and Matthew:

LUKE	MATTHEW
It is clear that *apostle* is a title, and the apostles are mentioned several times (9:10; 17:5; 22:14; and 24:10).	The Twelve are called "apostles" only here, and it is not clear that the word is used as a title here.
—	Peter is said to be "first."

The Twelve are arranged in pairs, perhaps reflecting the missionary arrangement we see in Mark 6:7.	The same.
—	The list is prefaced with mention of the power given them and is followed by a charge to them.
—	We are told that James and John are brothers.

Do these differences tell us anything about the different foci of Matthew's and Luke's testimonies?

Luke 4:14–32

Verse 17: Why do you think Jesus chooses Isaiah 61 for the scriptural passage that he will use for his sermon? (*Esais* is the Greek form of the Hebrew *Isaiah*. Remember that the name Isaiah means almost the same thing as the name Jesus, "the Lord is salvation.")

We don't know how synagogue worship in Christ's day was conducted, but a century or so later it was like this: two formal prayers, a reading from the Torah and a reading from the Prophets, a sermon that consisted of an explanation of a scriptural passage, and a priestly blessing on the congregation. It was probably similar in Christ's time. It seems, then, that Jesus was asked to give the sermon. Presumably following custom, he stands to read from the Old Testament prophets; then he seats himself to comment on the

73

passage. Why would the custom be to stand when they read the scriptures but sit when they commented on them? What is there in these verses that reinforces Luke's themes in his Gospel? Why might Luke want to draw these themes to the attention of his readers near the beginning of his Gospel?

Verse 18: As you read this quotation from Isaiah, think of how its parts apply to Jesus. What does it mean to say that the Spirit of the Lord is on him? (See Luke 3:22; 4:1, 14). Remember that *Christ* and *Messiah* are the Greek and Hebrew words, respectively, for "anointed one."

The Greek word translated *poor* in this quotation does not refer to individual poor people. Instead, it refers to the state of being poor.

The phrase "he hath sent me" uses a verb that indicates that the action is completed: he has sent me and I have arrived. What does that tell us about Jesus's preaching?

This is one of the few places, perhaps the only one, where Luke uses the Greek word translated *heal* for anything other than physical ailments. What does "heal the broken-hearted mean" in a gospel context? What does it mean to free the captives? To whom or what are they captive? Who are the blind whom Jesus says he has come to heal? What can they not see?

Notice that Jesus has inserted a line that is not in Isaiah 61:1–2: "to preach deliverance to the captives." That line comes from Isaiah 58:6.

Verse 19: Here is another way to translate this verse: "To proclaim the Lord's year of grace [i.e., the Jubilee year; see

Leviticus 25:8–55]." How are the practice of the Jubilee year and the preaching of the gospel related? How is the message that Christ has come the message of a Jubilee year?

Verse 21: Jesus begins his commentary with "This day is this scripture fulfilled in your ears." What would his listeners have understood him to say?

Notice that, as with the verb translated "hath sent" (verse 18), the verb translated "is fulfilled" indicates that the fulfillment has been completed.

Luke gives us only the beginning of his sermon. Many ancient writers did this as a way of naming an entire work, though usually they did so when the material they referred to was well known, just as we often refer to hymns by their first line rather than by their title. Jesus's sermon may have been well known in Luke's time, so he didn't feel he needed to repeat it. Or it may have been interrupted and not finished. Which do you think likely? Why?

Verse 22: How do the people respond to Jesus's sermon?

The verb translated "bear witness" means "to testify," "to acknowledge the truth of something," or "to speak well of." How do those who hear him bear witness of him?

The verb translated *wonder* is in a tense that means that its action continued indefinitely. We might translate it "continued to wonder." What point is Luke making?

The word translated *gracious* also means "favorable, pleasurable, beneficial, pleasing," but this isn't so much a comment about Jesus's preaching style as it is about the content of his preaching: "words of grace" rather than "graceful words."

What do his hearers find truthful and pleasing? Why are they surprised? If they are surprised that Joseph's son can do what he has done in their synagogue, how do you think they are most likely to explain what has happened?

Verse 23: Given the villagers' response to his sermon, what is surprising about his response to them? How do you explain his response? What does "Physician, heal thyself" mean, and how is it related to the sentence that follows: "Do here in your region whatever we have heard that you did in Capernaum"? Isn't that a reasonable request? Of what is Jesus accusing them?

Verse 24: Why does Jesus begin this pronouncement with "amen," translated *verily*?

Haven't we, in verse 22, seen them accept him? What point is he making? How does this apply to us today, or does it?

Verses 25–26: Jesus compares himself to Elijah ("Elias" in Greek). Notice that 1 Kings 17:1 says that the drought lasted three years, but Luke has Jesus say that it lasted for three years and six months. (Compare James 5:17.) Three years and six months is a standard number used in apocalyptic literature for times of persecution, stress, and struggle. (Compare Daniel 7:25; 12:7; Revelation 11:2; 12:6, 14.) Either Luke or Jesus seems to be using the standard number to make a point rather than to be historically accurate. What is that point? How does this story illustrate Jesus's relation to Nazareth? Does it also say something about his relation to Israel?

Verse 27: Jesus compares himself to Elisha ("Eliseus" in Greek). What is the significance of the fact that in the story of Elijah the woman to whom he goes is a Sidonite? (Where is Sidon?) Why is it significant that Naaman is a Syrian? What do these stories say to those who hear them?

Verses 28–30: What part of Jesus's sermon seems to have angered his fellow villagers enough to make them want to kill him? Why?

Notice the restraint of Luke's description of Jesus's escape: he simply passed through their midst and went on his way. What do you make of that restraint? What is its effect in the story as a whole?

Verse 31: Jesus moves from Nazareth to Capernaum (which means "village of Nahum"), a reasonably large fishing village on the northwest coast of the Sea of Galilee. Archaeologists are quite certain that they have uncovered the house of Peter in Capernaum, which they think might have included a room in which Jesus lived.

Verse 32: Does the people's reaction in Capernaum differ from that in Nazareth? Why?

Lesson 7
Mark 1–2; 4:35–41; 5; Luke 7:1–17

For purposes of this lesson, I take Luke 7:1–17 to be a supplement to the miracle stories we read in the material from Mark. So I will make my notes and questions on Mark, assuming that reading and thinking about them will be appropriate to understanding Luke.

Mark's Gospel

This is the first lesson to use the book of Mark, so some review of what we think we know about the Gospel of Mark may be in order.

Most non-LDS scholars believe that Mark was the Gospel written first and that the other two synoptic writers used his Gospel as a kind of first draft. In contrast, probably most LDS scholars believe that Matthew was written first because Matthew's version of things is what we find in Christ's teaching to the Nephites.

We are not certain who Mark was, but a strong and very old Christian tradition says that he was the John Mark mentioned in Acts. There he is Paul's assistant in missionary work (Acts 12:25; 13:5). He appears to have been a member of a wealthy Jewish-Christian family in Jerusalem and the cousin of a wealthy landowner, Barnabas (Acts 4:36–37; Colossian 4:10). Based on that, some have speculated that his family owned the Garden of Gethsemane and that he was the young man who escaped capture when Jesus was arrested in the garden, but the evidence for that speculation is not very strong. The fact that he gets Palestinian geography wrong is reason to believe that if he was from a Jerusalem family, he did not live there long himself.

For a reason that we do not know, Paul refused to continue to work with Mark at the end of the first mission, though Barnabas used Mark (Acts 15:37–39). However, Mark and Paul seem to have been reconciled later, for his name appears throughout the letters of Paul (e.g., 2 Timothy 4:11 and Philemon 24).

Mark also seems to be the person to whom Peter refers as "my son" (1 Peter 5:13). Tradition has it that he was Peter's interpreter, though that can mean "the person who explained Peter's teaching" rather than "the person who translated what Peter said from one language to another," and it may be he rather than Peter himself who wrote down 2 Peter after Peter's death. That letter appears to be a collection of Peter's sayings comparable to *The Teachings of Gordon B. Hinckley* rather than an original speech by Peter. If this is correct, then Mark might also be a collection of Peter's recollections recorded by Mark, perhaps after Peter's death.

According to the early Church historian, Eusebius, Clement (the bishop of Alexandria in the second century AD) said that Mark's Gospel was written for those being taught in Rome and that, after it was completed, Peter read it and ratified it for use in church. Though that seems to be reasonably possible, some other early writings say that Mark completed his gospel after Peter's death. If so, he may have been writing down the things he had learned from Peter. The Greek of Mark is much less sophisticated than that of the other Gospels, and he focuses on a series of brief and self-contained stories that prepare the reader for his lengthy treatment of the Garden of Gethsemane, the crucifixion, and the resurrection of Jesus. For Mark, events are the focus rather than doctrines. Eusebius also says that Mark did not put the events of his gospel "in order," but he is unclear as to what he means by "order."

Outline of Mark 1–5[1]

Mark 1:1–15	Jesus's mission was divinely ordained and he is in conflict with Satan
Mark 1:1	The title/theme of the work
Mark 1:2–8	John the Baptist
Mark 1:9–11	Jesus's baptism
Mark 1:12–13	The temptation in the wilderness
Mark 1:14–15	A summary of Jesus's mission: "Jesus came into Galilee, preaching the gospel of the kingdom of God, and saying, 'The time is fulfilled and the kingdom of God is at hand: repent ye and believe the gospel.'"

Mark 1:16–3:35	**Jesus has power from God (to which there is opposition, though he is always victorious)**
[Mark 1:16–20	Jesus calls Peter, Andrew, James, and John]
Mark 1:21–28	He heals a man of unclean spirit
Mark 1:29–31	He heals Peter's mother-in-law
Mark 1:32–34	He heals many others
Mark 1:35–39	He preaches throughout Galilee, healing many
Mark 1:40–45	He heals a leper
Mark 2:1–12	He heals a man of palsy and says specifically that he does so "that ye may know that the Son of Man hath power on earth to forgive sins" (Mark 2:10)
[Mark 2:13–28	Jesus calls Levi (Matthew) and confronts the Pharisees]
Mark 3:1–6	Jesus heals the man with the withered hand, drawing the Pharisees' criticism and enmity
Mark 3:7–12	Because of his healing—recognized by unclean spirits—he withdraws to a private place
[Mark 3:8–19	He teaches and ordains the Twelve]

Mark 3:20	The multitudes demand more miracles
Mark 3:21–30	His friends think he is mad and, urged on by scribes from Jerusalem, try to stop him. But he rebukes them
Mark 3:31–35	His family asks him to come out of the synagogue to meet with them. (The context suggests that they may also wish him to discontinue preaching.) He refuses and denies that they are his family
[Mark 4:1–34	The kingdom of God]
Mark 4:35–5:43	**Jesus has power from the Father, but his disciples do not understand that power**
Mark 4:35–41	Even the elements of the earth must obey him
Mark 5:1–20	He casts evil spirits out of a possessed man and into a herd of swine
Mark 5:21–43	He heals the daughter of Jairus and a woman with a hemorrhage

As you read Mark, you will notice that he concentrates on events, particularly conflict (between Christ and Satan, for example), more than he does on teachings. What might that say about how to understand his Gospel?

Mark 1

Verse 1: The first verse of Mark is ambiguous. It could mean that he is going to start with the beginning of Jesus's ministry: "This is how Jesus Christ's preaching began." Or it could mean "Here are the basic principles of the gospel of Jesus Christ." The phrase can also mean "the beginning of this book, which is the gospel of Jesus Christ." The phrase is ambiguous because the Greek word *archē* can mean either "beginning" (as it does in John 1:1)—and there are two ways to understand what is beginning here—or "basic principles," as it does in the Greek version of Psalm 110:10 (the Septuagint). Which reading do you think most fruitful?

Does Mark's focus on events, and especially conflict, suggest anything about how to understand verse 1?

Mark is the only evangelist to speak of "the gospel" without a qualifying adjective or pronoun. On that basis, however, we have come to describe the first four books of the Bible as gospels. Clearly Mark isn't merely telling the story of Christ's life. However we understand verse 1, Mark is proclaiming the gospel of Jesus Christ, the Son of God. When Mark tells us that he is writing the gospel, the "good news" or the proclamation, how is he telling us to read what follows?

To get a better feel for how Mark's audience would have heard verse 1, substitute "Jesus Messiah" or "Anointed Jesus" for "Jesus Christ." Does that substitution shed a different light on what we are to listen for as we read the Gospel of Mark?

Verse 8: John the Baptist tells us that he has baptized with water, a cleansing agent, but here he says that "the greater one" will baptize with the Holy Ghost. Does he intend us to see a parallel here: I baptize you with water, which cleanses in one way; he will baptize with the Holy Ghost, which cleanses in another way? (Does the use of fire as a metaphor for the Holy Ghost, as in Matthew 3:11 and 2 Nephi 31:13–14, suggest that parallel, or is something else going on?) If the baptism of the Holy Ghost is also a cleansing, what kind of cleansing is it?

Verse 9: Why does Mark begin with Jesus's baptism rather than with his birth?

Verse 15: Paraphrasing, we could say that Jesus's message is "The appointed time has arrived, the kingdom of God is near; repent and believe the gospel." What is Jesus speaking of when he refers to the appointed time? In what sense or senses is the divine kingdom near?

The Greek word translated *repent* is *metanoein*. Robert Guelich argues that *metanoein* is the equivalent of *šub* in the Hebrew Bible, usually translated as "return."[2] To repent is to return to God; it is to return to the covenant he made with Israel. How might that understanding of repentance and Jesus's message compare and contrast with our usual way of describing repentance and the cessation of particular bad acts?

Verses 17–20: Most of the time disciples choose their teachers/masters. In these verses, however, the master, Jesus, chooses his disciples. What significance does that reversal have?

The outline on pages 81–83 helps us see that Mark interrupts (indicated by brackets) his story of Jesus's power and the illustrations of that power, his miracles, to tell of the call of the disciples, the teaching and ordination of the Twelve, and the parables of the kingdom of God. So we could say that the primary theme of this section (indeed of Mark as a whole) is Jesus's power, but the secondary theme is the Church. Why would the theme of the Church be important for Mark? How is that theme related to the theme of power? Where is the power that we see in Christ manifest?

Verses 21–28: Mark does not often describe the works that Jesus does as miracles. (See, for example, Mark 6:2, 5, and 14.) When he does speak of miracles, he uses a Greek word that means "power" (*dynamis*), which is not the same word that the other evangelists use when they speak of miracles. They use a word that means "sign" (*semeion*). Does that difference say anything about how Mark sees Jesus's mission differently than the other writers see it? Why might Mark avoid using the word *sign* and instead use a word meaning "power" or "works" to describe Jesus's miracles?

What power has Jesus demonstrated in his works? How does his exhibition of power show who he is? For example, what can we understand his healing power to represent? His power over the wind and waves?

We see several instances where someone or something contests Jesus's power: in the temptation, when he healed the palsied man, in Levi's house, when he healed the man with the withered hand, when his friends and—perhaps—even some of his family try to stop him from preaching, and when he calmed the sea. Why does Mark tell us of these contests? What does he want us to learn from them?

Mark 4

Verses 3–23: N. T. Wright argues that those living at Jesus's time would have understood the parable of the sower as a description of the judgment of Israel similar to Isaiah 6 (and, therefore, also to Jacob 5).[3] Reading the parable with that in mind, can you reconstruct Wright's interpretation for yourself? What do you think of that interpretation? Does it teach us anything about our day?

Verses 1–33: Suppose that each of the parables in chapter 4 (the parable of the sower, of the candle under a bushel, of the seed growing secretly, and of the mustard seed) is a parable that teaches us about the Church. Do they all teach the same thing? If so, what is it? If not, what does each teach?

Why are these four parables followed by the story of Jesus stilling the winds and waves? What does the latter event have to do with those parables?

Mark 6

Verses 7–13: Notice that the stories of Jesus's power in the face of Satan's opposition lead, eventually, to Jesus sending the Twelve out as missionaries. How is the mission of the Twelve a culmination of the story of Jesus to this point?

Overall

Mark offers a testimony of Jesus. In the chapters we have read so far, who has Mark also shown offering a testimony

87

of who Jesus is? What do you make of that? What has Mark tried to show us by choosing to tell us of the particular testimonies he chooses to recount?

Lesson 8
Matthew 5

This lesson picks out the first part of a longer sermon. Matthew 5–7 give us Jesus's Sermon on the Mount. Even if you are preparing for only the Sunday School lesson, it is best to read the entire sermon to see the context of chapter 5.

During Jesus's time there seems to have been considerable controversy over who was "in" and who was "out" when it came to being the children of God. This controversy had been ongoing for some time, at least since the time of the return from exile. The Samaritan community was one of the earliest to be excluded, but they were not the only ones. We know of other groups, such as the Essenes who lived in Qumran and who left us the Dead Sea Scrolls. They thought of themselves as in, in other words as true to Israel's covenant, and everyone else as out. But, of course, everyone else thought the Essenes were out and their own group was in.

The controversy centered on a number of issues, but perhaps most prominent among them were questions like who had the right to be the temple high priest, whether the temple ritual had been corrupted, and what lineage had to do with being one of God's people. Besides the Essenes, this controversy had resulted in several often overlapping, more dominant groups (those supporting the temple priests, the Sadducees; the scribes, those who taught the Law; and the Pharisees, those who sought to reform Judaism by strict obedience to the Law and who rejected the Roman and Greek influences on Jewish culture). Though these groups were at odds with each other over such things as the resurrection and the importance of the temple, each claimed to be the authority on what salvation meant as well as who would be saved and who would not.

According to the Gospels, Jesus seems most often to have found himself at odds with the Pharisees. Contrary to what we sometimes hear, the Pharisees were not, as such, the leaders of the Jews, though some of them were among the leaders of the Sanhedrin and other leaders. The Pharisees were more or less comparable to a modern political party or lobby group, influencing those who govern. There were other parties also influential in Palestinian life, particularly the Sadducees. (The *Anchor Bible Dictionary* has excellent entries on the Pharisees, the Sadducees, and the Sanhedrin.) Many contemporary Jews consider the Pharisees to have been the forerunners of what became rabbinic Judaism, the kind of Judaism that most of us are most familiar with.

The Pharisees' answer to "Who's in?" was "Those who have the right lineage and who keep the Law as we interpret it." You can easily see why Jesus was often in conflict with these parties, particularly the Pharisees: their understanding of the Law was quite different from his—and LDS teaching makes that difference of understanding ironic because we teach that Jesus was Jehovah, the one who had given the Law to Moses. This difference over the question of lineage and over what obedience means makes more clear John the Baptist's rebuke of the Pharisees: "Bring forth fruits meet for repentance: and think not to say within yourselves, We have Abraham to our father" (Matthew 3:8–9). The Pharisees were preaching the Law and birthright rather than repentance. I think this also explains Jesus's ministry to so many of those who were excluded: those the Pharisees had decreed to be sinners, Samaritans, and so on. You might wish to reread Jesus's encounter with the woman at the Samaritan well (John 4:5–30), keeping in mind that she and her people were excluded from Judaism because of their lineage and because they understood the Law differently than did those in power.

Verse 1: In Matthew's Gospel, mountains are places where important things happen. (See Matthew 4:8; 17:1; and 28:16.) As he tells the story, Jesus seems deliberately to give the Sermon on the Mount in a way that compares him to Moses: he goes up on a mountain and delivers a "new" law for a multitude who are gathered at the base of the mountain waiting for his return. In Matthew 4:23, Matthew tells us "Jesus went about all Galilee, teaching in their synagogues, and preaching the gospel of the kingdom." In the chapters that follow, Matthew 5–7, we are given the gospel that he preached.

Joseph Smith's inspired emendation of Matthew 5:1 adds an interesting prologue to the sermon[1]:

KJV	JST
1 And seeing the multitudes, he went up into a mountain: and when he was set, his disciples came unto	1 And Jesus, seeing the multitudes, went up into a mountain; and when he was set down, his disciples came

him: 2 And he opened his mouth, and taught them, saying,

unto him; 2 And he opened his mouth, and taught them, saying,

3 Blessed are they who shall believe on me; and again, more blessed are they who shall believe on your words, when ye shall testify that ye have seen me and that I am.

4 Yea, blessed are they who shall believe on your words, and come down into the depth of humility, and be baptized in my name; for they shall be visited with fire, and the Holy Ghost, and shall receive a remission of their sins.

3 Blessed *are* the poor in spirit: for theirs is the kingdom of heaven.

5 Yea blessed are the poor in spirit, who come unto me; for theirs is the kingdom of heaven.

Joseph Smith's addition makes it even more clear that the Sermon on the Mount is an exposition of the gospel. It also changes the way we can understand verse 3: that verse becomes a summary of the gospel. Rather than the first in the list of beatitudes, it is the summary of the gospel, followed by the Beatitudes.

Seeing the sermon this way creates a chiasm, with mercy at its center:

> A They that *mourn* shall be *comforted* (verse 4)
>
>> B The meek shall *inherit* the earth (verse 5)
>>
>>> C Those who hunger and thirst for righteousness will be *filled [with the Holy Ghost]* (verse 6; compare 3 Nephi 12:6)
>>>
>>>> D The merciful will obtain *mercy* (verse 7)
>>>
>>> C' The pure in heart will *see God* (verse 8)
>>
>> B' Peacemakers will be the *children of God* (verse 9)
>
> A' Those who are *persecuted* for righteousness will *receive a great reward, the kingdom of heaven* (verses 10–12)

Why might the Beatitudes center on mercy? How is the theme of mercy related to the additions that Joseph Smith made to the beginning of the sermon? How is Jesus's message of mercy a challenge to the Pharisees and scribes? What would that message have meant to Jesus's audience? What does it mean to us today?

Verse 3: The word translated *blessed* is a poetic word that can also be translated *happy*. In Greek literature, it was used to describe the happy state in which the gods lived. What word in the Book of Mormon might be equivalent to blessed?

What does it mean to be poor in spirit? It cannot mean that one has a spirit that is poor or wanting, so what does it mean? Compare this verse to Isaiah 61:1. Does that comparison give you any ideas about how to understand this beatitude?

The Greek of this verse is usually translated as the King James translators have translated it: "for theirs is the kingdom of heaven." However, it could also be translated "for the kingdom of heaven is made up of them." Does this different translation add any meaning?

Verse 4: Compare this verse to Isaiah 61:2. What does that comparison suggest?

Verse 5: Notice the footnote in the LDS edition of the Bible for the word *meek*. The meek and the poor in spirit seem to me to be the same people. Later in the sermon, Jesus will give examples of meekness. (See Matthew 5:39–42.) Note, too, that this verse is a quotation of Psalm 37:11 (in the Greek version of first-century Judaism). Why would Jesus quote from the Old Testament so much in this explication of his gospel?

Verse 6: The word that is translated *righteousness* could also have been translated *justice*. One way to think about what it means to be righteous is to ask, "What would it mean for me to be just?" How does changing the question in that way change our thinking?

As the word translated *righteousness* is used in Greek, it most often refers to one who has right relations with God. What did the Pharisees believe was required for righteousness? When might our righteousness be like that of the Pharisees? What does Jesus teach about righteousness?

Verse 7: Is it significant that the previous beatitudes had focused on something like attitude and that this beatitude begins a focus that is more on action?

What does *mercy* mean? What does it take to be merciful? How are the requirement to desire justice (verse 6) and the requirement to be merciful related to each other?

Verse 8: The word translated *pure* could also have been translated *cleansed*. What does it mean to have a heart that has been cleansed? Is Jesus contrasting the cleansing of the heart with the various kinds of cleansing that the Pharisees required? How do the two differ? What does it mean to see God?

Verse 9: Who do you think that Jesus has in mind when he speaks of the peacemakers? Do verses 23–26 give us an idea of what he means?

What does it mean that the peacemakers *will* be called the children of God? Aren't we already his children?

Why might Jesus have associated being a peacemaker with being a child of God? In what senses is God *the* peacemaker? How do you square the understanding of God as peacemaker with the stories of God in the Old Testament?

Verses 10–12: Verse 10 speaks of being persecuted "for righteousness' sake." Verse 11 speaks of being persecuted "for my sake." What do you make of what appears to be the identification of righteousness and Jesus, a person? How does that contrast with the Pharisaic understanding of righteousness? When you preach obedience, do you do so as Christ did or do you do so as the Pharisees did?

Is the beginning of verse 12, "Rejoice, and be exceeding glad," parallel to "Blessed are [. . .]" in the previous beatitudes? Does it help us understand what it means to be blessed?

We can see a division in the sermon at verse 11: The Beatitudes give us the general description of the gospel, and the verses that follow expand on that general description.

Verses 13–16: Verse 16 explains the other verses in this group. Compare 3 Nephi 18:24. What does verse 16 teach us about good works? What is their purpose?

Verses 17–20: What does it mean to say that Jesus did not come to annul the Law? What does it mean to say that he came to fulfill it, to bring it to perfection?

How does Jesus's understanding of perfect obedience to the Law differ from the Pharisees' understanding? Verses 21–48 seem to be illustrations of the point that Jesus is making in verse 20: he gives concrete illustrations of how our righteousness ought to go beyond the righteousness of the Pharisees. How are we tempted to be Pharisaic? How can we go beyond, exceed, or overflow (to use another translation of the Greek idiom) our own Pharisaism?

Verses 21–26: Jesus seems to be giving examples of what he meant when he spoke of peacemakers in verse 9.

The word translated *judgment* in verse 21 means "to be cast off."

Notice that the Book of Mormon and the JST omit "without a cause" in verse 22—as do almost all Greek manuscripts. How does that change our understanding of the verse?

In verse 22 the word *raca* means the same thing as the Greek word translated *fool* at the end of the verse. It isn't any stronger than the kinds of things we sometimes say to each other when we are angry, such as "You idiot!" What does Jesus mean, then, when he says, paraphrasing, "Whoever calls his brother a fool is in danger of the community's judgment, but whoever says 'You fool' is in danger of hell fire"? Does it make a difference that the first case is about anger towards a brother and no one is specified in the second?

What is the point of verses 21–22?

To a Jew of Jesus's day, worship was the most sacred duty that one could have. So what is Jesus saying about reconciliation in verses 23–24? Notice that we begin with the prohibition of murder in verse 21, move to the prohibition of anger in verse 22, and, in verse 23, find a prohibition of hard feelings. Can you think of particular adversaries that Jesus might have in mind in verses 25–26? How do these examples apply to us?

Verse 28: What does this teach us about going beyond the righteousness of the Pharisees?

Verses 29–30: Jesus is obviously speaking hyperbolically. What is the point of his hyperbole?

Verses 31–32: The scripture to which Jesus refers (Deuteronomy 24:1) is unclear about the grounds for divorce. It says that a man can put away his wife if he finds something shameful in her ("some uncleanness" in the King James Version). In the late classical and early medieval texts that we have, the rabbis debated that phrase, some arguing that it meant only adultery, others arguing that it could be something as trivial as bad cooking. Presumably the same kinds of debates were had in the early first century.

It also isn't easy to know how to understand the exception that Jesus allows here, because it isn't clear what Matthew means by the word translated *fornication*. The Greek word that he uses literally means "prostitution." How do you understand these verses? Are they a higher standard than we presently are required to live, or has the standard changed?

Verses 33–37: The part of the Law that Jesus has in mind here seems to be that found in places such as Exodus 20:7, Leviticus 19:12, Numbers 30:3, and Deuteronomy 23:22. How does the teaching in these verses go beyond the righteousness of the Pharisees? How does the teaching of these verses apply to us?

Verses 38–42: It appears that the Mosaic law, "an eye for an eye," was not a directive as to how much punishment to inflict, but a limitation on the retribution one could seek: if someone puts out your eye, you have no right to demand more than the recompense for that eye.

A more accurate translation of the first part of verse 39 might be "resist not the one who troubles you (or 'the one who defies you')."

What do these verses teach us about how we are to respond to physical violence? How does this teaching compare to what we find in D&C 98:16–48? How does it compare to the way that the Book of Mormon prophets dealt with violence?

What do these verses teach us about how we should deal with others in legal contention? The demand of verse 41 is one dictated by Roman law: a Roman soldier could compel others to carry his baggage a mile, so the general topic seems to be something like "the demands of the government." How would people in Jesus's day have understood this part of his message? What do these verses teach us about how we should respond to the demands of government?

Compare verse 42 to Mosiah 4:16–23. What obligation is Jesus teaching us in verse 42?

Verses 43–47: The Old Testament teaches that we must love our neighbor. (See Leviticus 19:18.) But nowhere does it teach that we should hate our enemies. However, it is not difficult to imagine that many believed that the command to love our neighbors (those close to us) implies the need to hate our enemies. It is easy to infer the latter, hate for enemies, from the former, the command to love neighbors, even though the inference is logically unjustified. What particular enemies does verse 44 suggest that Jesus may have had in mind?

What reason does verse 45 give for loving our enemies? What does verse 45 suggest that it means to be one of God's children?

Verse 48: This verse marks a significant break in the Sermon on the Mount. It is the culmination of the sermon to this point. As such perhaps we should understand it as a restatement of verse 3—as well as a follow-up to verses 43–47. Can you think of ways in which those verses mean the same? How does the commandment in this verse sum up the teaching that we should love our enemies?

Pay attention to the footnote that explains what *perfect* means: whole, complete, finished, developed. A better translation of the verse might be "Be ye therefore whole, even as your Father in heaven is whole." Is the perfection or wholeness of which Jesus speaks here a perfection of love?

99

Or perhaps Jesus is quoting or paraphrasing Leviticus 19:2 here: "Ye shall be holy: for I the Lord your God am holy." What does it mean to be holy? The Hebrew word in Leviticus means "sacred" or "set apart." What does that suggest about what it means for us to be holy? For us to be whole? How has Jesus been teaching the answer to that question in the preceding verses?

James speaks of the double-minded person and his spiritual instability (James 1:8). What does it mean to be double-minded? In contrast, what does it mean to be whole? Can we be whole in this life? If not, then why has Jesus commanded us to be whole?

Is wholeness something that pertains only to myself—I must be undivided—or is it something that also pertains to my relationships with others, including God? What would it mean for a relationship not to be whole? How do we make our relationships with other persons whole?

Taken in its entirety, how does the Sermon on the Mount teach us to be perfect?

Does the chiasm that centers on verse 7 suggest anything about how we are to be perfect, about what constitutes our wholeness?

Is it possible to use the concept of mercy to restate or rethink each of the specific discussions that we saw in verses 11–47?

Lesson 9
Matthew 6–7

As is true for many of the Sunday School lessons, there is a lot of material to cover in this lesson. But the material in these chapters is so important that it would be a shame to focus on only part of it. So I will focus on the Lord's Prayer (Matthew 6:5–15), but I will also make notes for the rest of both chapters.

Matthew 6

Jesus continues to teach about true righteousness, a righteousness that goes beyond mere obedience. He first discusses three basic acts of piety in first-century Judaism: almsgiving, prayer, and fasting (verses 1–18). Then he teaches where we will find our treasure (verses 19–23), and he teaches us that we ought to serve God without taking thought for ourselves (verses 24–34). Is there a connection between these three teachings (piety, treasure, and not taking thought)?

Verses 1–4: In verse 1 the Greek word translated "to be seen" is a word related to the theater. We might loosely translate it "to be a spectacle." In verse 2 the word translated *hypocrites* could also be translated *actor* in other circumstances. Rather than "someone who pretends to be something good that he is not," the word had more to do with being an interpreter of words and ideas. For most Greek-speaking people, hypocrisy didn't have the negative meaning that we associate with it until long after Jesus's time. However, in the Greek translation of the Hebrew Bible the word *hypocrite* is used to denote someone who profanes or pollutes holy things.[1]

What is Matthew emphasizing by using these words to tell us Jesus's teaching? Why would the charge of hypocrisy—causing pollution—be particularly galling to the Pharisees?

What does Jesus mean when he says that those who give in public "have their reward"? It is easy to condemn those whom Jesus describes in verses 1 and 2, but how difficult is it to live the teachings of verses 3 and 4? In other words, how tempting is it, when we do good, to tell someone, to get our reward from other people's recognition of our good deed? What about when we do something because "it gives me a good feeling"? Are we doing it for reward, and if we are, what does that say about our deed?

Some may see a conflict between the doctrine taught in these verses and that taught in Matthew 5:13–16. How would you reconcile that seeming conflict?

Verses 5–15: In the Greek it is clear that the Savior is making a strong contrast here: They pray that way, but *you* should pray this way. To learn more about the Savior's teaching here, compare the Lord's Prayer in the Book of Mormon and in Matthew.

Joseph Smith said, "I have a key by which I understand the scriptures. I enquire, what was the question which drew out the answer, or caused Jesus to utter the parable? . . . To ascertain its meaning, we must dig up the root and ascertain what it was that drew the saying out of Jesus."[2] In Matthew, to whom is the Lord speaking and why? What's the occasion? Ask the same questions about the Nephi version of the sermon. Do the different answers to those questions for the Book of Mormon and the New Testament give the two versions different meanings? What might some of those differences in meaning be? What advantages are there for us to have two almost identical versions of scriptural passages?

Here is a side-by-side comparison of the Matthew prayer and the Nephite prayer, with some notes about language inserted in a smaller typeface. I have followed each section with questions that the comparison raised for me.

3 NEPHI 13:5–15	MATTHEW 6:5–15
5 And when thou prayest thou shalt not do as the hypocrites, for they love to pray, standing in the synagogues and in the corners of the streets, that they may be seen of men. Verily I say unto you, they have their reward.	5 And when thou prayest, thou shalt not be as the hypocrites are: for they love to pray standing in the synagogues and in the corners of the streets, that they may be seen of men. Verily I say unto you, They have their reward.

hypocrites: See the earlier discussion of this word.

reward: "pay" or "wage"

What kind of prayer is the Savior condemning here? How is it a matter of acting? Of polluting holy things? Of dissembling? Does that condemnation apply to our public prayers, such as those in church? If not, why not?

How is pay a good description of what the hypocrites receive?

The previous verses were about almsgiving. How does this discussion of prayer follow from the previous verses?

To the Nephites, the Savior says "thou shalt not *do* as the hypocrites." Matthew's version says "thou shalt not *be*." What does each teach? How is public prayer a reward?

3 NEPHI 13:5–15	MATTHEW 6:5–15
6 But thou, when thou prayest, enter into thy closet, and when thou hast shut thy door, pray to thy Father who is in secret; and thy Father, who seeth in secret, shall reward thee openly.	6 But thou, when thou prayest, enter into thy closet, and when thou hast shut thy door, pray to thy Father which is in secret; and thy Father which seeth in secret shall reward thee openly.
	closet: an inner chamber, a storeroom
	secret: hidden, concealed
	reward: literally, "give forth"; a strong way to say "give"
	openly: "clearly" or "publicly"

Given the problem of doing good for a reward, why does the Lord follow this exemplary prayer with a promise of reward? What question is he addressing? What kind of reward might this refer to?

This verse is parallel in structure to verse 4: the teaching about prayer is like the teaching about almsgiving. Verse 4 tells us that the Father sees in secret. What does that mean? This says the Father is in secret (using the same Greek word). What does that mean?

3 Nephi 13:5–15	Matthew 6:5–15
7 But when ye pray, use not vain repetitions, as the heathen, for they think that they shall be heard for their much speaking.	7 But when ye pray, use not vain repetitions, as the heathen do: for they think that they shall be heard for their much speaking.
	vain repetitions: The Greek word means "stammering, babbling"
	heathen: a foreigner
	heard: have their requests granted

Who were the heathen? They were not the same as those Jesus called hypocrites. Against what is Jesus warning? Why warn against the prayers not only of the hypocrites but also of the heathen? Could the parallel suggest that those who pray using vain repetitions are like those who do not recognize the God of Israel?

3 Nephi 13:5–15	Matthew 6:5–15
8 Be not ye therefore like unto them, for your Father knoweth what things ye have need of before ye ask him.	8 Be not ye therefore like unto them: for your Father knoweth what things ye have need of, before ye ask him.

Compare verses 24–35 and D&C 84:80–84. How are the two parts of this verse related? In other words, what does the connective *for* mean here?

Verse 8 may give us hints for understanding verse 7 better. The word *therefore* suggests that verse 8 is an explanation of verse 7. How does the fact that our Father already knows our needs explain why we should avoid vain repetitions?

3 Nephi 13:5–15	Matthew 6:5–15
9 After this manner therefore pray ye: Our Father who art in heaven, hallowed be thy name.	9 After this manner therefore pray ye: Our Father which art in heaven, Hallowed be thy Name.
	after this manner: translates a Greek phrase that literally means only "this"
	hallowed: holy

What does it mean to pray that the Father's name be holy? Do we do that? When?

3 Nephi 13:5–15	Matthew 6:5–15
10 Thy will be done on earth as it is in heaven.	10 Thy kingdom come. Thy will be done in earth, as it is in heaven.
	will: what one wishes to happen.

The Greek of verses 9 and 10 emphasizes the word *thy*. Why?

What does it mean to pray that the Father's kingdom "come"? Why does the Lord omit "Thy kingdom come" when he gives the Lord's Prayer in the New World? What is the kingdom of the Father? What does it mean to pray that the Father's will be done on earth as it is in heaven? Do perhaps the first three petitions of this prayer mean essentially the same thing? If so, why are they repeated? How do we pray for these things in our personal and public prayers?

MATTHEW 6:5–15

11 Give us this day our daily bread.

daily bread: the meaning of the Greek word here is uncertain, but it is usually taken to mean the bread that is sufficient for a day. Compare the story of manna (see Exodus 16 and John 6:48).

Why does the Lord omit "Give us this day our daily bread" in the New World? To what does this part of the prayer correspond in our own prayers? What might its omission in the 3 Nephi version suggest? Some have suggested that "daily bread" really refers to the bread that will be shared at the Messianic banquet. (See Matthew 8:11.)

To what else might it refer? Is this petition at odds with the teaching we will see in verses 25–34?

3 Nephi 13:5–15	Matthew 6:5–15
11 And forgive us our debts, as we forgive our debtors.	12 And forgive us our debts, as we forgive our debtors.

forgive: The Greek word means "send away" or "abandon."

debts: This is a literal translation: "something owed."

debtor: This is another literal translation: "one who owes."

How are our sins debts? What does this verse tell us about how our relation with others affects our salvation?

3 Nephi 13:5–15	Matthew 6:5–15
12 And lead us not into temptation, but deliver us from evil. 13 For thine is the kingdom, and the power, and the glory, forever. Amen.	13 And lead us not into temptation, but deliver us from evil: For thine is the kingdom, and the power, and the glory, for ever. Amen.

lead: "to bring into," "to lead"

temptation: The Greek word, from a word meaning "to pierce," means "going beyond the limits." Therefore, the word means "to sin."

deliver: a middle-voiced verb (similar to our passive) meaning "to flow" in the active voice.

Thus it means "draw us away from."

evil: The Greek word means "that which causes pain" or "that which is lacking"; it could mean either "evil" or "the evil one."

power: This could also be translated *virtue*.

Why does the Lord speak of the Father *leading* us into temptation in both versions? What are we to make of that metaphor?

Paraphrased, the final clause says "because the kingdom and the power and the glory belong to thee forever." Why does this begin with *because*? In other words, what does that clause explain?

3 Nephi 13:5–15	Matthew 6:5–15
14 For, if ye forgive men their trespasses your heavenly Father will also forgive you; 15 But if ye forgive not men their trespasses neither will your Father forgive your trespasses.	14 For if ye forgive men their trespasses, your heavenly Father will also forgive you: 15 But if ye forgive not men their trespasses, neither will your Father forgive your trespasses.

forgive: "cancel"

trespass: literally, "falling aside"; therefore, "false step" or "sin"

These two verses aren't part of the prayer itself, but a comment on it. Why do you think that the only part of the prayer commented on is the part about asking for forgiveness?

Verses 16–18: In the early books of the Old Testament, fasting is a sign of mourning or repentance, accompanied by wearing sackcloth and ashes. These verses parallel the form used in discussing almsgiving and for the beginning of the discussion of prayer. As in each of the previous cases, the emphasis is on going beyond what was then considered to be the standard of righteousness. What would it mean to go beyond the standard of righteousness for fasting in Jesus's day? What would it mean in our day?

Do we have community or cultural standards of righteousness? Are we expected to go beyond those? How? Does this mean, for example, that rather than paying a 10 percent tithe, we should pay 12 percent or 15 percent? Or that we should fast all three meals on the first Sunday of the month rather than the two required by the Church? How do we distinguish between good forms of going beyond the requirements of the law and bad forms?

Verses 19–23: Only righteousness—about which Jesus is giving a new teaching—results in anything of lasting value, and what we treasure tells us what we value. How do we recognize righteousness and avoid Pharisaism?

Verses 24–34: Verse 24 provides a transition to a new theme: we cannot serve both God and possessions (mammon).

Verses 25–31 give various examples of what that means: we need not take thought for ourselves and our provisions because God will provide. "Take no thought" might be better translated "don't be anxious" or "don't worry." How does that change your understanding of these verses and what Jesus commands?

President John Taylor once taught that these verses do not apply to people generally, but to those who serve in the Church through the priesthood.[3] How do these verses apply to them? If that is right, does it follow that the rest of us *ought* to worry? In what ways? *Are* there healthy ways of worrying about the things we possess?

How does verse 33 explain verses 24–32?

What does "Sufficient unto the day is the evil thereof" mean? It isn't a quotation from scripture, but seems to be a proverb of the time.

Matthew 7

The sermon concludes with a series of sayings that are not necessarily related to one another. These may not have originally been part of the Sermon on the Mount itself. Matthew may have known about these teachings from other times and added them as a collection to the end of the sermon.

Verses 1–5: The Greek word translated *judge* is a very strong word. It means "condemn or cut off." When are we guilty of the kind of judgment of which Jesus speaks here? Notice the insertion that Joseph Smith makes in these verses. How does that clarify or change their meaning?

Verse 6: What is Jesus teaching here? Whom is he thinking of?

The terms *dogs* and *swine* were among the most derogatory terms of the time. Some have thought that he is prohibiting the disciples from preaching to the Gentiles. What do you think of that explanation?

When would we be giving holy things to the dogs or casting our pearls before swine? How do we avoid doing so?

Verses 7–11: The Lord's Prayer in Matthew 6:9–13 keeps petition to only one line (verse 11), and the version that the Savior gave to the Nephites in 3 Nephi 13:9–13 omits it altogether. What does that say about the form our prayers ought to take?

Here in Matthew 7, however, we see that we are commanded to petition for our needs. Is there a contradiction between the Lord's Prayer and these verses? Explain what you think.

In these verses, is Jesus emphasizing what the Father gives or what we ask? What difference does your answer to that question make?

If the Father already knows our needs (Matthew 6:8, 32), why should we petition at all?

In verse 11 Jesus calls those to whom he speaks evil. Is he being hyperbolic? Why does he use that term?

Verse 12: This is one version of the Golden Rule. How is it related to Leviticus 19:18? Can a person who is not pure in heart use the Golden Rule as an accurate standard of his conduct? What problem might he encounter using it?

Verses 13–14: Remember that the word *strait* means "narrow": the gate leading to destruction is wide and the road to destruction is spacious, but the gate leading to life—eternal life—is narrow. What does it mean to say that few find the strait gate? Why don't we find it?

Verses 15–20: We can recognize prophets by their fruits. Notice that verse 19 is a word-for-word repetition of John the Baptist's teaching (Matthew 3:10). Why was this teaching particularly important at Jesus's time? How is it important to us today? Where do we encounter false prophets?

Verses 21–23: To whom is Jesus referring when he speaks of those who say "Lord, Lord" to him? Of those who prophesy in his name? Of those who do miracles in his name? Why would some who did these things be excluded from his presence? How can prophesying in Jesus's name and working miracles be iniquitous? Do any of the teachings that have come before this in the sermon answer that question?

Verses 24–27: What does it mean to hear the sayings of Jesus and to do them? What does it mean to hear them and not do them? How do these verses relate to Deuteronomy 6:4–9? How do they relate to Matthew 7:21–23?

Verses 28–29: There have been debates about when Jesus was talking to the crowd and when he was talking to his disciples in the Sermon on the Mount. Verse 28 suggests that whatever the answer to that question, the people gathered at the bottom of the hill were listening, for his teachings amazed them. The Greek word translated *authority* means "authority by commission," so they heard his teachings as the teachings of God rather than as merely the scriptural interpretations of the scribes. Compare this to Alma 17:3.

Lesson 10

Matthew 11:28–30; 12:1–13; Luke 7:36–50; 13:10–17

Matthew 11

Verse 28: What does it mean to come to Christ? Has he already told us how we can do that in readings from some of the previous lessons?

The word translated *labor* means "wearying labor." The phrase "heavy laden" translates a Greek word that means "weighed down." What wearying, taxing work does Christ have in mind here? From what does he offer relief? Why is that described as something that wears us out? As something that burdens us? The word translated *rest* literally means "cessation." It is used to mean "refreshment," "ease," or "rest." How does the Savior offer cessation from taxing labor? How does he offer refreshment?

Verse 29: The word translated *take* means literally "lift up." The Greek word translated *yoke* could also have been translated *scales* (the kind of scales one sees in statues representing justice). Does that suggest what kind of yoke Jesus has in mind? How would it be different from a yoke used on oxen?

Do you agree with the KJV decision to translate the term as *yoke*, or do you think *scales* would have been more meaningful? Why?

In the Old Testament the yoke was often used as a symbol of tyranny. (See, for example, 2 Chronicles 10:4.) Why do you think that was? Why do you think Jesus uses an image that is usually associated with being subjugated by a tyrant?

How do we learn of Christ? In other words, when he commands us, "Learn of me," what is he commanding? The root of the Greek word translated *learn* means "to direct one's mind toward something." That results in a variety of meanings, including "to experience" and "to learn a skill" as well as "to know." In the Greek translation of the Old Testament (the version many used at the time of Christ), the word translated *know* is used almost exclusively to mean "learn the will of God." Might that tell us something about what Jesus is teaching in this verse?

Should we understand "come to me" and "learn of me" to be parallel?

The word translated *meek* means "mild," "gentle," "friendly" and occurs in Matthew's writings more than in the other Gospels. Why does Matthew use the word so often in comparison to other writers?

The word translated *lowly* means not only "lowly" but also "modest," "humble," "obedient," "compliant," and the verb from which it comes can mean "to level." Is "meek and lowly of heart" a hendiadys, a case of saying the same thing twice (as in Genesis 1:1: "without form and void"), rather than a case of saying two different things?

In the Hebrew Bible (e.g., Proverbs 16:19) meekness and lowliness are associated with each other, and Daniel 3:87 speaks of lowliness of heart, using the same Greek phrase used here in the Greek translation of the Old Testament, the Septuagint. Do those connections to the Old Testament tell us anything about how to understand this verse?

Verse 30: The Greek word translated *light* means "serviceable" or "useful." How might that change our ordinary understanding of what Jesus is teaching here?

Verses 28–30: Both the *Hermeneia* volume on Matthew on Matthew 8–20 and the first volume on Matthew in *Word Biblical Commentary* suggest that this saying is part of the Old Testament Wisdom tradition.[1] (That is the literary tradition that produced works such as Proverbs, Ecclesiastes, and Job.) Here Jesus speaks as Wisdom herself has spoken. See, particularly, Sirach 6:23–31, which has many similarities to this saying. Sirach is part of the Apocrypha. Does that connection to Wisdom literature suggest any fruitful interpretations of this passage?

What makes the Pharisaic law a burden? How is the way of Christian life (life following the law of Christ, following Wisdom) an easy one? After all, Jesus has already said that he doesn't preach a less strict law than the Law of the Torah (Matthew 5:17–20). If we feel that living as a Christian is burdensome, what should we conclude from these verses?

Do these verses advocate that we respond to the trials of our life merely inwardly, seeing trouble as something pertaining to the world and thus seeking peace only in our hearts but not necessarily in our external circumstances? If not, how do we square these verses with the truth that, as Ernst Bloch says, Jesus "is anything but an artful dodger into invisible inwardness, or a sort of quartermaster for a totally transcendent heavenly Kingdom"?[2]

How would you use your own words to paraphrase these verses? How would you explain what they teach to someone who didn't understand them?

Matthew 12

Are the stories that follow supposed to illustrate what Jesus meant by the easy yoke?

Verses 1–9: This story is one of a number of stories that center on the controversy between Jesus and the religious authorities. (See Matthew 9:1–8 for the beginnings of that controversy.) If you've been on a grain farm, you probably know that you can pluck a head of grain and rub the kernels between your palms to get rid of the husk. Then you can blow away the chaff and chew on the threshed grains for a snack. This practice was permitted by the Mosaic law. (See Deuteronomy 23:26.) But the rabbis had decided that, though it was permitted, it was a kind of work and so was not permitted on the Sabbath. Jesus replies to the scribes (in other words, the rabbis) with a good rabbinical argument, namely an argument from scripture: first, David ate what was unlawful for him to eat (see Leviticus 24:5–9), but that violation of the Law was justified because he had nothing else to eat (see 1 Samuel 21:2–7); second, the priests in the temple work on the Sabbath, and that work is justified by the fact that it is done for a holy purpose.

This last example becomes an affront to the scribes, for Jesus explicitly says that what the disciples are doing is justified by the fact that they are in the service of someone—or something, the Greek could be translated either way—greater than the temple. Which do you think Jesus is saying is greater than the temple, some*thing*, presumably the principle of mercy, or some*one*, perhaps Jesus himself?

Jesus quotes Hosea 6:6 in verse 7: "For I desired mercy, and not sacrifice; and the knowledge of God more than burnt offerings." He tells the scribes that if they had understood that scripture they wouldn't have accused the disciples. How would understanding that have saved them from their mistake? In other words, what does understanding that mercy is more important than sacrifice have to do with this particular case?

Verses 10–13: The first disagreement with the religious authorities over the Sabbath is immediately followed by a second. Why do you think the dispute over the Sabbath was so important?

It appears that the rabbis allowed for healing on the Sabbath if death was likely, but not otherwise. Jesus heals a withered hand, something that *could* have waited until the next day. Jesus heals the man's hand in response to a challenge from the scribes: "Is it lawful to heal on the sabbath days?" Why does he take up their argument? Why not just ignore them? Why does he respond with a deed rather than an argument?

How do we know when we should respond to the challenges of those who attack us rather than ignore them? How do we know what kind of response is most appropriate?

Verses 9–14: One contemporary commentary understands these verses as chiastic:[3]

119

A 9 And when he went away from there, he came into their synagogue.

B 10 And behold, (there was) a man with a rigid hand.

C And they asked him and said, "Is one permitted to heal on the Sabbath" so that they might accuse him.

D 11 But he said to them: "Who among you will be the person who has a single sheep, and if it falls into a pit on the Sabbath will not grasp it and lift it out? 12 How much more than a sheep is a person?

C' Therefore, one may do good on the Sabbath."

B' 13 Then he said to the man: "Stretch out your hand." And he stretched it out, and it became whole again, like the other.

A' 14 But the Pharisees went out and took counsel against him to destroy him.

What does this chiasmus make most important to the story? So what?

Luke 7

Verse 36: Given the Pharisees' hostility to Jesus, it was brave of this Pharisee, named Simon, to invite Jesus to his house for dinner. (See Luke 7:36 and 11:37 for two other occasions when Pharisees do this.) What do you think might have motivated Simon? What do you make of the fact that each time he was invited to dine with a Pharisee, Jesus did something that scandalized his host?

Verses 37–38: The word translated *sinner* isn't used to describe the general condition of human beings: we are all sinners, but that is not the point of this word. (See verse 40.) Most have assumed that the woman was engaged in a dishonorable profession (an occupation that the Pharisees assumed disposed one toward sin), and there were many such occupations. Among the dishonorable professions were shepherds and shopkeepers, weavers and launderers, tax collectors and copper smelters. For women the most common was arguably prostitution. Perhaps Luke is implying that the woman is being described as a prostitute. That he adds "in the city" to her description may suggest as much. But that isn't necessarily the case. She could also be someone married to an outcast, such as a publican or a weaver. Given the Pharisees' interpretation of the Law, there was no significant difference between the alternatives.

But Jesus and his disciples didn't follow the Pharisaic interpretation of the Law, as we have just seen and as we will see in Matthew 15:2, where they do not observe the handwashing rituals of the Pharisees. Thus, the word *sinner* would equally have described them. We don't know what ointment the woman used. The Greek word translated *ointment* refers to any oil rendered from animal fat or any vegetable oil except olive oil, for which there is another word. Mark may tell us that it was spikenard, a musky-smelling perfume ointment made from a plant found in India. (This assumes that the incident in Mark and this incident are the same; they may not be.)

What is the significance of the woman's washing of Jesus's feet? Is it significant that she washes them with her tears? What does anointment suggest? Can we understand what she does symbolically as looking forward to the crucifixion? If so, how so?

Verses 39: On what grounds does this Pharisee believe that Jesus cannot be a prophet? What kinds of similar arguments are made today regarding modern prophets? What is the proper response to such arguments?

Verses 40–42: In verse 39 we saw that Simon was thinking to himself. What does Jesus's answer to his complaint show? How is that relevant to Simon's accusation?

Verse 43: What kind of attitude does Simon's "I suppose" suggest? Has the parable brought him to repentance?

Verses 44–47: The translation of these verses makes it appear that the woman is forgiven because she loves. That translation, however, is problematic. A better translation would say that she loves because she is forgiven. What is the difference?

What does Jesus's rebuke of Simon tell us about how Simon has treated Jesus? Why didn't Simon provide water to wash Jesus's feet, kiss him in greeting, or anoint his head?

Verses 48–50: Why do the onlookers ask, "Who is this that forgiveth sins *also*?" When did the woman exercise faith?

Luke 13

Verses 10–13: Luke often shows Jesus showing regard for women, especially for women in difficulty. Given the culture of his day, how is that significant? What lesson is in this for us today?

Verse 14: Why does the head of the synagogue address the crowd rather than Jesus? It is obvious that his reproach is aimed at Jesus.

Why is healing on the Sabbath such an issue? Is there any symbolic significance to the fact that Jesus insists on healing on the Sabbath? In fact, he is portrayed as flaunting before the scribes and Pharisees the fact that he heals on the Sabbath. Why?

Verses 15–17: Why does Jesus call the head of the synagogue a pretender, a dissembler? What is his pretense?

Though they are not the same, the Greek word translated *loose* here is related to the Greek word translated *loosed* in verse 12. What point is Matthew making by using related Greek words? It appears that tying and loosing knots were among the forbidden kinds of work on the Sabbath, though some knots were exempt. Does that matter to our understanding of these verses?

The Greek verb translated *ashamed* can also be translated *dishonored* and it can also be used to describe someone whose hopes have been dashed. How might each of those meanings give us a different understanding of verse 17? What is the point of the contrast that Luke makes between the response of Jesus's adversaries and the response of "all the people"?

Lesson 11
Matthew 13

We get the word *parable* from a Greek word (*parabolē*) meaning "to set aside" or "to compare." It is a translation of a Hebrew word (*mashal*) that we usually translate as *proverb*, but we might better translate that word as *wise saying*. The Hebrew word covers a wide range of things, from what we call proverbs and what we call parables to what we might call a sermon.

During Jesus's time parables appear to have been used by many teachers. Usually they were given in answer to a question, often a question asked by a follower; and they not only answered the question asked but did so by showing that there is more to the answer than the follower thought. Used that way, parables are a way of making the questioner think about his question.

As Joseph Smith pointed out, it is often very helpful to ask ourselves what the question was that produced the answer (see the study materials for lesson 8), what answer might have been expected, and how the parable goes beyond the answer that might have been expected. We may also want to ask ourselves what question *we* might have to which the parable is an answer and how that answer goes beyond what we might have expected.

N. T. Wright argues that Jesus's hearers would not have heard the parable of the sower as we do. Instead, they would have heard it as a parable about Israel's exile and return, comparable to Isaiah 6 and Jacob.[1] For them the point would have been that Israel has been sown in Palestine, but only some have hearkened to Jesus's revelation of the kingdom of God. However, if Wright is correct, why doesn't this parable begin, as others do, with "The kingdom of God is like . . ."?

Whether Wright's interpretation of the parable is correct or not, he makes what I think is an insightful remark: "The parable itself is a parable about parables and their effect: this is the only way that the spectacular truth can be told, and it is bound to have the effect that some will look and look and never see, while others find the mystery suddenly unveiled, and they see what God is doing."[2]

Verses 1–2: Chapter 12 seems to begin in a grain field, but it ends indoors, perhaps in a synagogue, perhaps in a private home. At the end of chapter 12, Jesus rebukes the Pharisees for thinking him evil and for asking for a sign, and he uses the visit of his family to make the point that anyone who does the will of the Father is Jesus's brother. Here in chapter 13, he goes back outside and sits by the seaside to teach. When a large crowd gathers, he moves to a boat slightly offshore. Why does do so? How will that help him teach?

As you read this chapter, think about how these teachings relate to what has come before them. What kinds of people are in the crowd? Are there likely to be scribes and Pharisees among them? Why? Who do you think would compose the majority of the multitude? Are the disciples also there? What teaching problem does this mixture of people present? How does Jesus deal with that problem?

Verses 3–8: Verse 3 begins, "He spake many things to them in parables, saying . . ." Then Matthew recounts the parable of the sower. How do you explain that introduction to the parable? Is Matthew doing more than merely recounting the parable Jesus told? In the parable Jesus seems to describe a very ordinary set of circumstances. The farmer has plowed his field. Remember that he did this by hand and that only the rich could afford an animal to pull the plow, so the audience probably doesn't have in mind someone plowing with an animal. The result is that he doesn't plow deep or evenly. But as he plows, not every spot in the field is equally good for planting: there are paths in it beaten down by those crossing the field, there are stony areas, some of the thorny weeds were not plowed under and have survived, and even the places with good ground have different yields. Though the farmer knows this, when he sows seed, he seems to sow it over the entire field, regardless of its quality for planting. Why? Is the yield—one hundred times, sixty times, and thirty times what was sown in the good soil—what the farmer would expect, or is it a surprising yield?

What does this parable teach? It doesn't come in direct response to a question, but what is the implicit question that it answers? Does it teach only one thing? Suppose you didn't have the explanation given in verses 18–23. To what could you compare the parable? Does it teach us anything about missionary work?

127

Joseph Smith gave an interpretation of this parable. How does Joseph's interpretation apply to our own day?[3]

Verse 9: Some read Jesus's remarks about parables here and in other places as telling us that Jesus wished to conceal his teaching. It is easy to see how one might come to that conclusion, but I think it is mistaken. I think he is telling us about revelation, not about concealment.

What does this verse tell us about the responsibility for understanding Jesus's teaching? What does that tell us about how we receive revelation? Given the conflicts we've seen in previous chapters and stories, what group is most likely not to have ears to hear (or, in our usage, "ears that hear")? In other words, whom do you think Jesus may have in mind? Why?

Are those who have been excluded—the "sinners" according to Pharisaic law—more likely to hear what Jesus has to say? If so, why?

Might this particular parable be intended to inspire the disciples who have seen the intense opposition of the scribes and Pharisees? How?

What does it take for us to have ears that hear? When are we most likely *not* to have ears that hear?

Are Jesus's parables supposed to work like the parable that Nathan told David so that, on hearing them, we will hear "Thou art the man" (1 Samuel 12:7)?

Verse 10: Has Jesus left the boat in which he was sitting?

Why do you think that the disciples ask this question? Is it significant that they ask why Jesus speaks to *them* (in other words, the other people, the multitude) in parables?

Verses 11–12: Verse 12 may have been a common proverb: "The rich get richer and the poor get poorer." Jesus applies it here to the disciples. What do the disciples have that has been given to them? In the context of the foregoing parable, what do others not have? Specifically, what does Israel not have? So what will be taken from them?

Verses 13–17: Can you put this explanation for why Jesus teaches in parables in your own words? Whom have we seen not hear what John the Baptist and Jesus teach, and what prevented them from hearing?

Jesus quotes scripture to them (the Greek version of Isaiah 6:9–10). Why does he quote scripture? Does it have anything to do with having ears that hear?

Does verse 15 tell us that God closed the people's eyes and ears so that they could not see and hear, or does it tell us that the people closed them so as not to see and hear? How do we close our eyes and ears to the teachings of the prophets? What blessing have the disciples received that many prophets and righteous people did not receive (verses 16–17)?

Verses 18–23: If the disciples have ears that hear and eyes that see, as Jesus has said in verse 16, why does he have to explain the parable to them?

Why is it important for the disciples to have this teaching about the different ways that people respond to the message of the gospel?

The images here are common in Jewish literature: trees by a stream with roots that sustain them (Jeremiah 17:8; Ezekiel 31:2–5; Psalm 1:3), trees with shallow roots that wither (Sirach 40:15; Wisdom 4:3–4; Isaiah 40:24). Those images were part of people's everyday experience. Are there contemporary images that might work for us as those images worked for them?

There is a progression in verse 23, from receiving to understanding to bearing fruit. What do you make of that progression?

Verses 24–30: Verse 24 tells us that Jesus spoke another parable unto "them." This time to whom does that refer, to the multitude or to the disciples? What clues in the chapter help you decide?

Matthew introduces this parable (and that which begins in verse 31) with language that is very much like that used by Moses when he gave the Law to the people. (See Exodus 19:7.) Why might he have done so?

Matthew could have placed the explanation of this parable immediately after the parable, but he doesn't. He gives Jesus's explanation (in verses 36–43) only after he tells two more parables. Why do you think he does that?

As he has done earlier, Jesus appears to be working from one of John's prophecies, amplifying it. (Compare Matthew 3:12.) Why might he have done so?

Jesus tells several parables that begin "The kingdom of heaven is like . . ." The word translated *kingdom* literally means "reign." In its earliest usages it meant "the king's power and dignity," and it continued to have those connotations. How does this word relate to the Israelite understanding of themselves? To their expectations of the Messiah? How is it relevant to John the Baptist's preaching that "the kingdom is nearby" (Matthew 3:2)? What word or words do you think would best translate the idea of the reign of God into contemporary English?

In what does the King of Heaven exhibit his power and dignity? Most commentators assume that the tares (weeds) were darnel, a weed that looks like wheat and sometimes carries a poisonous fungus. Does that add anything to your understanding of the parable?

We usually understand this parable as a parable about the Church in the last days. Some, however, have understood it originally to have been about Israel: it is important not to force too soon the separation of those in Israel who believe in Jesus from those who have not done so. Which interpretation do you think most reasonable? Why?

Verses 31–32: What question might Jesus be answering? Why answer with a parable in this particular case? What does this parable address that many people might have found scandalous about the early Christian church?

The mustard seed is indeed small, but it isn't the smallest of seeds. And the mustard shrub, though large, isn't gigantic. It grows to about ten or twelve feet. Jesus is using hyperbole here. Can you think of other places where he does so or may do so? Why would he use hyperbole?

Joseph Smith also gave an interpretation of this parable.[4] Is that the only way we can legitimately interpret the parable?

131

Why or why not? The kingdom of God is often referred to as a tree in scripture, but this is perhaps the only time it is compared to an herb. Those who heard Jesus probably would have been surprised at his use of a mustard seed and the mustard plant. Why do you think he might have used a metaphor that they wouldn't have expected?

Verse 33: Compare 1 Corinthians 5:6. Is leaven used as a symbol in the same way in both places? How is this parable the same as the immediately previous one? How is it different?

This is one of the few places where leaven is used as a positive symbol. See, for example, Matthew 16:6, and remember that every house had to be completely free of leaven during Passover. How is leaven a good symbol for evil? In this parable, how is it a good symbol of the reign of heaven?

We have an interpretation of this parable by Joseph Smith as well.[5]

Verses 34–35: Matthew says that Jesus teaches only in parables when he teaches the multitude, but that hasn't been the case from the beginning. Jesus gave some parables in the Sermon on the Mount, but he didn't speak *only* in parables. Why do you think his teaching method has changed?

Verses 36–43: Compare the explanation that Jesus gives here with the explanation in Doctrine and Covenants 86:1–7. What do you make of the differences in explanation? Do those differences help us better understand how to think about parables? According to this interpretation, what is Jesus trying to explain, evil persons in the world or evil persons in the kingdom? What do you learn if you think it about it each way? What do you learn if you think about it as the Doctrine and Covenants does?

Verse 44: To whom do you think Jesus is speaking in this verse? Is he still speaking only to the disciples, or has he turned back to speak to the multitude?

What do we learn about the kingdom of heaven from this parable that we didn't learn from the previous parables (verses 24–33)?

Verses 45–46: Does this parable teach anything different from the last one? If not, why did Jesus tell two parables, one after the other, with the same meaning? If it does have a different meaning, what is it? If it doesn't, why does Matthew repeat it?

Verses 47–50: Does this parable differ significantly in its teaching from the parable of the wheat and the tares?

Do we learn anything from the order of these parables: the sower, the wheat and the tares, the mustard seed and the leaven, the treasure hidden in a field and the pearl of great price, and the fishing net? Can you attribute a primary teaching to each of these and then see any coherence to their order?

Verse 51: Jesus introduces the final parable in this series with a question: "Have ye understood all these things?" Why does he think he must ask that before telling the next parable?

Verse 52: Pay attention to the footnote for "which is instructed." With the possible exception of the parable of the sower, all of the previous parables have been about the kingdom of heaven. This one is about someone who becomes a disciple in that kingdom. Why does Jesus end this series of parables with this one?

Do you think that the disciples would have been surprised by the person Jesus uses as an example of someone who becomes a disciple? Why? Why do you think Jesus uses that example?

What would a scribe (a rabbi, a recognized interpreter of the Law) treasure? What old things would be in his treasury? What new things? Is what Jesus says here and his way of doing so related to the method he used when he delivered the Sermon on the Mount: "you have heard it said [something "old"], but I say [something "new"]"?

Verses 53–58: Jesus returns to Nazareth (presumably) and teaches in the synagogue. People are amazed at his wisdom (probably referring to the parables, his wise sayings). When they ask how he got this wisdom and how he does these mighty works or miracles, why are they amazed? Why are they offended? (The Greek word translated *offended* could also have been translated *scandalized* or *caused to stumble.*)

How does this event relate to the teaching at the beginning of the chapter (verses 13–15)?

Lesson 12

John 5–6; Mark 6:30–44; Matthew 14:22–33

As is often the case, there is far more here than a person can prepare for one lesson. These materials will focus on John 5, but I will also include questions on John 6.

John 5

Some have suggested that the Gospel of John is constructed around seven wondrous works or miracles. With each, Jesus gives a sermon that illustrates the significance of what he has done. The seven are:

1. Turning water into wine at the wedding feast and the discourse on being born again (John 2:1–12; 3:1–21)

2. Raising the nobleman's son to life and a discourse on Jesus as the living water (John 4:43–51; 4:1–42)

3. Healing the man by the pool of Bethesda on the Sabbath and explaining that Jesus is Lord of the Sabbath (John 5:1–14; 5:19–47)

4. Feeding the five thousand and teaching that Jesus is the bread of life (John 6:1–15; 6:22–66)

5. Walking on the sea of Galilee, Jesus comes to Capernaum mysteriously and the discourse on the

inability of the Pharisees to understand him (John 6:16–21; 7:14–39)

6. Healing the man born blind and the teaching that Christ is the Light of the World (John 9; 8:12–59)

7. Raising Lazarus from the dead and the teaching of the resurrection (John 11; John 10:1–18)

Three of the seven are included in the readings for this lesson, one in this chapter and two in the next. Why do you think John might choose to give his testimony using that method of organization? What explanatory function do marvelous works play in John's narrative?

Verse 1: What feast do you think is referred to? (See the footnote.) Is that relevant to the story that follows? If so, how?

Verses 2–16: John seems to use water as a symbol of what the life-giving water of Christ—his word—can do that the ritual cleansings of Judaism cannot do. The name of the pool (the Aramaic word *Bethatha* is probably more accurate than *Bethesda*) may be "house of the two springs," referring to the springs that fed the pool—or it may mean "house of divine mercy." There are good arguments for both meanings.

Besides being near the Sheep Gate (the gate through which sheep were taken into the temple precincts, on the north side of the temple), archaeological evidence shows that there were actually two pools, a larger one and a smaller one. It also suggests that the pools were near a Greco-Roman temple to Aesclepius, the god of healing. Temples to Aesclepius always contained a pool; those who went to the temples looking to be cured offered sacrifice—which they had to buy from the temple priests—and then slept in the temple waiting for a dream to tell them whether they would be cured. It is possible that the Bethesda pools were used by those too poor to afford the Aesclepian sacrifice, but hoping that they could have a similar experience at Bethesda.

Do you see any symbolic significance in the pool's location? What kinds of parallels and differences do you see between Jewish ritual and what Jesus does? Between Greco-Roman practice and what Jesus does? How does what Jesus does demonstrate his difference from the other two major religious understandings?

On the Sabbath (verse 9) at about the time of Passover (verse 1), Jesus goes to a pool where many infirm people gather (verses 2–4). He approaches a man among those gathered at the pool and heals him (verses 5–9). Then he immediately leaves, undetected (verse 13). When the healed man is questioned because he is breaking the Sabbath (verses 10–12), he doesn't know who healed him (verse 13). However, later in the temple, Jesus finds the man and makes himself known (verse 14). Then the man reports to the authorities that Jesus healed him (verse 15). This is a strange story. What is going on here?

Why do you think Jesus went to these pools on the Sabbath? Why did Jesus initiate the healing rather than, as usual, wait for the suffering person to ask for help? Why did he tell the man to pick up his bed? Doesn't Jeremiah 17:21 specifically forbid what Jesus commands?

What quarrel do "the Jews" have with the man who was healed? What is his justification for carrying his bed? Did

Jesus search the man out or just happen to meet him? How do you understand Jesus's warning in verse 14?

Is Jesus suggesting that the man's sins caused his problems and warning him that he may have a worse illness if he sins again? Doesn't John 9:1–4 make that interpretation difficult? What else might Jesus be saying?

What is worse than physical illness?

Do you think Jesus was planning on or even precipitating what happens as a result of this miracle? If so, why?

Notice that John lumps a lot of events together in verse 16 and then moves to Jesus's response to those events in the following verses. As a result, though at first glance we seem to be seeing one continuous story, if we look carefully we can see that a good deal of time might have passed between the miracle at the pool and Jesus's answer to their charge. Note also that no early New Testament manuscripts contain the last part of verse 3 ("waiting for the moving of the water") or verse 4, so many scholars believe that the original manuscript went directly from speaking of the great multitude gathered at the pool (the first part of verse 3) to verse 5. If they are right, does that change the meaning of these verses? How so?

Verse 17: How does Jesus respond to the charge that he works on the Sabbath? We could translate this "My Father is still working and I work." What does "My Father is still working" mean? How does the Father continue to work? Is this an admission that his accusers are right about his Sabbath breaking? Explain how what Jesus says is an answer to their charge.

Is Jesus saying that the Father works on the Sabbath day? If so, how do you explain the apparent contradiction between that claim and Genesis 2:2? If not, how does Jesus's answer justify healing on the Sabbath?

According to the Hermeneia commentary on John, *Exodus Rabbah* (part of the Jewish tradition, written down about 200 years after Christ, but assumed to reflect at least some teachings from Christ's time) argues that carrying something around in your own house is not a breach of the commandment not to work on the Sabbath.[1] (The argument is based on the wording of Jeremiah 17:21–22.) It follows that since the earth is God's footstool, part of his house, he can do things on the Sabbath without breaking the commandment.

Verse 18: How do the authorities respond to his explanation? All of the Gospel writers agree that the authorities were initially offended by what they took to be Jesus's Sabbath breaking and subsequently by his claim to be equal to God (though the latter was more serious). *Has* Jesus made himself equal to God by referring to himself as the Son? Why do you think Jesus made the Sabbath rather than some other disagreement about the Law the initial point of contention between himself and the authorities?

Verses 19–21: Traditional Christians use this verse (among others) to justify their belief in Trinitarianism. How do Latter-day Saints understand what Jesus says in verse 19? How do 2 Nephi 31:12 and 2 Nephi 18:24 relate to verse 19? Might they help us understand what that verse means?

How does Jesus explain his imitation of the Father? Does that teach us anything about our imitation of the Savior?

How does love make command and obedience possible? How is that different from the command and obedience that we usually think of?

What does verse 21 tell us about the resurrection?

Verses 22–23: What does verse 22 tell us about the judgment? The word translated *judgment* in verse 22 and the word translated *condemnation* in verse 24 are variations of the same word. So we could insert *condemn* here in place of *judge* or we could insert *judgment* in verse 24 instead of *condemnation.* (However, see verse 24 and the notes on it.)

Verse 23 is given as an explanation of verse 22. What is the explanation? Why is honor (or according to another translation, valuing) so important in our relation to the Father and the Son? *How* do we honor them, value them? How is honor related to worship? How is honor related to what we saw when we looked at the Lord's Prayer (Matthew 6:9–13; lesson 9)? Is honor important in our culture? If so, in what ways? How do we show honor? Do we honor things we ought not to honor? What are some examples?

Verses 24–25: Does verse 24 answer some of the questions I asked about verse 23?

What does verse 24 teach about what will happen to the person who follows Christ? (I take it that verse 24 demonstrates that, in the New Testament, *judgment* most often means "condemnation" rather than "decision.")

What does it mean to *hear* the word of Christ? Does our discussion of Matthew 13:9 and related verses shed light on this verse?

When do we pass "out of death, into life"? Is that something that happens only with the physical resurrection, or can it occur before that? (Compare Romans 8:1–13, especially verses 8–10.)

To what event or events was Jesus referring in verse 25? Is that a verse only about those who are physically dead, or might it also be a verse about the spiritually dead? What does it mean to be spiritually dead?

Verses 26–27: What does it mean to say that the Father has life in himself? To say that he has given the Son life in himself? It might seem that we, as intelligences, have life in ourselves. However, if we did, then this statement wouldn't say anything particularly interesting about the Father and the Son; it wouldn't say anything about them that isn't also true of everyone. Presumably, then, we *don't* have life in ourselves. So what does that mean?

These verses say that the Father has given the Son two things: life in himself and the authority to judge. Are those two related in some way?

Jesus says that the Father has given him these things because Jesus is "the Son of man." What does that phrase mean, and how does it explain what the Father has given the Son?

Verses 28–29: We can paraphrase verse 28 in this way: "Don't wonder at the fact that the Father has given me life in myself and the authority to judge, because there will be a resurrection of the dead." What does this mean? How are the two parts of that sentence related to each other? Is Jesus saying that the resurrection is even more amazing than these two gifts of the Father to the Son? Or is he saying something else?

How are these two verses related to verse 22? Do they say the same thing or something different? Are verses 28–29 perhaps an expansion of the teaching in verse 22?

If, because we sin, we are all unworthy to enter the kingdom of heaven, what does it mean to say that we will be judged by our works (verse 29)?

Verse 30: How is the teaching of this verse related to that of verse 19?

What does Jesus mean when he says, "As I hear, I judge"?

Is this verse a summary of the theme Jesus announced in verse 17: "The Father is still working and I work"?

What guarantees that Jesus's judgment is right? How is that relevant to us?

Verses 31–47: Jesus tells his audience who his witnesses are: John, Jesus's works, the Father, and the scriptures. Who is the audience? How do you know? How are those witnesses relevant to them? To us?

Verses 32–35: John has testified of Jesus; he was a light in darkness—but that is not the witness to which Jesus will appeal. Why is Jesus not satisfied with the testimony of human beings (verse 34)?

What does he mean when he says, "These things I say, that ye might be saved"? To whom is he speaking? To what does "these things" refer? How will those things save? From what will they save?

Verses 36: A greater witness than John is the mighty works that Jesus has performed, works that he was given by the Father to bring to completion ("to perfect" in the King James Version). Why are Jesus's works a greater testimony of who he is than is the testimony of John the Baptist?

Verses 37–38: The true witness of Jesus is the Father. If Jesus's audience has not seen or heard the Father (verse 37), how has he been a witness?

What is the "abiding word" that his audience does not have?

When Jesus refers to "whom he hath sent," who is he talking about? Is it only himself, or is he also talking about others who have been sent? If the latter, who might that be?

For the scribes and Pharisees, who was the most important person who had been sent? How do the authorities show that they don't believe those whom the Father has sent?

Verses 39–40: We sometimes quote the first part of verse 39 as if it were a command, but a closer look at the context shows that to be unlikely. This verse probably means "You search the scriptures in which you think you find eternal life, but they testify of me." In other words, even though the scriptures, which you believe have the words of eternal life, bear witness of me (see Galatians 3:21–24), you don't see it. Putting verses 39 and 40 together, what is Jesus saying? To whom is he speaking?

Verses 41–44: Verse 41 seems to say that no one honors Jesus, but it really means that he does not seek the honor of men. Whom do the people that Jesus is addressing honor?

Verses 45–47: What does Jesus mean when he says that Moses, not he, will accuse them? What is the irony of Jesus's accusation?

John 6

Verses 1–13: That this occurs just before Passover (verse 4) suggests that it has been a year since the healing of the man at the pool of Bethesda. Why do you think Jesus performs this miracle, and what does John hope to show us by telling us of it? How was it a benefit to the crowd? To the disciples? What does it teach us? Is this miracle a representation, a type, of the sacrament? (See verse 51.)

Verses 15–21: Why does Jesus withdraw from the crowd?

What does the miracle of Jesus walking on the water teach us? Why do Mark and John tell so much less of the story than does Matthew? (Compare Mark 4:35–41 and Matthew 14:24–31.)

Verses 22–27: Why did the crowd follow Jesus to Capernaum?

Notice how the little parable in verse 27 leads the crowd to ask a question that goes further than the question they began with. They move from "How did you get here?" to "How do we do God's work?" (verse 28). Does that change of their question suggest anything about how we should understand the story? About how we should understand our own questions?

Verses 28–29: Why is believing on him whom the Father has sent a work? (The word translated *believe* could also have been translated *trust* or *have faith in*.)

Verses 30–40: Why don't the crowds understand Jesus's teaching here? What has that to do with the fact that he taught in parables? Given Jesus's explanation for why he taught in parables, what does their misunderstanding show us? Are we ever like the crowd, misunderstanding and, so, asking the wrong question? When? (We might wish to change the old saw to "Seeing is not necessarily believing.")

Verses 40–51: We've seen the crowd misunderstand; now we see the authorities misunderstand. Why do you think John shows us this comparison? How do their misunderstandings differ?

Verse 44 says that no one comes to the Son unless the Father has drawn him (literally "dragged him") to the Son. What does that mean?

Eating human flesh is in direct contradiction to the Mosaic law, so Jesus's statement in verse 51 would be shocking. What is the symbolic significance of that shock? Ought we perhaps to be more shocked by the symbols of the sacrament? Would we learn anything from that shock? What kinds of meanings do you see in the symbolic act of eating Christ's flesh and drinking his blood?

Verses 52–59: The authorities were shocked by Jesus's statement that those who wish to live must eat his flesh, but he shocks them even more: you cannot live unless you eat the flesh of the Son and drink his blood. Not only was human blood forbidden, *all* blood was forbidden, so the idea of drinking human blood was doubly offensive. (See Genesis 9:4 and Deuteronomy 12:16.) Verse 57 tells us that if we eat his flesh we shall live. To live in a fallen world is to live by

145

killing other living beings, vegetable or animal; as mortal human beings, we cannot avoid that fact. How does verse 57 use that fact, and what point does it make?

Verses 60–66: When the disciples say, "This is a hard saying," it is as if they are saying, "This parable is too difficult." (The word translated *hard* could also have been translated *harsh* or *violent*.) Why does the teaching of verses 40–59 cause many to cease following Jesus? Why does Jesus ask, "Does this offend you?" when he must know that it did?

When Jesus says "the flesh profiteth nothing" (verse 63), is he using the word *flesh* literally or as a symbol? How do you explain your answer? How is he using the word *spirit* in that verse?

Verses 67–71: How are the apostles different from the disciples? Can you answer that question using only the New Testament? Why does Jesus point out that one of them is a devil?

Lesson 13
Matthew 15:21–17:13; Luke 12:54–57

I have omitted the reading from Mark since it is a parallel of the same stories. There is a good deal of merit in studying each version on its own. It is a mistake to think that these stories are simply repetitions of the same events and, therefore, the writers are telling us the same thing. However, space and time make it difficult to look at both Mark's version and Matthew's in one lesson. I omit notes for Luke 9:18–36 for a similar reason: it too covers the transfiguration.

There are a number of stories in the reading from Matthew, and they appear not to be given in a haphazard way. Matthew arranges them as he does for a purpose. Notice the progression from one to the other:

1. Jesus heals the Canaanite woman's daughter (Matthew 15:21–28).

2. Then he heals many and multitudes come to him (Matthew 15:29–31).

3. He not only heals them, he feeds 4,000 (Matthew 5:32–39).

4. Having just given a miraculous sign, Jesus warns the Pharisees and Sadducees against sign seeking (Matthew 16:1–4).

5. And he tells the disciples to beware the leaven, the teaching of the Pharisees and Sadducees (Matthew 16:5–12).

6. Then he asks the disciples who he is, and Peter testifies that Jesus is the Christ (Matthew 16:13–20).

7. However, when Jesus tells the disciples that he will be killed and resurrected, Peter denies that teaching and is rebuked (Matthew 16:21–23).

8. Following that rebuke, he teaches the disciples what it means to be a disciple (Matthew 16:24–28).

9. Then, taking Peter, James, and John as witnesses, Jesus is transfigured and speaks with Moses and Elijah; the Father testifies of him (Matthew 17:1–9).

10. Finally the disciples ask whether this vision of Elijah was a fulfillment of the prophecy that Elijah will come to restore all things (Malachi 3:23–24), and Jesus answers that he has already come in the person of John the Baptist, distinguishing between the prophet Elijah and the priesthood calling that has that same name. (The names *Elijah* and *Elias* are the same in Greek. We make that distinction by using the name *Elijah* for the prophet and *Elias* for the calling.)

In these stories, how do we see Jesus preparing for what is soon to come? How is he preparing the disciples? Do they understand what he is teaching, or is he teaching them something that they will understand only later, on reflection? How often do we understand only on reflection? What does that suggest about how we should approach doctrine, revelation, and scripture?

Matthew 15

Verses 21–31: What comes before the healing of the Canaanite woman's daughter, and how is that related to the story of her healing?

Matthew calls the Gentile woman who comes to Jesus a *Canaanite*, using an Old Testament term that doesn't have a specific reference in New Testament times and occurs no place else in the New Testament. Why do you think Matthew uses that Old Testament name rather than a contemporary name? (Mark says that she is Greek speaking and from Syro-Phoenicia; see Mark 7:24–30.)

What do we see in the story of that healing that is similar to the second story, in which the multitudes follow Jesus to be healed? What is different?

Verses 32–39: How is the story of feeding the multitude related to the two previous stories?

What do the first three stories show us about Jesus? Does Alma 7:11–12 give any insight into these stories? What do they say to *us*?

Matthew 16

Verses 1–4: What does the discussion with the Pharisees and Sadducees about sign seeking have to do with the previous three stories?

Verses 5–12: The Pharisees and Sadducees were not usually in agreement. The former believed in the necessity of the Oral Law (in other words, the Pharisaic interpretation of and tradition concerning the Written Law) as well as the Written Law; the latter believed that only the Written Law was law. The former believed in the resurrection; the latter did not. The Pharisees believed that it was sinful to adopt Hellenic (Greco-Roman) culture; the Sadducees did not and for some time had been advocates of it as long as it didn't interfere with temple worship. The former believed that the temple priesthood was corrupt; since the latter were composed primarily of temple priests, they did not.

Jesus warns against the teaching of *both* the Pharisees and Sadducees. Against what teaching is he warning the disciples? Think about how his warning is a response to what the Pharisees and Sadducees have just demanded and how this story fits with the stories in the previous chapter.

Verse 13: How is the warning against the leaven of the Pharisees and Sadducees connected to Jesus's question about who the disciples think he is? Why do you think Jesus asks that question at this particular point in his ministry?

Verse 14: What do these answers tell us about the apostles? Do they believe in reincarnation, for example? If not, how do you explain what they say?

Verses 15–16: The word *Christ* means "Messiah," in other words "the Anointed One." Who was anointed in Israelite history? Does the anointment implied by the title *Christ* have anything to do with that anointment?

In what ways does Peter's addition of "the Son of the living God" clarify his reference to Jesus as the Christ? What might the phrase "son of God" have meant in Israelite history? Look at the use of the phrase "sons of God" and "Son of God" in the Old Testament to see whether that is helpful. What does it tell us that the Davidic king is called "son of God" three times in the Old Testament (2 Samuel 7:14; Psalms 2:7; 89:26)?

Is Peter doing any more than saying, "You are a rightful heir of King David"? Presumably so, but how do you know? What is the connection between being the Messiah as Christianity understands Jesus and being the Davidic king?

Verses 17–20: Why does Jesus call Peter "Peter, son of Jonah" (*bar-Jonah* means "son of Jonah")? How were Peter and Jonah alike?

As the footnote indicates, Jesus gives Peter a name, *Petros*, that is the masculine form of the Greek word for rock, *petra*. The Aramaic word would have been *Cephas*, also meaning "stone," a name that occurs several times in the New Testament.

Why does he give Peter the name "rock" when Peter is going to need rebuking immediately afterward and when he knows how Peter will behave at Jesus's trial?

We often teach that the rock Christ has in mind is the rock of Peter's testimony. But that doesn't seem to be the plain sense of verse 18: "Thou art Peter ["rock"], and upon this rock I will build my church." Can you give an explanation of our interpretation, perhaps by putting it into context? Or is the plain sense the correct one: Peter is the leader on which the Church will be built?

Against what will the gates of hell not prevail, the Church or the rock? If the Church, then how do you explain the apostasy? If the rock, then how do you explain Peter's martyrdom?

The word translated *church* was a general term meaning "assembly," a place in which people met to judge cases, debate issues, and come to decisions. The word did not yet have the specific meaning that it has for us. Why do you think this word came to be the word for *church* as we understand it?

What are the keys of the kingdom?

Are *church* (verse 18) and *kingdom* (verse 19) parallel? If so, what does that teach us? If not, how do they differ?

Why does Jesus want to hide his messiahship from the public?

Verses 21–23: What does Peter's denial of Jesus's coming death suggest about his testimony?

Why does Jesus rebuke Peter *so* severely, calling him Satan and an offense? The name Satan comes from a Hebrew word meaning "accuser." The word translated *offense* means "stumbling block." What meaning does that add to what Jesus says?

What does Jesus mean when he says that Peter's mind is on the things of men rather than God? The Greek word translated *savourest* means "to give careful attention to something," "to set one's mind on."

Verses 24–26: Why is Peter's denial of Jesus's coming execution followed by the teaching about discipleship?

What does it mean to "take up one's cross"? What is the image? Why does Jesus use that image in particular as an image of discipleship? Why not, instead, an image of resurrection? How do we take up the cross today?

To deny oneself, as the term is used in verse 24, seems not so much to be to give up one's goods, but to give up one's self. How do we do that? Why would we *want* to do it?

When verse 25 teaches that we ought not to try to save our lives, what does it mean? What does it mean that we must lose our lives "for my sake"? In what sense do we find our lives if we lose them for Jesus's sake?

Verse 27: Is verse 27 a threat or a promise? In Romans 3:10 Paul quotes Psalm 14:1, "There is none that doeth good." If that is true, should we fear being judged by our works?

How does the teaching of this verse follow from the teaching of verses 24–25?

Verse 28: How do you explain this promise to the disciples? How do you explain it when it has been given in patriarchal blessings to people who have since died?

Matthew 17:1–13

How do the previous eight stories lead up to the transfiguration?

Verse 1: Why does Jesus take Peter, James, and John to the mount to witness his transfiguration? What does that experience have to do with Jesus's teaching about the leaven of the Pharisees and Sadducees and with Peter's testimony?

Verses 2–5: How does this incident relate to Moses's experience on Mount Sinai? Are we supposed to see a parallel between them?

Moses and Elijah have symbolic as well as literal significance: Moses can stand for the Law (God's first revelation of himself) and Elijah for the Prophets, the second major part of Old Testament scripture (God's second revelation of himself). Understood that way, Jesus stands for the fulfillment of God's revelation.

In verse 4 Peter suggests that they build tabernacles, reflecting the Feast of the Tabernacles, a commemoration of the Israelite stay at Mount Sinai. Why does he make that suggestion?

Peter is prevented from erecting tabernacles by the voice of the Father commending his Son. What might that interruption signify?

How does what the Father says differ from what he said at Jesus's baptism? How is that difference significant to Peter, James, and John?

Verse 7: Why is it significant that Jesus touched them? Why did Matthew think it important to include that fact?

Verse 9: Why does Jesus tell the disciples not to speak of what they have seen until after the resurrection? How would it have been important to the early Church after the resurrection? Why do *we* need to know of the transfiguration?

Verses 11–13: How does the experience on the Mount of Transfiguration lead to the question about Elias? Why do you think the disciples asked that question? How do you think they understood Jesus's answer? How do we understand it today?

Lesson 14
Matthew 18; Luke 10

Matthew 18

Verses 1–4: Why do the disciples ask the question that they pose in verse 1? What does it suggest about their understanding of Jesus's message? What do you make of the fact that they are arguing about who shall be first so shortly after Jesus has talked about his coming death (Matthew 17:22)?

In verse 3 the verb phrase "be converted" translates a Greek verb that means "turn." To be converted, to repent, is to turn back, to return. In what sense is repentance a return? To what might it be a return?

Christ says that no one can even enter the kingdom (or reign) of heaven without becoming like a child. Then in verse 4 he says that if a person humbles himself and becomes as a child, then he or she is the greatest in the kingdom of heaven. A logical conclusion from the two claims (though rhetoric may trump logic here) is that everyone who enters the kingdom of heaven is the greatest in the kingdom of heaven. How do you make sense of that conclusion?

In Israel and Rome at this time, the child was not a legal person. Children were the property of their parents. Is that relevant to understanding what Jesus meant when he said that we must become as children to take part in the reign of heaven? How is what Jesus says an answer to the disciples' question?

Verses 5–6: Having answered the disciples' question very briefly, Jesus moves to a discussion of offenses. Why? How are the two discussions connected?

Is Jesus speaking only of children here, or does the context suggest that he is speaking also of those who have become as little children? Does the use of the phrase "little ones who believe in me" in verse 6, rather than *children*, suggest that he has in mind a wider meaning? Many commentators believe that the first fourteen verses are about believers rather than children. They take the child to be an example of what the disciples are to become. What do you think of their interpretation?

The Greek word translated *offend* means "to cause to stumble." What do you think that Jesus is speaking of?

Verses 7–9: What does it mean to say, "It must needs be that offences [stumblings] come"? Does it mean that stumbling/offending is unavoidable, or is Jesus speaking hyperbolically?

What is the point of verses 8 and 9? Does the JST help us see that point more clearly?

In verses 6–7 Jesus speaks of one person who causes another to stumble. How is it significant that he now speaks of being caused to stumble by one's own hand, foot, or eye? Does the JST answer that question?

Verse 9 refers to "hell fire" and may be a reference to Isaiah 66:24. Mark 9:47 gives it a name, *Gehenna*, the name of the valley south of Jerusalem where trash was burned, the city dump. Isaiah seems to have that place in mind when he speaks of hell, into which Israel's enemies would be cast. Does knowing these things add any meaning to these verses?

These verses seem to be addressed to those who are or will be leaders in the Church. How do they compare to the things he has said about the Pharisees and other leaders of the Jewish community at the time?

Verses 10–14: In verse 10 Jesus returns to the discussion of offending the little ones, though now he warns against despising them. The word translated *despise* could also be translated "not concerned for." I prefer the second translation because it shows better the connection between verse 10 and verses 11–14. Why do you think Jesus returns to the earlier discussion of the little ones?

What does Jesus mean when he says "in heaven their angels do always behold the face of my Father which is in heaven"? Who are "their angels"? What does it mean always to behold the face of the Father?

The word translated *face* can also be translated *person*, and in Greek "those who see the face of a king" is used as a title for court officials.

How are verses 11–14 connected to verse 10? The first word of verse 11 is *for*, suggesting that there is a connection, that somehow verses 11–14 explain verse 10.

Sheep naturally stay together in a herd. How would one of the sheep have become lost? By stumbling? Does the parable teach that the one lost sheep is more important than the ninety-nine? We often use this parable to teach the duties of a Church leader, but is this a parable about Church leaders or about Jesus?

Verses 15–17: How does Jesus's advice here relate to the parable of the lost sheep? What does forgiving those who trespass have to do with lost sheep?

Explain verses 16–17. What does it mean to say that someone who will not deal with your complaint about his fault should, after all else, be dealt with as a Gentile unbeliever and a tax collector?

Verse 18: How does this verse fit with the theme we have seen so far in the chapter, that of offense and resolving offense? Is it an expansion of the last part of verse 17? If not, how is it related to what comes immediately before it?

Verses 19–20: Jesus seems to be speaking of shared prayer. What do these verses have to do with the theme of the previous verses?

Verses 21–35: The number seven was considered to be a perfect number, a number that showed completion. So when Peter asks Jesus whether he should forgive his brother seven times, he is implying that there is a limit to the number of times he must forgive: to the point at which the forgiveness is complete. Then if the offender continues to offend, forgiveness isn't required. How should we understand Jesus's response?

Notice that Jesus gives the explanation of the parable first and then the parable. Why do you think he does that?

The parable tells of a king who begins to check the account books of those in his court. In this case the word *servant* probably refers to a high official in the court. Otherwise he couldn't have amassed such an incredible debt.

We can't be sure of how to convert ancient money to contemporary values, but some have estimated that 10,000 talents would have been about 650,000 pounds of silver. (That's about $1,750,000,000 in modern prices, but the value of silver has dramatically decreased over the last 600 years. In Jesus's time it might have been worth as much as $3,250,000,000 in today's dollars, perhaps more than all the wealth of the existing nations of the ancient world.) However accurate our estimates of the value of that much silver might be, the point is that the servant owed the king an *enormous* amount of money, and the implication is that he may have obtained it fraudulently. Standard practice was to sell into slavery a debtor who could not pay, and also his family, and to sell all of their possessions. That wouldn't have paid the debt, but it would have punished the servant. How realistic was the servant's promise to pay the debt?

What reason does Jesus give for the king forgiving the debt? The word translated "moved with compassion" means literally "inner organs were moved." Jews and early Christians believed that the inner organs—intestines, liver, stomach, heart, and so on—were where our deep emotions are felt. What does that tell us about the king's response to his servant?

As the LDS footnotes point out, 100 pence was about three months' wages for a laborer. What point is Jesus making by making the discrepancy in the debts so enormous? When the king learns of how the servant has treated his fellow servant, why does the king have the first servant tortured? Since the debt the servant owes cannot be repaid (in other words, it is too large, and as long as he is being tortured, he has no way to get the money for payment), how long will the torture last? Why does Jesus include the point about torture in the parable? Does God torture sinners?

What is the point of this parable as a whole? I have pointed out before that parables often answer a question that the disciple didn't ask but that was a more important question. Does this parable do that? If so, what might that more important question be? Ask yourself that question and consider what your answer would be.

Luke 10

The assignment is only for verses 25–37, but the first part of the chapter is interesting enough to warrant our attention, though it doesn't directly fit into the lesson's theme "Who Is My Neighbor?"

Verse 1: Some interpreters see a connection between the seventy elders sent out to preach the gospel and the list of seventy nations in Genesis 10. Note that 70, like 7, is a number used to denote perfection or completion. "The seventy nations" in Genesis means "the whole world." If there is a connection between this seventy in Luke and the seventy in Genesis, what does it tell us about the seventy elders?

Verses 2–16: What is the point of verse 2? What are we admonished to pray for?

In verse 3 Jesus shifts the metaphor from laborers in the field to sheep among wolves. What is the point of that shift?

The word translated *scrip* in verse 4 means "a traveler's bag." What is the point of verse 4?

What does Jesus mean when he tells the Seventy not to greet people along the way? Does the reference in footnote 4b suggest an answer?

What does verse 6 mean by "the son of peace"? Most interpreters do not think that the phrase refers to the Lord. What else could it mean?

Verses 7–8 don't stand out for us, but they probably did for these seventy elders, for "eat what they give you" contrasts sharply with the Pharisaic dietary laws. What might this commandment foreshadow?

What is Jesus commanding when he tells them to "go not from house to house"? Is he telling them not to go tracting?

Notice that in verse 9 Jesus commands them to do two things, to heal the sick and to preach that the kingdom of God "approaches" or "comes near." Though the English verb phrase "is come nigh" has something of a static sense, the Greek verb that it translates (*engiken*, the third-person, singular, active, indicative of *engizō*) does not. "Is coming near" is a more literal translation. What does it mean to say that the kingdom of God is near us or is coming near us?

Does the last part of verse 1 give one way to answer the question? Are there other ways? Is there a difference between preaching that the kingdom or reign is approaching and what the disciples are to teach after the resurrection?

Some have seen these commandments (take no money, salute no one, speak peace, eat what you are given, heal the sick) as an attack on Satan's reign. Can you understand that interpretation? Can you explain it to someone else?

How have healing and preaching been related in Jesus's mission? How are they related in the mission of the Seventy, in our own life in the gospel?

What point is Jesus making in verses 10–16? What is the symbolism of wiping the dust of the city from the feet?

Verses 17–20: When the Seventy return, what has most impressed them?

In verse 18, why does Jesus begin his response to them by saying, "I beheld Satan as lightning falling from heaven"? Is he saying something about the success of their mission?

In verse 19, why is the second thing he says to them "I have given unto you power (or authority)"? The verb that we translate "have given" could also be translated "have already given." Is that significant? In what does Jesus say the Seventy should rejoice (verse 20)? Why?

Verses 21–22: For what is Jesus thankful? Explain.

Is Jesus's use of the word *babes* related to the discussions of children in Matthew 18?

Some believe that the words of these verses were used in a hymn in the early Church. If they were, how do they apply to the early Saints? Is this a song that Latter-day Saints could sing?

Verses 23–24: Previous kings and prophets lived in hope, but the disciples see the fulfillment of their hopes. Why did Jesus tell the disciples this? Why does Luke tell us?

Verses 25–37: Is there a conceptual connection between the first part of this chapter and what follows? What might it be?

The parable of the Good Samaritan is perhaps the most famous of all Jesus's parables. There are many interesting ways of reading it and more than enough questions to ask to fill several pages. But I will confine myself to a few notes and questions.

In verse 25 the word translated *lawyer* refers to Jewish leaders insofar as they were concerned with administering the law. They could be members of any of the contemporary parties—Sadducees, Pharisees, or scribes—but they were not lawyers in our sense of that word.

Luke says that a lawyer questioned Jesus, though he could have used one of the other, more specific terms to describe the one asking the questions. (Matthew describes him as a Pharisee, and Mark describes him as a scribe. Those terms overlapped.) Why does Luke use the word *lawyer*?

How is the lawyer's question a test?

In verse 26 Jesus responds to his question with another question. Why? The lawyer's answer (verse 27) combines Deuteronomy 6:4 and Leviticus 19:18, and Jesus's response (verse 28) echoes Leviticus 18:5. What does this teach us about the Old Testament and its relationship to Jesus's teaching?

The word *neighbor* in verses 27 and 29 (as well as in the verses that follow) translates a Greek word that means "ones nearby," as does the English word. However, the Hebrew equivalents in the Old Testament refer to someone who was a fellow member of the covenant. What is the lawyer asking in verse 29?

What does verse 29 mean when it says that the lawyer was "willing to justify himself"? The word translated *justify* could also be translated "make righteous." Do we ever try to justify ourselves, make ourselves righteous? If so, how do we do it?

The Greek word translated *thieves* is the same word used to describe Barabbas (John 18:40) and the thieves crucified with Christ (Mark 15:27). Is that significant to our interpretation of the story?

A priest would be one of the religious leaders; a Levite was one who assisted in the temple. Why might they have seen the wounded man and passed by? Who would be comparable in our own culture? Is it likely that those who passed by were just insensitive to his problem?

The contrast between those who held important positions in Israel and the outcast and hated Samaritan is something no one who heard the parable could have missed.

Why do you think Jesus told a story that so explicitly condemned Jewish leaders?

The word translated *compassion* in verse 33 is the same word used in Matthew 18:27. So what?

What kind of assistance does the Samaritan offer in verses 34–35?

In verse 37 the lawyer seems to be unable to simply say "the Samaritan." I imagine the name sticking in his throat, so he used the description to avoid having to say the name. But the result is that he says something more significant. How is what the lawyer said significant?

In the Old Testament, the word *mercy*, as it is used here, means the attitude that God requires that each human being show to other humans. What does the lawyer's response teach us about the Samaritan? How does this prefigure the preaching of the gospel to the Gentiles?

How does Jesus's answer in verse 37 differ from his answer in verse 29, or does it?

Verses 38–42: Why does this story follow so closely on the heels of the parable of the Good Samaritan? What contrasts are we supposed to see? How are both Mary and Martha different from the lawyer?

In the parable that Jesus has just told, the focus is at least partly on the practical response of the Samaritan to the wounded man. How is practical service dealt with in this story? What does the juxtaposition of these two stories teach us? How does this story fit into the theme of the chapter?

Why would Martha have been engaged in "much serving"? Would Martha have understood Jesus's comment to be a remark about the meal she was preparing? How else might she have understood it? We often read this short story as Jesus rebuking Martha, but is he? How might he be coming to Martha's defense as well as Mary's?

What kinds of things worry us, keeping us from sitting at Jesus's feet?

Lesson 15
John 7–8

John 7

Verses 1–5: In verse 1, to what is John referring with the phrase "these things"? Look at chapter 6 to remember what things happened that caused him to be in danger.

A more accurate translation of the word *Jewry* is *Judea*. The theme of Jewish opposition to Jesus is frequent in these chapters (verses 1, 13, 19, 25, 30, 32, and 44; and in chapter 8, verses 37, 40, and 59). John is setting the stage for Jesus's entry into Jerusalem and his crucifixion.

The Feast of the tabernacles, an autumn harvest feast, was the most popular feast of the year.[1] The city would have been filled with pilgrims, and a triumphal procession of pilgrims was met and welcomed by temple priests as it entered the city. Perhaps John tells us that these events happened at the time of the feast to help us understand Jesus's brothers' advice to him. Why do they want him to go to Judea? What are they asking Jesus to do? Does verse 5 shed any light on their advice? How do the brothers understand Jesus's work? Is it significant that one of them, James, will later not only become a Christian but will be the head of the Church in Jerusalem? Is John drawing a parallel between the unbelief of the multitudes in chapter 6 and the unbelief of Jesus's brothers? What might that parallel demonstrate?

Verses 6–10: What does Jesus mean when he says "it is not yet time for me" in verse 6?

What does he mean when he says that their time is "always ready"? What is their time?

Why won't the world hate the brothers? (Compare John 15:19.)

There may be a wordplay in verse 8: the word translated *go up* (*anabainein*) is a variation of the word for resurrection (*anabasis*). What might John be doing with such a wordplay?

Is there a contradiction between what Jesus said in verse 8—"I go not up yet unto this feast"—and what he does in verse 10? When he told the brothers that he wasn't going up to Jerusalem, what was he telling them he wouldn't do? (Remember what they were asking him to do.)

Verses 11–13: Like Jesus's brothers, many in Jerusalem are expecting him to make an appearance at the festival. Why would they expect him to come?

Almost everyone in the festival was a Jew, so what does it mean to say that they did not speak openly "for fear of the Jews"? What must the phrase "the Jews" mean in this story in order for it to add information to what John tells us?

Verses 14–16: A better translation of the beginning of verse 13 is "Now when the feast was already half over."

In verse 15, what do people find amazing, Jesus's appearance at the festival or his teaching? Is what the Jews (and remember whom you think this phrase refers to) say in verse 15 a compliment or an insult? How would we expect someone to respond to whom this had been said? How does Jesus's response in verse 16 differ from what we might expect?

Verses 17–19: Verse 17 gives us a test, as it were, for deciding the origin of Jesus's teaching. (Compare Mosiah 5:13.) What is unusual about this test if we compare it with other ways that we test what people teach?

In verse 18 Jesus repeats the point that he is not his own witness. (Compare John 5:31.) The Greek and Hebrew words translated *true* in usages like those we see in verse 18 both suggest trustworthiness, truthfulness, and righteousness. Jesus reminds them that he is not unrighteous, and the evidence is that he does not seek his own glory.

Then in verse 19 he describes the Jews in a way that compares them to what he has just said of himself. What contradiction between their behavior and their claim to keep the law of Moses does Jesus use as evidence that they do not keep that law?

Verses 20–27: Compare verses 20 and 25. Are these two different groups asking these questions? If so, who do you think each might be? What do you conclude about those who charged Jesus with being possessed by an evil spirit when he said that the Jews were plotting to kill him?

Only one miracle by Jesus is recorded as happening in Jerusalem, the healing at the pool of Bethesda. Presumably that is the miracle that he refers to in verse 21 as "one work."

Remembering that circumcision was understood as a purifying ritual, explain Jesus's argument in verses 22–23.

How would the Pharisees have understood verse 24? How would the Christians come to understand it after the resurrection? How should we understand it today?

In verse 26, how do some begin to explain the Jewish leaders' failure to silence Jesus? Are they speaking honestly or ironically? What does verse 27 tell us about the Jews' understanding of how the Messiah would come among them?

Verses 28–30: The people speaking may think they know Jesus, but whom do they *not* know?

What does it mean for a person, divine or otherwise, to be true?

In this context, what is the significance of verse 29? How would those in the crowd have understood it? How would the leaders have understood it?

Verses 31–32: Can you paraphrase what the people are saying in verse 31? Verse 31 tells us the basis of the faith of those who believed on Jesus, namely his miracles. But chapter 6 has already shown us that those who believe because of miracles may not really understand Jesus or his teaching. For us, what is comparable to believing because of miracles? What more than miracles must we have if our faith will allow us to understand who Jesus really is?

John makes it clear in verse 32 that the two forces in Jerusalem who opposed each other for leadership, namely the Pharisees and the temple priests, were united in their opposition to Jesus. Why? Why would the political leaders have responded as they do in verse 32?

How does the attempt to arrest Jesus in verse 32 differ from that in verse 30? What motivates the first attempt? The second?

To see what happened to those sent to arrest Jesus, read verses 45–46.

Verse 33–36: When the leaders say what they do in verse 35, do you think they are being sarcastic, or are they genuinely puzzled? Could they have imagined that the Messiah would teach the Gentiles?

Verses 37–39: Does the Bible Dictionary's description of the Feast of the Tabernacles help us understand better why Jesus chooses the figure that he does—water—and how those who heard him would have understood what he was saying?

In Greek there are two ways of reading the end of verse 37 together with verse 38. One way: "If any man thirst, let him come to me; and [let him] drink, he that believeth on me. As the scripture says . . ." On that way of reading, the living waters flow from Christ. Another way is the way that the King James translators decided to read it: the scripture describes the believer rather than Christ. Which reading do you think is most likely? Why?

Verses 45–49: Why haven't the temple guards brought Jesus to the priests and the Pharisees? What has prevented them?

What does the leaders' reply show about them? Why should it matter that—as far as they know—none of the Pharisees have believed Jesus?

To what people are they referring in verse 49? What is their evidence that they don't know the Law? Why would they be a cursed people?

Verses 50–53: Nicodemus's interjection at this very point is telling, for he is a person learned in the Law, one of those who they assume has not believed Jesus. But as John points out, we know that at some level Nicodemus has been affected by Jesus's teaching. (See John 3:1–13.) Perhaps he was a convert. But what do you make of the fact that Nicodemus neither mentions his interaction with Jesus nor defends him? Instead, he insists that they follow the Law.

What do you make of their response to Nicodemus? Why was Jesus's geographic origin so important to them? How did their learning cause them to stumble with regard to the question of where Jesus came from?

John 8

The story of the woman caught in adultery (John 8:3–11) seems originally not to have been located in this part of John's text. Most good manuscripts of John do not include the story at all. Many scholars believe that the story was originally part of Luke. Others believe that it was part of John, but located someplace else in the book. Few doubt that it is an authentic story, but few believe it belongs where it is. However, there is no way to know where it might have been if it weren't here. We can only guess. Since whoever put it here did so for some reason, we will deal with it as part of the sequence of events that John describes.

Verses 1–2: The chapter and verse divisions, created thousands of years after the Gospels were written, can sometimes cause us to miss things we might see otherwise. Compare John 7:53 and John 8:51. When John wrote his Gospel, these two sentences were right next to each other, with no break between them. What contrast do you see between them? What reasons might Jesus have had for going to the Mount of Olives at night? What does verse 1 tell us about Jesus at this time? Why did Jesus return to the temple the next day, the day after the feast was over?

Verses 3–11: This story and the parable of the good Samaritan are probably the two favorite stories of the New Testament? Why? What do they have in common? What do they show us about Jesus? Why is their message important to us?

In what ways are we like the woman of this story? In what ways are we like the scribes and Pharisees who bring her to Jesus?

The scribes and Pharisees bring the woman to Jesus and put the question to him in a legal way: "Moses commanded . . . , what sayest thou?" Deuteronomy 22:23–24 decrees stoning for a betrothed virgin who has committed adultery. (Joseph worried that this was the case with Mary: Matthew 1:18–19.) Deuteronomy 22:22 decrees death for a married adulteress but says nothing of how the penalty is to be carried out. (Most rabbis believed it should be done by strangulation.) What do you think they are asking Jesus to decide, and how do you think his answer might allow them to accuse him?

In verse 6, Jesus seems to ignore them, tracing something in the dirt. (The word translated *wrote* does not necessarily mean that he wrote words. It could equally describe doodling.) Why do you think he refuses to answer their question?

Deuteronomy 17:7 says that the first witness against a person also had to initiate the execution of the death sentence. When the scribes and Pharisees continue to demand an answer, how does Jesus use that scripture against them?

What does verse 9 mean when it says that the accusers were convicted by their own consciences? The word *convicted* translates a Greek word that means "to show someone his sin and to bring him to repentance." In verses 10–11, the word *condemn* translates a Greek word that means "to cut off."

Does Jesus excuse anyone in this story? He doesn't condemn the woman, but does he condemn the scribes and Pharisees? How are John 7:24 and 8:15–16 related to this story?

Verse 12: Light and water were centrally important in the Feast of the Tabernacles. In John 7:37–38, he used water to talk about himself (though he did not say, "I am the living water"). Now he uses light to talk about himself. Why was it important for him to connect the people's thinking of him to the Feast of the Tabernacles? How is Peter's offer to build tabernacles on the Mount of Transfiguration related to all of this (Matthew 17:4)?

Verses 13–14: To whom is Jesus speaking in these verses? To whom does *them* refer in verse 12? See John 8:20.

How might the people of Jesus's time have understood "I am the light of the world"? How might they have understood "shall have the light of life"? Could they have made any connection to things found in the Hebrew scriptures?

Why does testifying of oneself mean that one's testimony is not true? I am the author of this book. Surely I could say, "I am the author of this book," and that would not be false. So what are the Pharisees saying? Of what are they accusing Jesus?

Is Jesus denying the principle that the Pharisees have invoked, or is he claiming that he is a special case?

From where have the Pharisees judged Jesus to have come earlier in the story? When he says that he knows where he came from and where he is going, where do you think he is referring to? Why can't the Pharisees tell where he came from and where he is going?

Verses 15–19: Why does Jesus seem to change the subject to judgment, in other words condemnation, in verse 15?

What does it mean to judge "after the flesh"? Do we judge otherwise? Can we?

What does it mean to say, "I don't judge, but if I do . . ."? What point is Jesus making with the statement that he doesn't judge followed by the hypothetical of what his judgment would be like if he were to judge?

When Jesus says he is not alone, is he saying that the Father also testifies of him? How does the Father do that?

Hasn't Jesus led them in a circle: I testify of myself, but the Father also testifies of me; you will know the Father (and therefore, presumably, his testimony of Jesus) only by knowing Jesus? Do you think the Pharisees were exasperated with

175

what he said? How would you have responded? Why does he speak to them in this way?

Verse 20: Why does John wait until now to tell us to whom Jesus has been speaking for the last nine verses?

Verses 21–24: It may be helpful to remember that the Greek word for *parable* (*parabolē*) translates a Hebrew word (*mashal*) that means both "parable" and "riddle." New Testament people seem not to have drawn any sharp line between parables and riddles.

Jesus continues to riddle his interlocutors in these verses. Why does he engage them at all? Why does he engage them in this way? Is this way of speaking with the Pharisees related to the reasons that Matthew tells us Jesus gave for speaking in parables (Matthew 13:10–17)?

When Jesus says, "Ye are from beneath," what does he mean? How would those listening probably have understood him?

How did the Pharisees understand what it means to be found righteous at death? What does Jesus say it means?

Verse 25: How do you square what Jesus says here with the fact that he told his disciples not to tell anyone who he was (Matthew 16:20)? Has he or hasn't he told them who he was from the beginning? If he hasn't, how do you understand what he is saying here? If he has, how do you explain Matthew 16:20 and numerous similar passages?

Verses 26–27: Here is another way to translate the first part of verse 26: "There are many things I could say about you and condemn." How does that alternative translation change the meaning of what Jesus says?

Of course the Father is true, though the Pharisees don't understand that Jesus is referring to the Father. But how is that connected to the first part of the sentence, "I have many things to say and to judge of you"?

Verses 28–30: Notice that in the King James Version the word *he* in verse 28 is in italics. That means that the translators added the word in order for the sentence to make sense grammatically in English. That's not an unusual thing to have to do when translating from one language to another. But in this case perhaps the word wasn't needed in English. In Greek Jesus says "then you will know that I am." (That translates a Greek word, *hoti*, which is a narrative marker. It tells us that what follows is the object of knowledge or understanding.) Used as it is here, "I am" doesn't take an object. Jesus is announcing himself as Jehovah of the Torah (compare Exodus 3:14).

Jesus's testimony is that he is Jehovah and does what the Father wills him to do. Why does that testimony convert many?

Verses 31–36: Who are "those Jews who believed on him"? Is the word *Jews* used here to refer to Judah in general, or is it used here as it often is to refer to the leaders in Jerusalem?

What does it mean to continue in the word of Christ? Why does he use the image of the word rather than say something like "If you do as I command"? What does that image convey that *command* might not? Another way to think about the same question: what is the difference between continuing in the word of God and obeying his commandments?

Who is speaking in verse 33? Is it those who have believed on him? How did you come to your conclusion?

If those referred to in verse 33 are "those Jews which believed on him," their faith must not have been very deep. Does that help you decide to whom Jesus is speaking here?

The word translated *continue* in verse 31 could also have been translated *endure*. What does it mean to endure in the word of God?

What does it mean to know the truth? How does knowing the truth make one free? Compare verses 32 and 36: the first says that the truth will make us free; the second says that the Son will make us free. We could read that to mean that "the truth" and "the Son" mean the same thing. Is that a reasonable reading?

How can the truth be a person rather than a set of facts? That raises the question of whether the truth that Jesus teaches is a body of doctrine or something else? If you say it is a body of doctrine, see if you can find places in Jesus's teachings where he speaks of it as that. If you say it is something else, what is it? What scriptural passages back up your conclusion?

Notice the connection of ideas in verses 31–32: if you endure in my word, then you are my disciples; if you are my disciples, then you know the truth; if you know the truth, then you are free. Why do you think that Jesus gives them this chain of ideas? Why not, instead, just tell them, "Endure in my word and you will be free"?

Given the fact that the Jews had spent the last several hundred years under the rule of one foreign nation or another, how could they say, "We . . . were never in bondage to any man" in verse 33? What must they understand by freedom, and what do they think makes them free?

In verses 34–36, Jesus uses a metaphor that becomes central to Paul's thinking later: the comparison between the servant (literally "slave") of the household and the son of the house. What would have been the difference between the servant and the son (verse 35)? What does it mean to be a servant of sin? (Compare 2 Nephi 2:27.) In the ancient eastern Mediterranean, servants—who were almost universally slaves—could be freed only by the master of the house or his son acting under the master's authority. How is that relevant to Jesus's teaching?

Verses 37–41: In verse 37 Jesus first compares those to whom he is speaking to seed, the seed of Abraham, and then he compares them to ground in which his word, his seed, cannot take root. Does that reversal of images mean anything to you?

In verses 38–39, who is Jesus suggesting is their father? How does Jesus say we can identify the true children of Abraham? What are the works of Abraham? Are they different from the works of Moses? Is there any place in the story of Abraham where we find him sparing the life of someone who has told him the truth?

Why do they respond to Jesus's criticisms by saying, "We are not children born of fornication" (verse 41)? Has Jesus suggested that they might be, symbolically? If so, why did he do so, and in what sense are they illegitimate children?

Verses 42–44: In verses 42–43, of what does Jesus accuse those he is talking with? How does he explain their inability to understand his riddling declarations?

What does it mean to say that Satan was "a murderer from the beginning" (verse 44)? The contrast is important to Jesus's message: Satan brings death, in fact murder; Jesus brings life.

Verse 48: Why do they call Jesus a Samaritan in verse 48? What is the import of that?

Verses 51–53: Taken at face value, Jesus's claim in these verses is astonishing, as his interlocutors point out: those who keep his saying will never die; but Abraham is dead; so the natural conclusion is that Abraham did not keep the sayings that Jesus taught. That conclusion is either a condemnation of Abraham or a condemnation of Jesus. But what ambiguity is Jesus playing on? What does he mean that is, once again, not what they hear?

Is Jesus intentionally provoking his audience to anger?

How has Jesus's audience understood what he says in verse 57? In verse 58 he makes clear what might have been unclear in verse 28. Why does he make this declaration to these people?

Lesson 16
John 9–10

John 9

Verse 1: Chapter 8 ends with the phrase "passed by" and chapter 9 begins with those words. Did the events of chapters 9–10 happen as Jesus was leaving the temple precincts, or did they occur later? (See verses 2 and 14 for some clues.)

Why is it important to the story that the man has been blind since birth?

As you read the story, ask yourself: "How we are like the blind man: in what ways are we or have we been blind from birth? How do we come to see? What do we see when we have been healed?"

Verses 2–5: How could the disciples believe that the man's sins could be responsible for his blindness since he was born blind?

What do you make of the fact that over and over again we see Jesus ignoring general, hypothetical, and legal questions such as the question that the disciples ask? (See, for example, Luke 10:25ff. and John 8:3ff.) What does he deal with instead?

How does Jesus explain the man's blindness? Does he say that is giving complete explanation? As you read the rest of this story, ask yourself what works of God are made manifest through this healing. What night might Jesus be speaking of in verse 4?

Light is that by which we see things and which makes it possible for us to do our work. Is Jesus the light by which we see the world? What would it mean for that to be true? Given the symbolism of verse 4–5, what can we conclude will be the case if we do not see the world by his light?

Verses 6–7: Do you see any symbolic meaning in the spit and the clay with which Jesus anoints the man's eyes?

The Siloam pool (also translated as "the waters of Shiloah" in Isaiah 8:6) was the pool from which the water for the Feast of the Tabernacles was drawn and that Jesus seems to have used symbolically in his sermon at that feast. (See John 7:37–38.) Is that relevant to understanding this story?

Why does John stop to tell us that the name *Siloam* means "sent"? (That etymology is perhaps inaccurate, but it is the one that those listening would have assumed.) Does the name have anything to do with the story? Is the comparison to Elijah sending Namaan to wash in the river Jordan (2 Kings 5) intentional?

Verses 8–12: Who is questioning the man who has been healed? The Greek word translated *neighbor* in verse 8 means, etymologically, "one who shares the earth or land." It and related words are most commonly used to speak of locality. John tells us that these are the people who lived around the blind man. Who else is asking?

What is the people's discussion like in verse 9?

In verse 11 the man describes Jesus as "a man that is called Jesus." What does this tell us about the healed man's relation to Jesus?

Why might those who question him want to know where Jesus is (verse 12)?

Verses 13–17: Why do the man's interrogators take him to the Pharisees? Which Pharisees might that have been?

Why does John think it is important to tell us that Jesus performed this miracle on the Sabbath? Why does Jesus do so many of his miracles on the Sabbath?

What division do we see in verse 16, and what does that tell us about these events? What does it suggest about the Pharisees?

In verse 17, why do they keep badgering the man who was healed? How does the man's answer compare with his description of Jesus at the beginning of verse 11?

What does the statement in verse 17 tell us about how the man's understanding has changed? What has brought about that change? Is the man's change of understanding perhaps one of the godly works that is to be shown by his healing? How does our understanding of Jesus and our relation to him change?

Verses 18–23: Notice that those referred to as "the Pharisees" are now referred to as "the Jews" in verse 18. Since we know that not all Jews were Pharisees, what does that suggest us about the term "the Jews" in John's Gospel?

Why do the Pharisees ask his parents about the man, and why do his parents hold back from saying how he was healed? Being blind, the man would have already been ritually outcast;

now that he is healed, he is in danger of continuing to be outcast. How might the Pharisees have put people out of the synagogue? (Formal excommunication seems to have been rare at this time.) Do we ever put people out of the Church unjustly? In what ways?

Verses 24–27: What is going on in verse 24?

When the Pharisees say that Jesus is a sinner, what are they saying about him?

Why does the man stand fast (verse 25)? Why not simply do as they've asked and give God the praise? What would be the harm?

What do we see about the man's understanding of the Pharisees in verse 27? What does the word *also* in the man's question of the Pharisees (verse 27) suggest?

Verses 28–29: Compare what the Pharisees say in response to John 1:17. What point is John making in these two verses? By what light do the Pharisees see? To what are they blind?

Verses 30–34: What gives the man the courage to argue with the Pharisees as he does? What does he find amazing (*marvellous* in the King James Version)? Has his understanding of Jesus changed since he declared Jesus to be a prophet in verse 17?

How do the Pharisees explain the man's blindness (verse 34)?

Is it significant that they give an answer to the disciples' question but Jesus did not?

Verses 35–38: Why does Jesus search out the man?

A better translation of the Greek word translated *believe* in verses 35 and 36 would be "trust in."

What does verse 36 tell us about the man's understanding of Jesus?

How do you think the man is using the word *lord* in verse 36? Is he using it differently in verse 38? What explains the change in understanding that we see in these few verses?

Verse 39: Explain Jesus's summary of the meaning of this event in your own words.

Verses 40–41: Under the circumstances, it is difficult to believe that the Pharisees didn't know whether Jesus was talking about them. Why, then, do they ask whether Jesus is calling them blind?

Why does saying "we see" mean that their sin remains? What would have taken away that sin?

John 10

As you read how Jesus is compared to a shepherd and to a door, ask yourself how these two comparisons are connected to the event of chapter 9. How do they continue the same theme?

Verses 1–6: One scholar suggests that "verily, verily" in verse 1, which literally is "amen, amen," is used when Jesus is going to talk about something that he has already spoken of and he is going to expand on what he said before.[1] Assuming that is true, where have we already seen this teaching, and how does Jesus expand on it? (Compare John 8:47 with verse 4.)

What point is Jesus making by talking about thieves and robbers in verses 1–2? (The distinction between *thief* and *robber* is similar to our distinction between shoplifter and armed robber.)

Do you think that Jesus has Ezekiel 34:1–16 in mind when he tells this parable? How would the Pharisees have responded to that comparison had they heard it?

Verses 7–19: In the past Jesus has been content to teach the disciples what his parables meant, but to leave the Pharisees in ignorance. Why does he now tell them explicitly what he meant?

How can Jesus be both the gate and the shepherd in the parable? (See verses 7 and 11.) Does the fact that he can be both teach us something about how to interpret parables?

In verse 8, who are "all that ever came before me"?

How would his listeners have understood verse 11? How do we understand it?

Who might Jesus be talking about when he refers to the hireling in verses 12–13? What does verse 13 say distinguishes the real shepherd from the hireling? For whom is the hireling concerned? When are we hirelings rather than shepherds?

The word translated *good* in verse 14 means not only "good" but also "morally praiseworthy" and "noble." What makes Jesus the good shepherd?

We understand verse 16 as referring to the descendants of Lehi, but how would the Pharisees have understood what Jesus says here? How would the disciples and the early Church understand this verse?

How do you explain the difference between verse 16 and Matthew 15:24?

There is a wordplay in Greek at the end of verse 16. We can translate that wordplay approximately like this: "There shall be one sheepherd, one shepherd." What point is Jesus making with that wordplay?

How are verses 15 and 17 related to each other?

In verse 18, to what does "this commandment" refer? To what he has said in verses 17–18 or to something else?

Almost the whole of the Pharisees' religious focus was on the commandments. How is Jesus teaching them something different in this parable and its explanation? What is he teaching them? How might that teaching help us understand what it means to be obedient?

Verses 19–21: Once again we see the division among the Jews, in other words, among the community leaders. Why does John think it is important that we know about that division?

Verses 22–30: The Feast of Dedication (known today as Hanukkah) typically occurs in December. It celebrates the rededication of the temple altar by the Maccabees in the second century BC. It was also called the Feast of Lights, ostensibly in remembrance of the oil that miraculously continued to burn in the temple candelabra even after it should have burned out, but (according to Josephus) more in recognition of the freedom that the Jews gained, "the light of liberty."

Several months have passed since the events of chapters 7–8. Perhaps that time passed between chapters 8 and 9.

Perhaps it passed after the parable of the Good Shepherd and its discussion (John 10:1–21). Why does John juxtapose these events that occur at different times?

What question do the leaders have (verse 24)? Jesus has yet to publicly declare that he is the Christ, in other words, the Messiah. Why do they demand that he tell them whether he is? Do they really want to know, or might they have another motive?

How is "the Jews'" demand like the demand of Jesus's brothers (John 7:3–5)? How might the demands be different?

When Jesus says "I told you" in verse 25, what is he talking about? What has he told them? How has he told them?

Why is it important to tell these questioners that no one can take Jesus's sheep from him (verses 28–29)?

Verse 30 seems to be offered as an explanation of verses 28–29. How does it explain them?

Verses 31–32: What do you make of the irony of Jesus's response in verse 32 to their threat to stone him in verse 31?

Verses 33–39: In verses 34–36, Jesus defends himself against the charge of blasphemy. What is his argument? (Compare Psalm 82:6.)

The word translated *sanctified* in verse 36 could also be translated *dedicated*. It is the same word used in the scripture for the Hanukkah lesson in the synagogue, Numbers 7:1. How is what Jesus teaches here related to the feast being celebrated?

What is Jesus telling the leaders in the first clause of verse 38?

How do Jesus's works show that the Father and the Son are in each other? Given what we see in these verses, what does it mean to say that the Father is in the Son and the Son is in the Father?

Verses 40–42: John begins the story of Jesus's public ministry at the place on the Jordan where John was baptizing. He ends the story of Jesus's public ministry by telling us that Jesus returned to that spot. Why does he go back to the site of his baptism before he begins the final stage of his ministry, the stage that culminates in his death and resurrection?

Lesson 17

Mark 10:17–30; 12:41–44; and Luke 12:13–21; 14; 16

Given the quantity of material in these chapters, rather than try to cover everything, I will focus my questions on the verses from Mark and selections from the verses from Luke.

As you read this material, be sure to ask how it applies to us who live in the latter days. What do these verses teach us about taking up our cross? (Compare Jacob 1:8; 3 Nephi 12:30; Alma 39:9.)

What do they teach about riches (not what do we recall others saying that they teach, but what do they *really* teach)?

What does the parable and explanation in Luke 16:1–12 teach us about our relation to the world?

Mark 10

Verses 17–22: How is the story of verses 13–16 connected to the pericope in verses 17–30?

Why does the fact that the man is running suggest? Why does he kneel? That is an unusual thing to do before a teacher, which is a more accurate translation of the word that the King James Version translates *Master*.

Why do you think the man employs the unusual title "good teacher"? Why does Jesus reject being called "good" (verse 18)?

What does this person want? Compare this story to that in Matthew 12:28–34. How is the scribe in that story like the person in this one?

In verse 19 Jesus says that the man knows the commandments. What does that tell us about the person?

Why might Jesus have reworded the commandment "Do not covet" as "Defraud not"?

Which of the Ten Commandments does Jesus *not* mention in his initial response (verse 19)? Is that relevant?

Are the first four of the Ten Commandments implied in his second response (verse 21)? If so, how so?

What do we learn from the first part of verse 21, "then Jesus beholding him loved him"? What does it mean to say that Jesus beheld him? Clearly he was already looking at him. And what does it mean to say that Jesus loved him? Doesn't Jesus love everyone?

In verse 21 Jesus tells the man that, in terms of observing the Torah, the Law, he lacks only one thing. What is that one thing?

Jesus commands the man to do three specific things: to go on his way, to sell everything he has and give it to the poor, and to then take up his cross and follow. Is any one of these more important to the other? Does one of them require that one do one of the others first?

What does "take up the cross" mean? Compare Matthew 16:24, Mark 8:34, and Luke 9:23.

How does this story compare to Matthew 8:18–22 (Luke 9:57–62)?

Jesus says little about property, but what he does say has a negative slant. Why? What does that mean for us? Might his teaching about property be a "hard saying" (John 6:60) for us? (The Greek word in John means "difficult to the point of being impossible.")

The King James Version translates the first part of verse 22 merely as "and he was sad at that saying," but a more literal and, I think, better translation is "but he, becoming gloomy at the word." What makes this man gloomy? Why did the prospect of giving away his possessions grieve (literally "pain") him?

When we read this story, we assume that the man is rich. Verse 22 gives us evidence for our assumption when it says "he had great possessions." What does it mean to be rich? Is that an absolute description or a comparative one? If it is comparative, to whom ought we to compare ourselves in deciding whether we are rich?

Verses 23–27: When Jesus exclaims, "How hardly shall they that have riches enter into the kingdom of God!" (verse 23), why are the disciples astonished (verse 24)? What does their astonishment show about their belief?

What do we really believe about riches and salvation? If we go behind what we say about riches, both publically and to ourselves, to our behaviors and attitudes, are we ever astonished that it is difficult for the rich to be saved? What might any such astonishment say?

How does this story relate to Jesus's admonition in Matthew 6:24 (Luke 16:13)?

Why does Jesus call the disciples children (verse 24)?

At verse 24 many New Testament manuscripts differ from the manuscripts used by the KJV. They omit "for them that trust in riches," so that instead the last part of the verse says merely, "How hard is it to enter into the kingdom of God!" What difference does that make to what Jesus is saying? Which version of the verse do you think is probably right? Why?

What is the point of verse 25?

Note this comment from a contemporary New Testament scholar about the eye of the needle:

> Many stories have been told to indicate that the "eye of the needle" is a small postern gate that was opened at night when the city gate had been shut, and that a camel could get through it provided it had been fully unloaded. It is a nice story but not true in biblical terms. The eye of a needle refers to a surgeon's needle. In both Matthew 19 and Matthew 23, the point was that the camel was the largest animal with which people of the day were familiar. Jesus was using the term much as we would use the word *elephant* as the largest creature in our experience. Jesus may also have used the camel as an illustration because it was ritually unclean.[1]

A century or two later in Judaism there was a similar rabbinic parable that spoke of an elephant rather than a camel.

In verse 26 the disciples are even more astonished, and they seem to ask, "If the rich can't be saved, then who can?" If that isn't what they are asking, what is it?

Is what Jesus teaches here related to his teaching about the narrow gate and how one enters that gate (Matthew 7:13–14; Luke 13:23–24)?

Verse 27 begins, "Jesus looking upon them saith . . ." Why is it important that he looked at his disciples? Is that parallel to him beholding the person in verse 21? What does Jesus see that caused him to say what he does in verse 27?

In verse 27 Jesus seems to be referring to Genesis 18:14. How might that reference be significant to what he teaches here?

Verses 28–30: Mark tells us that Peter began to say something (verse 28) and was interrupted by Jesus (verse 29). What was Peter trying to say? What does Jesus's interruption show?

In verses 29–30, Jesus promises that those who deny themselves will receive a hundredfold "in this time." What does that phrase mean? What does it mean to receive a hundredfold "with persecutions"?

Mark 12:41–44

Two mites were approximately one-hundredth of a day laborer's wages,[2] no more than about three dollars, or even less, in today's wages. How does this story contrast with the rest of chapter 12? How might it have given the disciples hope?

What do you make of the comparison between the *abundance* referred to in verse 44 (which could also be translated *excess*) of the wealthy and the *want* (or "lack") of the widow?

Luke 12

Verses 13–15: In verse 13, what is the man asking Jesus to do? It seems that rabbis were often called to settle family disputes. Many recognized Jesus as a rabbi. Why, then, does he refuse to settle this (verse 14)? Isn't he the ultimate Judge? (Compare John 3:17–18, remembering that the word translated *condemn* could also be translated *judge*.)

Why does the man's demand cause Jesus to speak to his disciples about covetousness? What is covetousness? The Greek word translated *covetousness* means "wanting more." Does that tell us anything about what Jesus is criticizing?

What does it mean to say "a man's life consisteth not in the abundance [excess] of the things which he possesses" (verse 15)? Explain that claim as carefully and as true to the wording that Jesus uses as you can.

Does the story of the young man in Mark 10 offer an alternative for giving life meaning? What is it? (See also Luke 9:23–25.) Why is that the only thing that can truly give life meaning?

Verses 16–21: How is what the farmer does in Jesus's story in these verses different from what Joseph did in Egypt? Does this story teach that we ought not to retire or to prepare for retirement?

What does God's reproof in verse 20 mean? Can you put that in your own terms as it might apply to someone today?

What would it mean to be "rich toward God" (verse 21)? The Greek word translated *rich* means also "to have abundance." How do we have abundance *toward* God rather than from him?

Jesus gives a brief sermon explaining this parable in verses 22–40. Compare the two and ask yourself what this means for your own life.

It is taught that these verses were directed at those called to full-time service in the kingdom of God, people such as missionaries and apostles. Does that mean that they have no applicability to us? If they are relevant to the rest of us, how so?

Luke 14

Verse 15: What has brought on the exclamation of this verse?

Do you think that the speaker is thinking literally of eating in the kingdom of God, or is he thinking metaphorically? If the latter, what would it mean to eat in God's kingdom?

Verses 16–24: How is this parable a response to the exclamation in verse 15? Can we infer anything about the man who spoke in that verse from this parable?

How are the excuses that the invitees offer like that of the young man in Mark 10:17–22?

Verses 25–27: How is the parable of verses 16–24 related to the teachings of verses 26–35?

The word *hate* in verse 26 is accurate, but it is probably hyperbolic. (Compare Proverbs 13:24 and 2 Samuel 19:6.) The Greek word can also be translated *disregard*. (Also see the JST.) How would those listening to Jesus probably have responded to this? Is he intentionally alienating them? If so, why? If not, how so?

Read the JST for verse 27. Does it change the meaning of these verses, or does it augment that meaning?

Verses 28–32: The comparisons that Jesus makes in verses 28–32 are to people who carefully take into account what their actions will cost them before they proceed: a builder and a king going to war. Why does Jesus tell two parables that make the same point?

What do these parables tell us about forsaking all and following Christ? Verse 33 says that if we do not forsake all, we cannot be disciples of Christ, or, conversely, if we are his disciples, then we have forsaken all. In our context, what does it mean to forsake all? How do we do so—and have we done so?

Look at the verses inserted in the JST. (They are in the JST material in the back of your Bible.) What do they mean in the context of forsaking all and counting the cost of discipleship?

Luke 16:1–12

A steward was usually a slave entrusted with the management of a household. What that might mean would depend on the type and size of the household he was to manage. Some speculate that the master in question would have been one who did not reside at the household managed by the steward, an absentee landlord, as it were. That isn't necessarily the case. A steward entrusted with money was expected to make a profit for his master, but stewards often also made money for themselves by manipulating the master's loans and by charging extra interest. Within limits, it seems that such practices were either tolerated or even expected. We might substitute the word *squandered* for *wasted* and understand the meaning more accurately.

The phrase "I am resolved" in verse 4 means "I've known all along."

What do we see the steward doing? In verse 8, why does his master commend the steward rather than condemn him?

In the same verse Jesus says "for the children of this world are in their generation [i.e., in their time] wiser than the children of light." What does that mean?

The word *mammon* (verse 9) seems to mean "that in which one trusts." What is Jesus recommending in verse 9? Is it related to any of the teachings of Ecclesiastes, for example, Ecclesiastes 2:24–26; 3:11–12?

How does verse 10 explain verse 9?

Are verses 11 and 12 parallel?

Can you see different ways of reading "if ye have not been faithful in that which is another man's, who shall give you that which is your own?" (verse 12).

Who might the "other man" be in this life? In the eternities?

Lesson 18
Luke 15; 17

Luke 15

Many years ago a friend, Bruce Jorgensen, convinced me that it is important to read the parables of Luke 15 together. He did that by reading them aloud as if they were a small drama. His reading took them as responses to those at the dinner, responses that build on each other and culminate in what we call the parable of the prodigal son.

Consider the setting that Luke gives us in verses 1–2 and then imagine Jesus telling each of these parables in response to what happens in those verses: he hears the Pharisees and the scribes complaining because he eats with sinners, so he tells the parable of the lost sheep. Evidently they don't understand his point, because he immediately tells another parable, that of the lost coin. I imagine a silent pause after the first parable, with Jesus waiting for the Pharisees and scribes to respond. But they seem not to understand the second one either, so he tells them a third, more complicated parable, the so-called parable of the prodigal son. Try duplicating Jorgensen's reading for yourself by reading the parables aloud in that way. Does that way of seeing them change your understanding of them?

Verses 1–2: Why would the publicans and sinners have come to hear Jesus? Why does it bother the Pharisees and the scribes that Jesus eats with publicans and tax collectors?

Verses 4–7: Why does Jesus use the figure of the shepherd so often? Are scriptures such as Isaiah 40:11 and 56:11 relevant? Would the Pharisees have seen a connection to such verses?

How is this parable a response to the murmuring of the Pharisees and scribes? If they understood what he was saying about himself in this parable, how would the Pharisees and scribes have reacted?

Do you think that verse 7 is hyperbolic, exaggerating the joy felt for the recovery of the lost sheep? If not, why doesn't this verse suggest that it is better to be a repentant sinner than one who never needed to repent?

Verses 8–10: Why would the woman have to light a candle to find a lost coin during the day? What would have made finding it difficult?

Who did Jesus intend the shepherd to represent to the Pharisees and scribes in the previous parable, and what does he intend the parable to teach them? Who does the woman represent? Is the lesson of the second parable the same as that of the first? Another way to think about these questions: what do the Pharisees and scribes fail to understand when Jesus tells them the first two parables? Do verses 7 and 10 explain how these parables are related? Do they tell us what the Lord wanted the murmurers to understand? If so, what is that?

Verse 11: What do you make of the fact that Jesus begins this story telling us that it is about *two* sons? What does that suggest about the name we usually give it, the parable of the prodigal son? As you read the story, think about how focusing on both sons rather than only one may change its meaning.

Verse 12: What is the young man asking for? Under inheritance practices of the time, how much of his father's estate would the younger son receive?

In response to the son's request, the father gives *both* of the sons their inheritance. What does this mean for the father?

The word translated *riotous living* is also used in Ephesians 5:18, where it is translated *excess*; Titus 1:6, where the King James translators have *riot*; and 1 Peter 4:4, where we also find *riot*. How is the second son spending his money?

We often imagine that he spent the money on immoral activities. What evidence do we have for that? In our own context and time, what kind of spending would count as riotous or excessive?

Verses 14–16: How does the famine figure in this story (verse 14)? Is it the cause of the younger son's repentance, for example?

When asked to recount this story from memory, those from poor countries almost always include the famine in their retelling while those from wealthier countries seldom do. What might that say about how we listen to and understand scripture?

What does it mean to say that the second son joined himself to a citizen of the country where he was (verse 15)?

How would Jesus's audience (verses 1–2) have responded to the idea that this young man has taken the job of feeding swine?

Does verse 16 say that he wanted to eat the carob husks that they fed pigs, but no one would let him? Or does it say that he wanted to eat the husks because no one would give him anything else?

Verses 17–19: "Came to himself" is a literal translation. What does it mean to come to oneself? What does it mean to be away from oneself? Have you ever been away from yourself? How did you come back? What does coming to oneself have to do with repentance?

What does the son remember about how his father treats hired servants? What does that tell us about the father?

Why does the son rehearse what he is going to say to his father? How has he sinned against heaven? How has he sinned before ("in the presence of") his father?

Verses 20–24: What would the father have to have been doing to see his son while the son was still a great way off? What does this suggest about what the father has been doing? How long has the father been waiting for the son to return?

The word translated *compassion* could also have been translated *pity*. What is pity? When is it appropriate, and how is it related to compassion? How does Jesus portray the father as responding to seeing his son return?

Why doesn't the son finish the little speech that he has prepared for his father?

Does the father treat the returned son as he would a hired servant?

How does he explain his joy in verse 24? How does that answer the Pharisees' murmuring?

Is the explanation also a reference to Jesus's coming death and resurrection?

Is there any sense in which Jesus has become, metaphorically, a prodigal son? If so, what inheritance did he take and spend excessively?

Whom would Jesus have expected the prodigal son to represent in the Pharisees' understanding?

Verses 25–27: We have here the second half of the story, about the second son. The story does not end at verse 24.

Whom would Jesus have expected the Pharisees to understand the second son to represent?

Why does the second son call a servant to find out what is going on in the house rather than go in and find out for himself? Who was the owner of the house at the time the son sent the servant to find out?

Verse 28: Why is the second son angry? Why won't he go into the house?

How does the father deal with the son's anger?

Verses 29–30: Is it true that the father has not given the older son anything?

Do you think it is true that the older son has never transgressed one of his father's commandments?

Is it likely that he has had these feelings about his brother before? If he has, would that have violated his father's commandments?

The older brother says that the younger one has used up the father's money "with harlots." Should we be at least somewhat skeptical about what the older brother says about the younger? Why?

Verses 31–32: When the father says "all that I have is thine," of what is he reminding the older son?

Compare verse 32 to verse 24. Why does Jesus have the father repeat this? Does this parable answer the Pharisees' murmuring differently than the previous two do? If so, how so?

Luke 17

Verses 1–6: What gives the sayings in these verses unity? Is it the theme of causing offense and strengthening faith?

Verses 1–2: In the King James Version, *offences* translates a Greek word that means "stumbling blocks." The word *offend* translates a word that means "cause to stumble." If you insert "stumbling blocks" and "cause to stumble" into the appropriate places in these verses, does that change their meaning for you? If so, how?

Who are the "little ones" to whom Jesus refers in verse 2? Is he speaking of children or of followers, *his* children? Or is he speaking of some other group?

Verses 3–5: In verse 5 the apostles ask Jesus to increase their faith. What about the teaching in the previous several verses has made them ask for this?

Can one person strengthen the faith of another? How?

Verse 6: Wouldn't this have rubbed salt into the wound the apostles felt because they need more or stronger faith? Why would the Lord do that?

In context, what is the point of this short parable?

Verses 7–10: Is what Jesus says in these verses a continuation of his response to the apostles' request in verse 5? If not, what motivates this teaching? If this does respond to their request, how does it do so?

What is the point of this parable? Is it anything besides what we see in verse 10: no matter how much you do what you are commanded, you will still be an unprofitable servant? How can that teaching possibly be part of a gospel of hope? If we can never do anything more than our duty, where does the value of our work come from?

Compare Jesus's teaching to that of King Benjamin in Mosiah 2:21–25, 3:19, and 4:5–7, 11–16. Does King Benjamin's longer sermon help us understand Jesus's teaching? How?

Verses 11–19: Is this story related to the parable in verses 7–10? How is it relevant that the leper who gave thanks was a Samaritan?

Verses 20–21: Why would the Pharisees have asked Jesus when the kingdom of God would come (verse 20)? What do you think they thought would bring that kingdom?

What does Jesus mean when he says that the kingdom doesn't come by observation (verse 20)?

What does it mean to say that the kingdom is within us (verse 21)? Does that mean that the answer is "The kingdom of God is already here, in you"? How could the kingdom of God be within those who were opposed him? Or is Jesus speaking only to the disciples here? How would you decide who his audience was?

Some have translated the Greek phrase we are looking at as the King James translators did: "within you." Others have translated the phrase as "in your midst" or "within your grasp." How does the meaning of each differ? Which of those translations seems most likely to you? Why?

Verses 22–23: Can you explain verse 22? The translation is straightforward. There is nothing to be cleared up by looking at another possible translation. But the meaning is not clear. What does it mean to say that there will be a time when the disciples will long to see one of the days of the Son of man, but they won't see it?

Why would they long to see a day of the Lord's reign when the kingdom is already within them, in their midst, or within their grasp?

What are those hypothetically speaking in verse 23 responding to? Why shouldn't a Christian pay attention to those who proclaim that they see the events of "the days of the Son of man"?

Verses 24–27: How are the various things that Jesus says in verses 24–27 unified? Do they have a common theme?

What point is the Lord making with his reference to Lot in verses 28–31?

How did Lot's wife seek to save her life (verses 32–33)? How is she a type of those who seek to save their lives?

Verses 34–37: In verse 37, what are Jesus's disciples asking when they say, "Where, Lord?" What are they trying to figure out?

Verses 24–36 focused on how quickly the day of the Son of man will come. In verse 23 Jesus warned against listening to those who would tell them where to see that day. Does that say anything about the disciples' question in verse 37?

Luke uses the generic term for body here, but the Greek of the parallel verse in Matthew 24:28 uses the word for a corpse, so we can assume that is what Luke means by the word *body*. This appears to be a variation of the same saying that we find in Job 39:30 which, speaking of the eagle, says "where the slain are, there is she."

How is this enigmatic saying of verse 37 a response to the disciples' question? In the context of this discussion of the second coming, what might the body stand for? The eagles? Is it relevant that the verb is passive, "will be gathered" by some agent rather than "will gather" themselves?

Lesson 19

Luke 18:1–8, 35–43; 19:1–10; John 11

Luke 18

Verses 1–8: The chapter division here (an artificial division not in the original text) makes us overlook the connection between the end of Luke 17 and the beginning of 18. Might Luke have any particular prayers in mind in verse 1? How about the desire mentioned in Luke 17:22? In other words, does the context of verse 1, which we know from the previous chapter, inform its meaning?

In verse 1 Luke portrays Jesus telling us the teaching of the parable before he gives the parable. Why? After reading the parable, ask yourself whether there are other ways to read it, perhaps ways that Luke wants to forestall.

We will later see that Paul particularly likes the language that Luke uses here, "pray always" (see, for example, 1 Thessalonians 5:17; Romans 12:12; and Ephesians 6:18) and "do not faint."

The word translated *faint* means "to become weary or exhausted" and can mean "lose heart." (For examples of places where Paul uses the term, see 2 Thessalonians 3:13; 2 Corinthians 4:1, 16; and Galatians 6:9.) What kind of fainting or exhaustion do you think Luke has in mind?

What does constant prayer have to do with being a Christian? Does it have anything to do with seeing the world with Christ as the light that makes sight possible (John 9)?

What does not getting exhausted have to do with being a Christian?

In verse 2 we find that the judge neither fears God nor regards man. What does the second mean? Are the two phrases parallel, and if they are, does understanding the first help us understand the second? What does "feared not God, neither regarded man" tell us about this judge? Is that a positive or a negative description?

The King James Version (verse 3) says that the woman "came unto" the judge, but a more accurate translation might be "she kept coming to him." A better translation than *avenge* is *defend, plead my case*. What is the woman asking, and why do you think she has to keep coming to the judge?

In verse 6, why does Jesus tell his listeners to pay attention to what the judge said? What is the import of verse 7 and the first half of verse 8? How does the parable explain God's defense of his elect? Why compare the Father to an unjust judge? Isn't that blasphemous?

The last part of verse 8 is poorly translated in the King James Version. As we have it, the verse says "though he bear long with them," but most agree that something like "Will he be slow to answer them?" is more accurate. How does that change of translation change the meaning of the verse?

How is the question in the second half of verse 8 related to the parable and its explanation? This is the only parable that ends with an explicit question. Why? What is the answer to the question? How is that answer relevant to the context in which Jesus has told this parable?

Verses 35–43: When Mark recounted this story, he placed it immediately after James and John's request to sit at the Lord's right and left hand and Jesus's discussion with the apostles about what it means to be great in the kingdom. Luke puts the event after Jesus's encounter with the rich young man who could not give up his riches, the discussion with Peter about what things those who follow him are blessed with, and Jesus's prophecy that he would soon be killed in Jerusalem. Do the different contexts into which Mark and Luke place this story give it different meanings?

How do Jesus's "handlers" deal with the blind man (verse 39)? To whom might we compare those people in our own experience? Are we, probably without knowing it, ever among those who tell people crying for the mercy of God to hold their peace? If so, how do we do so?

To whom might we compare the blind man with his cry for mercy? Are we blind? Do we need mercy? What can heal our blindness?

The blind man calls Jesus "Son of David" (verse 39). What did he mean by that title? How is it relevant to the coming events, such as Jesus's entry into Jerusalem?

Verse 43 describes the response of both the blind man and the people who saw him cured as praising and glorifying God. Is that part of our worship? If so, where and when does it occur?

Luke 19

Verses 1–10: The name Zacchaeus (Zaccai in Hebrew) means "pure" or "innocent." Is that relevant or irrelevant to the story?

213

Why does Luke tell us that Zacchaeus was the chief publican and that he was rich? Does that suggest anything about his character? Which suggestion, that of his name or that of his occupation, turns out to be more accurate? When we hear his occupation, "rich tax collector," how does Luke expect us to think of Zacchaeus?

Compare this parable to that of the blind man. How are Zacchaeus and the blind man in the same position relative to their culture?

Do you think that Luke places this story near the story of the rich young man so that we can contrast the two? If so, in how many ways do you see a contrast?

Of what significance is it that Jesus calls someone to him whom it would seem impossible for him to know about (verse 5)?

Why was Zacchaeus joyful (verse 6)? Who do you think murmured (verse 7)?

What does verse 8 tell us about Zacchaeus? Is he describing what he *has* done all along or what he *will* do from now on? How do you decide? Compare Numbers 5:5–7, which gives the law of restitution. What does that tell us about Zacchaeus's offer?

In verse 9, what does Jesus mean when he says, "This day is salvation come to this house"? Is he using the word *salvation* to refer to himself or to what has happened to Zacchaeus? If the latter, why does Jesus say "to this house [or household]" rather than "to Zacchaeus"?

Explain Jesus's explanation of what has happened: "forsomuch as he also is a son of Abraham" (verse 9).

The language of verse 10 suggests that this event is related to the parables of the sheep, the coin, and the two sons (Luke 15). What specific connections can you see? (Notice, for example, the parallel between Luke 18:7 and Luke 15:2.) How does remembering that parable help us understand this event? How does understanding this event help us read that story?

John 11

Recall from the study questions for lesson 12 that many see the first part of the Gospel of John as organized around seven miracles and accompanying sermons:

1. Turning water into wine at the wedding feast and the discourse on being born again (John 2:1–12; 3:1–21)

2. Raising the nobleman's son to life and a discourse on Jesus as the living water (John 4:43–51; 4:1–42)

3. Healing the man by the pool of Bethesda on the Sabbath and explaining that Jesus is Lord of the Sabbath (John 5:1–14; 5:19–47)

4. Feeding the five thousand and teaching that Jesus is the bread of life (John 6:1–15; 6:22–66)

5. Walking on the Sea of Galilee, Jesus comes to Capernaum mysteriously and the discourse on the inability of the Pharisees to understand him (John 6:16–21; 7:14–39)

6. Healing the man born blind and the teaching that Christ is the Light of the World (John 9; 8:12–59)

7. The material for this lesson: raising Lazarus from the dead and the teaching of the resurrection (John 11; 10:1–18).

Why do you think John uses miracles as the signs of Jesus's ministry and of his teaching?

Four of the seven miracles are healings. Why is healing such an important sign of Jesus's ministry? Does it have symbolic significance as well as physical benefit?

The second part of John's Gospel focuses on Jesus's entry into Jerusalem, trial, death, and resurrection. How do these seven signs and sermons prepare us for that story?

As you read the story of the raising of Lazarus, ask yourself how Lazarus is a type for every person: in what various ways can we be said to be dead? Brought back to life?

Verses 1–2: The name Lazarus (Eleazar: "God has helped") was a common name at the time.

Why is it important that we know that Jesus has gone to the town where Mary and Martha live? Why is it important that we know which Mary it is? (See John 12:3; it does not seem to be the woman in Luke 7:37–38.)

Verses 3–6: What do the Gospels mean when they describe a person as someone whom Jesus loved? Didn't he love everyone? Does Jesus love the true Christian differently than he does the unrepentant person? If not, why not? If so, how?

In verse 4 Jesus says, "This sickness is not unto death." Since Lazarus does, in fact, die, what could Jesus have meant by that? To what does this sickness lead?

What would you normally think of someone who delayed coming to the bedside of an ill person whom he could heal? What would you think if that person said, "Waiting and letting him get worse before I heal him will show what a good doctor I am"? Is that what Jesus was doing?

How do you think a non-Christian might respond on hearing this much of the story? Why would John tell the story this way? (Notice that he is the only Gospel writer who tells the story at all, though the other Gospels tell of other persons restored to life.) Why don't we think the same things of Jesus that we might think of another person who acted in a similar way? Why is it important for Jesus to bring someone to life at this particular point in his ministry?

Verses 7–10: How is what Jesus says in verses 9–10 an answer to the disciples' worry in verse 8? How would you explain what Jesus is saying in verse 9? (Note that there were twelve hours in the daylight during Jesus's time, regardless of the season. So during the winter, daytime hours were shorter than they were during the summer.)

What does Jesus mean by "There is no light in him" (verse 10)? Do you think that the disciples understood Jesus's answer? Why or why not?

Verses 11–15: How do the disciples misunderstand Jesus? How is their misunderstanding nevertheless a kind of prophecy? Does that misunderstanding teach us anything about our relation to the Father and the Son?

217

Verse 16: When Thomas says, "Let us also go, that we may die with him," is he speaking of dying with Christ or with Lazarus? (See the footnote in the LDS edition.)

Why does John put Thomas's exhortation at this point in the story, where it seems out of place, rather than earlier?

Verses 17–19: There appears to have been a common belief at the time that the spirit of a person hung around its body for three days after death. The idea was that a person might die but revive during the first two or three days afterward. If that was a common belief, would that help us understand why Jesus waited as long as he did?

It seems that Jesus came to Bethany on the seventh day after learning of Lazarus's illness. Are those seven days significant? If so, how?

Why is it important that we know how far it was from Jerusalem to Bethany? How far was it from the Jordan, where Jesus was baptized, to Bethany? (See the map in the LDS edition of the Bible.)

Who are "the Jews" who came to comfort Martha and Mary? To whom does John often refer with that name? (See passages such as John 2:6; 3:25; 5:10–18; 6:41, 52; 7:1, 11–13; 8:48, 52, 57; and 9:18–22; also compare verse 18 to verse 13.) It is important to recognize that in John's Gospel the term "the Jews" does not refer to all who were from the tribe of Judah. Rather, it refers to a specific group of people in Jerusalem at that time, a particular social caste or political power. (Failure to see that has caused countless deaths and horror: Christians killing and otherwise tormenting those whom they took to be among "the Jews.")

What does the fact that many of the Jews came to comfort Martha and Mary suggest about their social standing? How is that relevant? Why is their presence in the story important?

Verses 20–22: Compare Martha's and Mary's behavior in Luke 10:38–42 to their behavior here. Do Luke and John portray them the same, or do you see differences?

Why does Martha go to meet Jesus? Why do you think Mary stays in the house?

Does Martha accuse Jesus in verse 21?

Verses 23–27: Why doesn't Jesus tell her straightforwardly that he will bring Lazarus back to life?

Is Jesus giving this event a double meaning, showing two ways that the miracle will glorify the Father and, therefore, the Son (compare verse 4)?

What are some of the purposes that this miracle serves? Do we see one of those purposes in these verses?

In verse 24 Martha confesses her belief in the resurrection and Jesus responds, "*I* am the resurrection." How would she have most likely understood that response? What is Jesus telling her when he says what he does?

Why does verse 26 say that everyone who is alive and believes in Jesus "shall never die"? Why do we need already to be alive? Alive in what sense? Why is it important that Martha believe this teaching? How is her belief related to the story as a whole?

Verses 28–32: Did Jesus call for Mary, or was this Martha's idea? What would the former suggest? What would the latter suggest?

Why does Martha go to Mary secretly? Can we see Mary as a type for the Christian in verse 28? If so, for whom is Martha a type?

Is Jesus waiting outside the town? If so, why?

Is Mary accusing Jesus in verse 32?

Verses 33–37: What troubled (and the best translation here is probably *angered* rather than *troubled* or *groaned in the spirit*) Jesus about this event (verse 33)?

If weeping at death is appropriate (D&C 42:45), what was wrong with the weeping of this group? Is 1 Thessalonians 4:13 relevant? Why did Jesus weep (verse 34)? Presumably he knew that he was going to raise Lazarus, so what was there to weep about?

Do some of the Jews accuse Jesus in verse 37? Is what they say different from what Martha and Mary have said (verses 21 and 32)? If so, how?

Verses 38–44: Why does John again tell us that Jesus was "groaning in himself" or angry (verse 38)?

Why does Martha think that Jesus wants the tomb opened?

When did Jesus tell Martha that if she would believe, then she would see the glory of God (verse 40)? If he is referring to what he said in verse 26, then "shall never die" and "shouldest see the glory of God" are parallel. Does that tell us anything about what he was saying in verse 26? What kind of life was he promising those who believe? What does it mean to believe?

In verse 41 we see them take away the stone from the tomb; then we hear Jesus speak to the Father as if he has *already* said a prayer asking that Lazarus be returned to life. Is that what has happened? If so, why doesn't John explicitly tell us about that previous prayer?

The word translated *people* in verse 42 could perhaps better be translated *crowd* or *multitude*. Is Jesus putting on a show for them? How do you explain verse 42?

John shows us Lazarus coming out of the tomb (verse 44), but nothing of his reunion with his sisters and friends. Why does John end the story so abruptly and move on to a related topic?

Verses 45–46: We've seen this division among "the Jews" before (e.g., John 9:16). What does it tell us about these events and about Christ's effect on those who experienced his earthly ministry?

Verses 47–48: At this time, what was the relationship like between the priests and the Pharisees? Does that relation shed any light on the gathering that we see here?

Do the priests and the Pharisees believe that Jesus performs miracles (verse 47)? If so, why are they opposed to him?

What two things are the priests and Pharisees worried about losing (verse 48)?

Why would they believe that if people follow Jesus the Romans are likely to take over the rule of Judea? The Romans already oversaw the Judean government and had troops in Jerusalem and other cities to enforce their power. So what would it mean for them to "take away both our place and nation"? When did the priests and Pharisees lose their place and nation? What brought that about?

Verses 49–52: In verse 50 Caiaphas uses the same reasoning—and perhaps exactly the same wording—that the Lord used with Nephi when he told Nephi to kill Laban (1 Nephi 4:13). How do you explain that? What do you make of it? Would Caiaphas have seen the two circumstances as different?

Verses 51–52: The first clause of verse 51 suggests that we could understand Caiaphas to have been referring to himself in verse 49. How so? What irony is John exploiting? When did the high priest ever die to save Israel? To think about that, consider that Hebrews speaks of Jesus as "the great high priest" (Hebrews 4:14). What Jewish ritual made that parallel explicit?

In verse 52, to whom would early Christians have thought "that nation" referred? Does it refer to the phrase "the children of God that were scattered abroad"?

How is Jesus's death related to the gathering? Given the importance of the resurrection, why does John speak here only of Jesus's death?

Verses 53–57: How is the raising of Lazarus related to the decision to kill Jesus?

Why does Jesus go to Ephraim to wait for Passover (verse 54)? How was Passover a purifying festival?

For what reason or reasons might Jesus's passion and resurrection have taken place at Passover rather than at the fast commemorating the atonement, Yom Kippur?

Lesson 20

Matthew 21:1–11, 23–46; 22:15–46; 23;
John 12:1–8

Matthew 21

Verses 1–7: The end of verse 3 could also be translated "and straightway he will return them." Does that make any difference to your understanding of the verse?

Verse 5 puts two scriptures together, Isaiah 62:11 and Zechariah 9:9 (as they appear in the Greek rather than the Hebrew version of the Old Testament). What does "daughter of Sion" mean? Why is it important that the Lord enter Jerusalem on the back of a donkey (rather than on a horse, for example)?

Verses 8–11: Why did the people put their cloaks and branches from the trees onto the road in front of Jesus?

Hosanna means "save, we pray." Do you think that the people were using it because of its meaning or only as a shout of acclamation (much as we use the word *amen* without usually thinking about its meaning)?

In Israelite history, who was first called "son of David"? What did that name signify? What does it have to do with the temple?

What does it mean to say "all the city was moved [i.e., shaken]"?

Why do the crowds describe Jesus as "the prophet of Nazareth of Galilee" rather than with the Messianic title they have been using?

Verses 12–16: Though the story of the cleansing of the temple isn't part of the readings for this lesson, I include study notes for it.

Why does Jesus go to the temple immediately upon entering Jerusalem?

In order to offer sacrifice, people had to be able to buy animals for sacrifice—in particular, the poor had to be able to buy the doves that they used for offerings—and they had to exchange their money for the temple money that was used for offerings. Scholars assume that the animal sales and money exchange occurred in the Court of the Gentiles, an outer court of the temple into which any person could enter. Since selling doves and changing money were necessary to the function of the temple and since it occurred outside the sacred part of the temple, why did Jesus drive out the money changers and the dove sellers?

In verse 13 Jesus combines two Old Testament passages: Isaiah 56:7 and Jeremiah 7:11. What do Jesus's actions show about his authority? To whom do you think Jesus refers when he uses the word *thieves*? Many believe that he is speaking of the high priest and those who rule with him. How might they justify that opinion? The word *thief* is a strong one, comparable to *armed robber*. (It is not the same word that John uses to describe Judas in John 12:6.) Josephus uses it to describe the Zealots and others who waged armed conflict with Rome. Why is it the right word in this case? Is Jesus's use of the word here related to his use of the word in John 10:1? What happens in a cave (the King James Version has *den*) to which armed robbers retreat? What is Jesus saying that those he condemns here have done to the temple?

In verse 15, why does Matthew describe as children the crowds who acclaim Jesus?

Why don't the chief priests and scribes complain about Jesus's cleansing of the Court of the Gentiles? Their complaint seems to be that the people are saying, "Hosanna to the Son of David."

What do you think they mean when they say to Jesus, in verse 16, "Hearest thou what these say?"

Jesus answers them by quoting the Greek version of Psalm 8:3. The word translated *perfected* means "completed," but it connotes restoration, putting something back as it was. How have the crowds "perfected praise"?

Verses 23–27: Why do the chief priests and elders wait until the day after Jesus has cleansed the temple (see verse 18) to question Jesus's authority to do what he has done? What things are they asking about—cleansing the temple or what he teaches?

Does Jesus respect the authority of those who question him about his authority? On what evidence do you base your answer?

Why can't the chief priests and elders answer his question about John's baptism? Why doesn't he answer their question?

Verses 28–46: After this confrontation with the chief priests and scribes, Jesus tells them three parables: that of two sons, one obedient and one disobedient; that of the wicked husbandman; and that of the king's son's marriage (Matthew 22:1–14). The last of these is not in our reading assignment, but I suggest you read it so that you see this story in its entirety.

As you read those parables, ask what Jesus was trying to teach the priests and scribes. Also ask yourself what the common theme of the three parables is.

Verses 28–32: To whom does Jesus compare the first son? The second?

How do you think the chief priests and scribes responded when Jesus said, "The tax collectors and prostitutes go into the kingdom of God before you"? How did he explain that? Can you think of anything that would be a comparable insult in today's society?

Verse 32 says that John the Baptist taught how to become righteous (he "came unto you in the way of righteousness"). In what did righteousness consist according to John? What have the chief priests and scribes ignored?

Verses 33–44: Compare verse 33 to Isaiah 5:2. What does the vineyard represent in the Isaiah passage? Does it represent the same thing here?

Who do the servants in the parable represent? Whom does the son represent?

What is the irony of verse 41?

What does the JST add to our understanding of these verses?

Matthew 22

Verses 1–14: Why does Jesus tell the chief priests and scribes, a group that probably also included Pharisees, three parables rather than just one?

What does this third parable add that we have not seen in the previous two?

In the context of these parables, what does "many are called, but few are chosen" mean? Is that meaning different here than it is in other places where we see the same phrase, such as D&C 121:40?

Verses 15–22: Why would Matthew's audience have been shocked by the coalition of Pharisees and Herodians? (To learn about the Herodians, see the Bible Dictionary.) What would the Herodians have thought about the tax (a poll or head tax) in question? How about the Pharisees? What position does verse 16 suggest that they think Jesus will take?

When Jesus asks them whose image is on the coin (verse 20), what point is he making about the coin? Does Jesus answer the question he has been asked?

Many have said that Jesus's response to the question is an early commandment to keep church and state separate. What do you think of that interpretation?

Verses 23–33: Now the Sadducees come to question Jesus. Luke describes them as the party of the high priest (Acts 5:17). Though most Sadducees did not believe in the resurrection, the primary difference between them and the other parties was that they thought that Israel should be ruled by the priesthood or, in other words, by them.

The various overlapping political parties of Jesus's day fought with each other about many things, such as the right relation of Judea to Rome and what was included in the Law, but they agreed in their antipathy for Jesus. Why did they agree on that? What might their agreement teach us about ourselves?

Does Jesus give his listeners any way to decide what belongs to Caesar and what to God? What is the point of his teaching in these verses?

Verses 34–39: Jesus's confrontation with the ruling powers continues.

How is the Pharisees' question a trial or test of Jesus? If we can infer from what we know of rabbinic teaching in the second and later centuries, the rabbis (scribes in the New Testament) taught that there were 613 commandments in the Law, 248 positive commandments and 365 negative ones. They ranked these commandments in terms of their greatness or heaviness. Do you think they would have disagreed with Jesus about which commandment is the greatest or heaviest (Deuteronomy 6:5)?

Why does Jesus continue the discussion by answering a question that the Pharisees have not asked: "Which is the second greatest commandment?"

What does he mean when he says that the second commandment (Leviticus 19:18) is "like unto" the first?

What does the phrase "the law and the prophets" mean? Is Jesus referring to the parts of Jewish scripture designated as "the Law" (or Torah) and "the Prophets"—so that the phrase means "scripture"—or is he using it in another way?

What does it mean to say that the law and the prophets hang or are suspended from these two commandments? Can you explain that metaphor?

Verses 41–46: The series of confrontations ends with Jesus questioning the Pharisees. He quotes Psalm 110:1 and poses a problem for them to solve. What is the problem that Jesus has raised, and why can't the Pharisees solve it? What is Jesus trying to show by giving them a problem that they cannot solve?

We can read the text in the first part of verse 44 as saying, "Yahweh said to the Messiah, 'Sit on my right hand.'"

Matthew 23

Where does this sermon occur?

Does Jesus deliver any other public sermons between this one and his death?

Why do you think he makes hypocrisy the topic of his last sermon? Was this sermon particularly important for Jesus's day but less so for our own?

Verses 1–12: In verse 2, what do you think "the seat of Moses" means?

What does Jesus mean in verse 3 when he tells the people to do what the scribes and Pharisees tell them, but not to do what they do? Is the example he gives in verse 4 particularly telling?

What does Jesus say motivates the scribes' and Pharisees' obedience (verses 5–7)?

The word *rabbi* means "my master." Why does Jesus tell them not to use that title (verse 8)? What does it mean that he tells them also not to use the title *father* or the title *teacher* (*master* in the King James Version)? What title or titles are they to use (verse 8)? How do the permitted titles differ from the forbidden ones? Does Jesus's injunction to the disciples suggest anything about our own practices? How, for example, can we justify some of the titles we use in the Church or in our society at large if we accept these verses? Ought we to rethink some of our use of titles whether in the Church or in the secular world?

How are verses 11–12 an explanation for what Jesus says about titles?

Verses 13–36: Jesus pronounces seven woes on the scribes and Pharisees. Why doesn't he include the Herodians or Sadducees—or does he?

How do the scribes and Pharisees shut up (in other words, lock up) the kingdom of heaven (verse 13)?

Is he saying anything about priesthood keys? What do they lock up? (Compare Luke 11:52.) What parallel might we find in our own lives for what he accuses the scribes and Pharisees?

Though after the destruction of the temple in AD 70 the Jews no longer proselyted, there is evidence that they were actively proselyting at the time of Christ. What might verse

15 condemn? Do we ever do anything like that? If so, how so? How can we avoid doing this?

What problem does Jesus identify in verses 16–22, the third woe? Is there a contemporary equivalent?

What practice does Jesus criticize in verses 23–24? How is this condemnation connected to his teaching in Matthew 22:39–40?

The fifth and sixth woes (verses 25–26 and 27–28) are similar in structure. What is their point? How would we avoid the sin that Jesus describes in them? Remember that dead things were considered impure, so anything that touched them was impure. That means that the interior of a tomb was as impure as anything could be.

Given the similarity of these two woes, why do you think Jesus pronounced both of them? Why not leave it at six woes by omitting one of these two?

The concluding woe (verses 29–36) is the longest of the seven. What does Jesus condemn in it, and why does he keep it for last and make it longest? Is there anything in our contemporary worship practices like this?

What does it mean to say that they witness to themselves that they are descended from prophet-killers (verse 31)? How is that relevant to Jesus's situation?

Explain what verse 32 means.

What does Jesus mean when he says that the blood of the righteous from Abel to Zechariah will come on them (verse 35)? (In the Hebrew Bible of the time, the first victim of murder mentioned was Abel, and Zechariah [2 Chronicles

24:20–22] was the last. We no longer arrange the books in the order that was used in Jesus's time.) When would early Christians have thought this prophecy had been fulfilled? (Consider verse 36.) Does it have a latter-day fulfillment?

What is the point of verse 37? Does it teach anything that applies to us? How does verse 38 explain prophecies such as that in Jeremiah 22:5? When will Israel see Jesus again (verse 39)?

John 12:1–8

Verses 1–3: Why is it important that we notice that what follows happens shortly after the raising of Lazarus, as verse 1 reminds us? Is it important that we know this happened in Bethany, or is that merely an incidental detail? If the latter, why did John include it?

Do you see any significance in the fact that this dinner is given for Jesus seven days before his death and resurrection, probably on Friday evening, at the beginning of the Sabbath?

Why is it important to John that he tell us what roles Mary and Martha played at the dinner? How is this story related to the two earlier stories that involve these two women? Does the fact that Martha serves at this dinner help us understand better the story in which Jesus remonstrates with her for being troubled about many things in her serving (Luke 10:38–42)?

The custom seems to have been to anoint the head of a guest with oil (though sometimes feet were anointed after being washed), but Mary and the Galilean woman (Luke 7:38) each anoint Jesus's feet (rather than wash them), and they dry his feet with their hair rather than with a towel. The work of washing feet was a servant's job, and it was probably unseemly for a respectable Jewish woman to let her hair down in public. What is the symbolic significance of what Mary does? The literal meaning of "the house was filled with the odour of the ointment" is obvious. What is its symbolic significance?

Verses 4–8: Isn't Judas's objection a reasonable one? Would it have been reasonable if Judas had been a person of good character? How can his character be relevant to our judgment of the reasonableness of his objection?

We could restate verse 6 loosely in this way: "Judas did not say this because he cared for the poor but because he was a thief and was in charge of the disciples' money." Does John give one reason or two for Judas's complaint? Does he intend us to remember John 10:1 or 10:8 when he describes Judas as a thief?

Why was it important for Jesus to explain the symbolic significance of Mary's act to his disciples (verse 7)?

What are we to make of Jesus's paraphrase of Deuteronomy 15:11: "The poor always ye have with you" (verse 8)?

Over and over again we have seen Jesus's love for those who are excluded from the community, those the Pharisees called sinners, most of whom would have been poor. Does what he says here contradict that love and concern? If not, why not?

Verses 9–11: Do you see symbolic significance in the fact that the Jewish leaders want to kill the person whom Jesus has raised from the dead?

Lesson 21
Matthew 24 (JST)

While studying for this lesson you will probably find it helpful to be able to see the revealed changes that Joseph Smith made to this chapter of Matthew. Here are the King James Version and the Joseph Smith Translation side by side:

KING JAMES

1 And Jesus went out, and departed from the temple: and his disciples came to him for to shew him the buildings of the temple.

2 And Jesus said unto them, See ye not all these things? verily I say unto you, There shall not be left here one stone upon another, that shall not be thrown down.

JOSEPH SMITH TRANSLATION

1 And Jesus went out, and departed from the temple; and his disciples came to him for to hear him, saying, Master, show us concerning the buildings of the temple; as thou hast said; They shall be thrown down and left unto you desolate.

2 And Jesus said unto them, See ye not all these things? And do ye not understand them? Verily I say unto you, There shall not be left here upon this temple, one stone upon another, that shall not be thrown down.

3 And as he sat upon the mount of Olives, the disciples came unto him privately, saying, Tell us, when shall these things be? and what shall be the sign of thy coming, and of the end of the world?

4 And Jesus answered and said unto them, Take heed that no man deceive you.

5 For many shall come in my name, saying, I am Christ; and shall deceive many.

6 And ye shall hear of wars and rumours of wars: see that ye be not troubled: for all these things must come to pass, but the end is not yet.

7 For nation shall rise against nation, and kingdom against kingdom: and

3 And Jesus left them and went upon the mount of Olives.

4 And as he sat upon the mount of Olives, the disciples came unto him privately, saying, Tell us, when shall these things be which thou hast said concerning the destruction of the temple, and the Jews; and what is the sign of thy coming; and of the end of the world? (or the destruction of the wicked, which is the end of the world.)

5 And Jesus answered and said unto them, Take heed that no man deceive you.

6 For many shall come in my name, saying, I am Christ; and shall deceive many.

there shall be famines, and pestilences, and earthquakes, in divers places.

8 All these are the beginning of sorrows.

9 Then shall they deliver you up to be afflicted, and shall kill you: and ye shall be hated of all nations for my name's sake.

10 And then shall many be offended, and shall betray one another, and shall hate one another.

11 And many false prophets shall rise, and shall deceive many.

12 And because iniquity shall abound, the love of many shall wax cold.

13 But he that shall endure unto the end, the same shall be saved.

14 And this gospel of the kingdom shall be preached in all the world for a witness unto all nations; and then shall the end come.

7 Then shall they deliver you up to be afflicted, and shall kill you; and ye shall be hated of all nations for my name's sake.

8 And then shall many be offended, and shall betray one another, and shall hate one another.

9 And many false prophets shall arise, and shall deceive many.

10 And because iniquity shall abound, the love of many shall wax cold.

11 But he that remaineth steadfast, and is not overcome, the same shall be saved.

15 When ye therefore shall see the abomination of desolation, spoken of by Daniel the prophet, stand in the holy place, (whoso readeth, let him understand:)

16 Then let them which be in Judaea flee into the mountains:

17 Let him which is on the housetop not come down to take any thing out of his house:

18 Neither let him which is in the field return back to take his clothes.

19 And woe unto them that are with child, and to them that give suck in those days!

20 But pray ye that your flight be not in the winter, neither on the sabbath day:

21 For then shall be great tribulation, such as was not since the beginning of the world to this time, no, nor ever shall be.

12 When ye therefore, shall see the abomination of desolation, spoken of by Daniel the prophet, concerning the destruction of Jerusalem, then ye shall stand in the holy place. (Whoso readeth let him understand.)

13 Then let them who are in Judea, flee into the mountains.

14 Let him who is on the housetop, flee, and not return to take anything out of his house.

15 Neither let him who is in the field, return back to take his clothes.

16 And woe unto them that are with child, and unto them that give suck in those days!

17 Therefore, pray ye the Lord, that your flight be not in the winter, neither on the Sabbath day.

18 For then, in those days, shall be great tribulations on the Jews, and upon the inhabitants of Jerusalem;

such as was not before sent upon Israel, of God, since the beginning of their kingdom until this time; no, nor ever shall be sent again upon Israel.

19 All things which have befallen them, are only the beginning of the sorrows which shall come upon them; and except those days should be shortened, there should none of their flesh be saved.

22 And except those days should be shortened, there should no flesh be saved: but for the elect's sake those days shall be shortened.

20 But for the elect's sake, according to the covenant, those days shall be shortened.

21 Behold these things I have spoken unto you concerning the Jews.

22 And again, after the tribulation of those days which shall come upon Jerusalem, if any man shall say unto you, Lo! here is Christ, or there; believe him not.

23 Then if any man shall say unto you, Lo, here is Christ, or there; believe it not.

24 For there shall arise false Christs, and false prophets, and shall shew great signs

23 For in those days, there shall also arise false Christs, and false prophets, and shall

and wonders; insomuch that, if it were possible, they shall deceive the very elect.

25 Behold, I have told you before.

26 Wherefore if they shall say unto you, Behold, he is in the desert; go not forth: behold, he is in the secret chambers; believe it not.

27 For as the lightning cometh out of the east, and shineth even unto the west; so shall also the coming of the Son of man be.

28 For wheresoever the carcase is, there will the eagles be gathered together.

show great signs and wonders; insomuch that, if possible, they shall deceive the very elect, who are the elect according to the covenant.

24 Behold, I speak these things unto you for the elect's sake.

25 And ye also shall hear of wars, and rumors of wars; see that ye be not troubled; for all I have told you must come to pass. But the end is not yet.

26 Behold, I have told you before, Wherefore, if they shall say unto you, Behold, he is in the desert; go not forth. Behold, he is in the secret chambers; believe it not.

27 For as the light of the morning cometh out of the east, and shineth even unto the west, and covereth the whole earth; so shall also the coming of the Son of man be.

28 And now I show unto you a parable. Behold,

wheresoever the carcass is, there will the eagles be gathered together; so likewise shall mine elect be gathered from the four quarters of the earth.

29 And they shall hear of wars, and rumors of wars. Behold, I speak unto you for mine elect's sake.

30 For nation shall rise against nation, and kingdom against kingdom; there shall be famine and pestilences, and earthquakes in divers places.

31 And again, because iniquity shall abound, the love of men shall wax cold; but he that shall not be overcome, the same shall be saved.

32 And again, this gospel of the kingdom shall be preached in all the world, for a witness unto all nations, and then shall the end come, or the destruction of the wicked.

33 And again shall the abomination of desolation,

spoken of by Daniel the prophet, be fulfilled.

34 And immediately after the tribulation of those days, the sun shall be darkened, and the moon shall not give her light, and the stars shall fall from heaven, and the powers of heaven shall be shaken.

35 Verily I say unto you, this generation, in which these things shall be shown forth, shall not pass away until all I have told you shall be fulfilled.

36 Although the days will come that heaven and earth shall pass away, yet my word shall not pass away; but all shall be fulfilled.

29 Immediately after the tribulation of those days shall the sun be darkened, and the moon shall not give her light, and the stars shall fall from heaven, and the powers of the heavens shall be shaken:

37 And as I said before, after the tribulation of those days, and the powers of the heavens shall be shaken, then shall appear the sign of the Son of man in heaven; and then shall all the tribes of the earth mourn.

30 And then shall appear the sign of the Son of man in heaven: and then shall all the tribes of the earth mourn, and they shall see the Son of man coming in the clouds of heaven with power and great glory.

31 And he shall send his angels with a great sound of a trumpet, and they shall gather together his elect from the four winds, from one end of heaven to the other.

32 Now learn a parable of the fig tree; When his branch is yet tender, and putteth forth leaves, ye know that summer is nigh:

33 So likewise ye, when ye shall see all these things, know that it is near, even at the doors.

34 Verily I say unto you, This generation shall not pass, till all these things be fulfilled.

38 And they shall see the Son of man coming in the clouds of heaven, with power and great glory.

39 And whoso treasureth up my words, shall not be deceived.

40 For the Son of man shall come, and he shall send his angels before him with the great sound of a trumpet, and they shall gather together the remainder of his elect from the four winds; from one end of heaven to the other.

41 Now learn a parable of the fig tree: When its branches are yet tender, and it begins to put forth leaves, ye know that summer is nigh at hand.

42 So likewise mine elect, when they shall see all these things, they shall know that he is near, even at the doors.

35 Heaven and earth shall pass away, but my words shall not pass away.

36 But of that day and hour knoweth no man, no, not the angels of heaven, but my Father only.

37 But as the days of Noe were, so shall also the coming of the Son of an be.

38 For as in the days that were before the flood they were eating and drinking, marrying and giving in marriage, until the day that Noe entered into the ark,

39 And knew not until the flood came, and took them all away; so shall also the coming of the Son of man be.

40 Then shall two be in the field; the one shall be taken, and the other left.

43 But of that day and hour no one knoweth; no, not the angels of God in heaven, but my Father only.

44 But as it was in the days of Noah, so it shall be also at the coming of the Son of man.

45 For it shall be with them as it was in the days which were before the flood; for until the day that Noah entered into the ark, they were eating and drinking, marrying and giving in marriage, and knew not until the flood came and took them all away; so shall also the coming of the Son of man be.

46 Then shall be fulfilled that which is written, that, In the last days,

47 Two shall be in the field; the one shall be taken and the other left.

41 Two women shall be grinding at the mill; the one shall be taken, and the other left.

42 Watch therefore: for ye know not what hour your Lord doth come.

43 But know this, that if the goodman of the house had known in what watch the thief would come, he would have watched, and would not have suffered his house to be broken up.

44 Therefore be ye also ready: for in such an hour as ye think not the Son of man cometh.

45 Who then is a faithful and wise servant, whom his lord hath made ruler over his household, to give them meat in due season?

46 Blessed is that servant, whom his lord when he cometh shall find so doing.

48 Two shall be grinding at the mill; the one taken and the other left.

49 And what I say unto one, I say unto all men; Watch, therefore, for ye know not at what hour your Lord doth come.

50 But know this, if the good man of the house had known in what watch the thief would come, he would have watched, and would not have suffered his house to have been broken up; but would have been ready.

51 Therefore be ye also ready; for in such an hour as ye think not, the Son of man cometh.

52 Who then is a faithful and wise servant, whom his Lord hath made ruler over his household, to give them meat in due season?

53 Blessed is that servant, whom his Lord when he cometh shall find so doing;

47 Verily I say unto you, That he shall make him ruler over all his goods.

48 But and if that evil servant shall say in his heart, My lord delayeth his coming;

49 And shall begin to smite his fellowservants, and to eat and drink with the drunken;

50 The lord of that servant shall come in a day when he looketh not for him, and in an hour that he is not aware of,

51 And shall cut him asunder, and appoint him his portion with the hypocrites: there shall be weeping and gnashing of teeth.

54 And, verily I say unto you, he shall make him ruler over all his goods.

55 But if that evil servant shall say in his heart, My Lord delayeth his coming; and shall begin to smite his fellow servants, and to eat and drink with the drunken; the Lord of that servant shall come in a day when he looketh not for him, and in an hour that he is not aware of, and shall cut him asunder, and shall appoint him his portion with the hypocrites; there shall be weeping and gnashing of teeth.

56 And thus cometh the end of the wicked according to the prophecy of Moses, saying, They should be cut off from among the people. But the end of the earth is not yet; but bye and bye.

Traditional Christianity finds this chapter ambiguous: in some ways it seems to refer to the destruction of Jerusalem that occurred in AD 70; in some ways it seems to refer to the second coming. As I see it, Joseph Smith's revisions make it more clear which passages refer to the destruction of Jerusalem and which refer to the second coming. You may also wish to read Doctrine and Covenants 45:60–75 as background for understanding the Joseph Smith version better. Unless I note otherwise, all references to Matthew 24 in these questions are to the JST.

From Matthew 21:3 to Matthew 24:2, Jesus has been in the temple confronting the temple hierarchy and other community leaders, a confrontation that seems designed to bring about his death. Why does the discussion of the destruction of the temple and the end-time occur now?

Verse 1: In the Greek text of the unrevised biblical text, the disciples want to show the temple buildings to Jesus. Apparently they are struck by its majesty or beauty. In contrast, in the JST version they ask Jesus to show them (tell them) *about* the buildings. What difference do you think that difference makes?

Jesus's sermon to the elders of Jerusalem and the temple hierarchy appears to go from Matthew 21:23 to Matthew 22:46, followed by a sermon to the multitudes (Matthew 23:1–12) that turns into a sermon directly condemning the leadership once again (Matthew 23:13–39). How does that series of sermons bring on the disciples' question in this verse? What are they curious about? Why do you think they have come to Jesus privately?

Verses 2–3: Does the fact that Herod's temple was still under construction (mostly complete, but not fully finished) help explain the puzzlement of the disciples to which Jesus refers? What is Jesus prophesying?

Verse 4: What are the disciples' two questions? Does Jesus answer both of them?

Do the disciples repeat themselves when asking some questions? If so, why? What does it mean to say that "the destruction of the world" and the "destruction of the wicked" mean the same? Given that identity of meaning, how many different events can "the destruction of the world" refer to?

If I die before the second coming, can it have meaning in my life?

The phrase "sign of thy coming" can also be translated "miracle of your appearance," and "end of the world" can be translated as "fulfillment of the age or generation." Do either of these help you understand the disciples' questions with more depth?

Verses 5–11: This is Jesus's last sermon to the disciples before the crucifixion. When do they seem to have understood it, before his death or afterward? If more afterward than before, why was it important for him to tell him these things before the crucifixion rather than during the forty-day ministry between his resurrection and his ascension?

In these verses, what is Jesus's first concern (verses 5–6)?

The JST revision moves the verses that correspond to the traditional translation of Matthew 24:6–8. (Verse 6 is found in verse 23, 7 is found in verse 29, and 8 is found in verse 19.) Why might that be so?

How are verses 7 and 8 (JST) parallel? How are they different?

When will the events of verse 7 occur? The events of verse 8?

Does verse 9 prophesy the same thing as verse 6? Does verse 10 speak of the same events as verses 7 and 8 or of different events? Are verses 9–10 perhaps a synopsis of verses 5–8? What is Jesus's answer to the problems he has described in verses 5–10?

How does the JST help us understand what it means to "endure to the end"?

Verse 12: Why do you think that the JST moves the equivalent of verse 14 in the King James Version to verse 31?

Daniel 9:27, 11:31, and 12:11 refer to the abomination of desolation. Up to this point in time, those living in Judea had understood Daniel's prophecy to refer to the desecration of the temple by Antiochus IV (168 BC), when he set up an image of Zeus in the temple and is said to have sacrificed a pig on the temple altar. To what is Jesus referring in this verse? Was the previous understanding wrong? If not, how can Jesus refer to it in the future tense?

What does it mean to "stand in the holy place"? Where is that place literally? What might it signify symbolically?

Is the admonition in parentheses something that Matthew has added or something that was in Jesus's sermon? How do you know?

Why does Matthew add the warning "Whoso readeth let him understand"? That suggests a hidden meaning in what Jesus has just said. If there is a hidden meaning, what is it?

Verses 13–17: To whom is this advice directed, to the disciples or to the Saints in general?

How do you reconcile the advice to flee (verses 13–15) with the advice to "stand in the holy place"?

If you were on the roof of a Palestinian house in Jesus's day, why wouldn't you be able to take things from the house with you? If you were in a field, stripped down to a loincloth if a man or to a light shift if a woman, to where might you be tempted to go to get your clothing?

Why does Jesus tell them to pray that their flight not be on the Sabbath? What does that warning tell us about Jesus's attitude toward the rabbinic interpretations of the Law? (Compare Matthew 23:2–3.) How would you explain that attitude, given his withering criticism of the Pharisees and scribes (rabbis) and their belief that he frequently violated the Sabbath?

Verses 18–20: In verse 18, is Jesus referring to Israel as the disciples might have understood it or to Israel as we understand it? What's the difference between those?

What covenant is he referring to when he says that the days of tribulation will be shortened "according to the covenant"?

Verses 21–22: Why does Jesus repeat in lengthier form what he has already told the disciples (in verses 5–6, 9)?

Are the false Christs and prophets in the Church or exterior to it? How do you justify your answer?

What does it mean to be elect? The Greek word that Matthew uses can also be translated *chosen*. Who are the elect or chosen? For what are they chosen?

What does it mean to be chosen "according to the covenant"? What covenant do you think Jesus has in mind here? How would the disciples, as first-century Jews, have understood the covenant? Is that the same covenant that we have in mind when we refer to "the covenant"?

Verse 23: If I were dividing the verses, I would probably have included the first part of verse 23, "Behold, I speak these things unto you for the elect's sake," as the last part of verse 23. (As we read scripture, it is important to remember that the chapter and verse divisions reflect the thinking of an editor rather than the understanding of the Prophet.) Would you divide these verses as I would? As the editor did? In some other way? How does each way of dividing them change the meaning slightly?

What would Jesus's warning about wars and rumors of wars have meant to his disciples? What does it mean to us?

Verses 24–27:

When did Jesus tell them these things before (verse 24)? In this sermon or another?

What is he telling them that he has told them before?

Against what is Jesus warning them when he tells them not to look for him in the desert or in "secret chambers" (in other words, in secret meetings or meetings in hidden rooms)?

What does verse 26 tell us his coming will be like?

In the King James Version, the word *eagle* in verse 27 would be better translated *vulture* or *carrion bird*. I assume that the same meaning is intended for the JST. What is the point of the metaphor in verse 28?

Verses 28–29: These verses repeat the warning of verse 23. How is the intervening material (verses 24–27) related to the theme of impending war?

Verses 30–36: Jesus repeats the message of verses 10–11. Why?

Why is the waning of love, its waxing cold, such a terrible thing? Why is the waning of love the consequence of iniquity? Isn't it merely natural that over time things like love and friendship have less power?

Does verse 32 tell us that there will be a second abomination of desolation, or is it referring to the same one referred to in verse 12? Given the meaning of that phrase when used to speak of what happened in 168 BC and then to speak of the events of AD 70, what might it refer to in the last days?

To what does "this generation" (in other words, this time period) refer in verse 34?

In what sense will the earth pass away? Heaven?

Why would all of the tribes of the earth mourn at the coming of Christ? Is it relevant that Jesus says *tribes* will mourn rather than all the people of the earth?

Verse 37: What does it mean to treasure up the words of Christ? How does doing so protect us from being deceived?

Why is protection from deception so important?

Verses 38–40: What is the point of the parable of the fig tree?

What does it mean to say that Christ is "near, even at the door"? In what ways can he be near?

Why is verse 40 important to us? (It is repeated in D&C 39:21 and 49:7.) In how many ways is it important? Is Alma 5:29 relevant to verse 40 or vice versa?

Verses 41–45: Do these repeat the same theme as verses 13–15 or a different theme? How are they the same? Different?

Does Jesus speak of signs in these verses—for example, in verses 42, 44–45? What do these verses suggest about what it means to be watchful?

Verses 46–55: We see the theme of diligent watching in this parable. How would one know if a thief were digging through (note the term "broken up" in the KJV) the mud-brick wall of his house at night? Does answering that help make more sense of the metaphor that the parable uses?

What is the point of verses 46 and 48? What does that teaching have to do with us?

What does the Lord find the servant doing when he returns (verse 53)?

What is the blessing that the Lord gives the diligent servant (verse 54)? What does that mean to us?

To whom is the evil servant (verses 51–52) comparable?

Jesus uses an extremely disagreeable metaphor to describe the punishment given the evil servant (verse 55):

dismemberment. How is that metaphor apt? The Mosaic law speaks of being "cut off from among the people" (verse 55) in many places (e.g., Exodus 30:33 and 31:14, as well as Leviticus 18:29). Is that also a version of this disagreeable metaphor, though one that we've perhaps gotten so used to that we no longer recognize its original meaning? Or does it mean something different? From what people will the wicked be cut off? How will they be cut off? In what variety of ways do we see or will we see this happen?

Lesson 22
Matthew 25

Verses 1–13: We call this the parable of the ten virgins. We know little about marriage ceremonies in Palestine during Jesus's time. As with other Palestinian Jewish customs of the day, most of what we say about such things is really a description of customs 200 years or so later. Perhaps those later customs reflect what happened in Jesus's day. It is likely that there was considerable continuity between the first and the second centuries. But we cannot know what the customs were like, and the tremendous social upheaval resulting from the destruction of the temple in AD 70 could have interrupted the continuity of traditions.

Nevertheless, we can infer some things from this parable itself: Wedding feasts seem to have been held at night; otherwise there would be no reason for the bridal attendants to bring their lamps. It seems that the bride's attendants went out to escort the groom to the wedding feast, presumably held at the bride's house. It may be that the groom did not arrive at a particular time, but the tarrying of the groom in this parable might be for the story rather than because it was a custom.

How do the scriptures use the symbols of a bride and groom in other places? (See, for example, Matthew 9:15 and 22:1–14, as well as John 3:29. For another example, see the first several chapters of Hosea.) What do they stand for? Given that symbolism, whom might the ten virgins, the bridal attendants, stand for?

Do the lamps and oil represent anything in particular? If so, what?

Does the parable criticize those who slept while they waited? Is their sleep symbolic?

Whom does the parable criticize and for what? Be careful that your answers are based on what the scriptures say rather than on what you have always heard.

Why do the wise virgins refuse to share their oil with the foolish ones (verse 9)?

Why might it be such a big deal that the door is shut (verse 11)? In other words, might there be a practical reason that guests could not expect to be admitted after the door was shut and barred?

Why would this parable have been particularly important to the disciples at this point in Jesus's life?

What would verse 13 have meant to them? What does it mean to us?

Verses 14–30: This, of course, is the parable of the talents. A talent is a weight, supposedly the weight you could expect a laborer to carry. It represented a large sum of money, almost 65 pounds of silver, and since silver was more scarce in biblical times than in our own, it was also more valuable. The *Word Biblical Commentary* says that a talent was worth about 6,000 days' work for a common laborer![1] If that is accurate, that is easily the equivalent of almost a million dollars in today's wages.

To understand the story better, remember what it is about: A very wealthy man is taking a long trip. Before he leaves, he takes his property and divides it among each of three stewards (who would have been his slaves), commanding them to take care of that property until he returns. Since the property is his to begin with and the servants are his slaves, when he returns, everything that he gave them will still be his, as will any profit they have made on his money. (This circumstance, giving money to slave-stewards and expecting them to make a profit, was covered in Roman law, so it seems to have been common enough that it would not have seemed strange to Jesus's listeners.) Given Jewish law against interest, perhaps the profit was not interest but profit from land or commodity speculation. Only verse 27 mentions interest. However, that reference suggests that the fictional lord whom Jesus has in mind is a Gentile, which would make interest a possibility.

What kind of return does each servant but the third get on the money that the lord gives him? Is the return low, normal, or high? What does each servant receive from his lord?

Why does the lord take from the slothful servant what he has been given? It seems unfair to take from those who have not and to give to those who already have (verse 29). Is that what is going on? How are we to understand this? What is it that those who receive already have? What is it that the others do not have and is taken away?

To understand the parable better, also think about its context: To whom does Jesus teach this parable? Given that audience and the fact that the parable is sandwiched between two parables about the second coming, what would you say is its point?

To the disciples as they listened to this parable, what would the talents have represented?

If the point of the earlier parable of the ten virgins is that the disciples must be prepared for the second coming, what does *this* parable teach them about the second coming? What does it teach us?

Verses 31–46: We say that this is a parable about the last judgment, but is it that or is it about the criteria for entering God's kingdom?

In what sense was the kingdom prepared before the world was founded or created?

What kinds of works does Jesus mention in verses 35–37? Are they obligations or duties?

Why are those speaking in verses 38–39 surprised? How do you account for the fact that they don't know when they did the things for which they are rewarded? What does that teach us about our own works?

Those who are condemned are equally surprised. Why? What might have given them the confidence that they *did* minister to the Lord when they should have?

Who are "the least of these" (verses 40 and 45) to whom Jesus was referring at the time he gave this parable? (*Least* is a good translation, but *smallest* would also be a good one.) Who might "the least of these" be to us? Is it easy for us to recognize "the least"? Why or why not?

Are we likely to be surprised by the results of the last judgment? If no, why not? If so, how?

Lesson 23
Luke 22:7–30; John 13; 14:1–15; 15

To give a better sense of the context, in a few places I have added notes for a few verses more than the lesson assigned. However, because most of John 13 covers the same material as Luke 22, I have provided notes only with verses 31–35. That is a dangerous thing to do because it may implicitly invite readers to assume that Luke and John are teaching the same things, and they may not be. If they both say the same thing, we really only need one; I assume they both testify of Christ, but that they say different things in those testimonies. So I assume that they teach different things. But I have risked the danger in order to keep this chapter of study materials approximately the same length as other chapters.

With this lesson we begin to read about the part of Christ's life that is traditionally called the passion, the time between the last supper and his death on the cross. The word *passion* and the word *passive* are related terms. To have a passion is to be affected by something. Why is this part of Jesus's life called the passion?

The longest part of each of the New Testament Gospels is the part describing the passion. As Latter-day Saints, our tendency is to focus on the resurrection rather than the passion. Why do you think the Gospels give so much attention to the passion and comparatively little to the resurrection? Does 1 Corinthians 1:17–2:16 explain that attention?

259

Why might the Book of Mormon focus its attention, instead, on the resurrection? What should our focus be?

The *Jerome Bible Commentary* says that in the passion stories of Matthew and John we are invited to worship Jesus as we see him completing his mission as the Son of God, that Mark's way of telling the story invites us to sorrow at the events that conclude his earthly ministry, and that Luke's Gospel asks us to accompany Jesus as he suffers and to see ourselves in people like Simon of Cyrene, Peter, and the "good thief."[1] Do you think that characterization of these accounts is accurate? How might each way of reading the story be important to us? Are there other ways of reading it? If you had been a witness of these events, how would you have written about them? What would have been your focus? Why?

Luke 22

Verses 1–6: Why does Luke introduce the story of the last supper by telling us of the plot to kill Jesus? What does this contrast show us?

Verses 7–13: The Feast of Unleavened Bread and the Feast of the Passover are two different but back-to-back feasts. However, some writers, such as Josephus, conflate the two, presumably because they are writing for a non-Jewish audience to whom the difference is irrelevant. Luke seems to be doing this in verse 7.

Is it significant that Jesus provides a place in which to eat the Passover meal through a miracle? Why do you think he did it that way?

Verses 14–20: In verse 15 the phrase "with desire I have desired" is a Hebrew colloquialism. It means "I have greatly desired." In the Gospels Jesus rarely says anything about what he desires, so the fact that he does so, and does so emphatically, is a way of underlining what follows. Why is his desire, rather than something else, the thing that creates emphasis on the story for the next several verses?

What does verse 16 mean? To what does the word *it* refer? When will Christ once again partake of the sacrament? What is the significance of that delay? How is our taking of the sacrament related to his?

In verses 16 and 19 Jesus says, "I will not," using a verb form that in Greek means something like "I definitely will not." How is that definitiveness important to what he is saying at this point?

Jesus tells those with him, "Take this, and divide it among yourselves." One way of understanding that is straightforward: "Take this wine and each of you have some." The fact that he does not say something similar with the bread (though, obviously, they share the bread) suggests that what he says here may have more than merely literal significance. What cup will Jesus's followers have to share? Is sharing in the sacramental cup a symbol not only of the sacramental covenant, but also of sharing in Jesus's and his followers' cup?

In verses 17 and 19 Jesus gives thanks for the wine and the bread before he shares it with his disciples. What is the significance of those prayers? Is it significant that Luke says that he gave thanks rather than a blessing?

In verse 19 the Greek word for *remembrance* is a word for forgetfulness with a negative prefix (*an* + *amnēsis*). It implicitly suggests that to remember is to no longer forget. What are we to stop forgetting? How do we forget the body and blood of Christ? How do we stop forgetting them?

Try to imagine how shocking the sentences "This is my body which is given for you" and "This cup is the new testament in my blood, which is shed for you" would have been for those at this meal. A non-Christian reading this for the first time could not escape seeing something like cannibalistic symbolism in verses 19–20. Could the disciples have heard anything else? What does that shocking symbolism teach us? On the other hand, what does the symbol of nourishment, also very much part of the symbol, teach us?

The Old Testament often speaks of the Lord remembering his people. What does that have to do with the sacrament? How is our memory of him linked to his memory of us?

How are the various parts of the sacrament ordinance significant? For example, if we think about Jesus's death, what might the cloth covering the bread and water represent? How is Christ's body symbolically significant in the ordinance? His blood? Why are eating and drinking important to the ordinance? What kinds of symbolic significance does eating have?

We use the word *testament* when we speak of a "last will and testament." What does the word mean in that case? How is that relevant to the use of the word in verse 20? The word translated *testament* could also have been translated *covenant*. How is the ordinance of the sacrament a covenant? What specifically do we covenant?

Why is the sacrament of the Lord's Supper a two-part ordinance? Why doesn't Jesus give us an ordinance instead that focuses on his body as a whole, flesh *and* blood? Is the covenant we make in each of the prayers any different? If not, why is it necessary to repeat it, once in remembrance of Christ's blood and once in remembrance of his body?

Verses 21–23: If it was necessary for Jesus to die on the cross, why does he condemn Judas for bringing that event to pass?

Do we learn anything about our own lives from the fact that Judas was one of the Twelve?

Verses 24–27: If we assume that the disciples are people like ourselves, what do we learn about ourselves from verses 23–24?

What do you make of the fact that the verses about Judas and about the argument over who will be greatest come immediately after the introduction of the sacrament of the Lord's Supper? (Mark and Matthew put it before. How might that change the meaning they are trying to convey?) What might that juxtaposition suggest about the ordinance? About us?

Note that the word *benefactors* (verse 25) translates a title that the Syrian kings gave to themselves. What point is Jesus making?

What does it mean for the greatest to "be as the younger" (verse 26)?

The Greek word translated "he that doth serve" (*diakoneō*, from which we get the word *deacon*) indicates one who waits on another and provides his or her necessities, literally a "waiter." What does it mean to say that Christ has come among us as one who serves? How does he wait on us? How does he provide our necessities? In verse 27 Jesus specifically compares himself to a table waiter. Think about the analogy between Christ and the waiter as literally as you can. What does that comparison suggest? Does it show you anything about what Christlike service means?

In John 13:4–5, do we see Jesus demonstrate the kind of service he means? Did the disciples understand what he was talking about then? (See John 13:6–10.) Does their inability to understand suggest anything about us and our understanding? What safeguards against misunderstanding do we have?

Verses 28–30: The word translated *temptations* in verse 28 can also be translated *trials* or *adversities.* How is the fact that the disciples have stayed with him through his adversities relevant to what follows in verse 29?

The Greek word translated *appoint* has the same root as the word *covenant,* so we could translate the beginning of verse 29 as "And I covenant unto you a kingdom." What would that mean? How has the Father covenanted a kingdom to the Son? How is our covenant with him like his covenant with the Father? What is the difference between being covenanted a kingdom and being promised one? Between being covenanted one and being contracted to receive one?

John 13

Verses 31–35: When Jesus says, "Now is the Son of man glorified, and God is glorified in him," to what time does *now* refer? To that very moment immediately after the departure of Judas? To the events that are just beginning?

What does it mean to be glorified? What does it mean for God to be glorified in the Son?

Neither the Jews nor the disciples can follow Jesus, but what is the difference between them?

Why does Jesus give the new commandment in the context in which he gives it? Specifically, why does he give it immediately after telling them that he is going to leave them? How is this commandment new? New compared to what? Compare Leviticus 19:18. Is this new commandment different from that commandment?

How has Christ loved us? The parable of the good Samaritan (Luke 10:30–37) teaches about neighborly love. Is Christ's love for us the same as the love for the neighbor that we see in that parable?

Compare verse 34 with John 15:12–13. Do those verses shed any light on the new commandment? How does verse 13 of John 15 add to the meaning of verse 12?

John 14

Verses 1–3: It is important to remember that these verses follow immediately after Jesus's prophecy to Peter that he will deny him three times. The break we perceive when we read the scriptures is an artificial one. It wasn't there when John wrote his Gospel. Read John 13:36–38 and John 14:1–3 without making a break between them. Does that make a difference in your understanding of the interaction between Christ and Peter?

Is Jesus teaching the doctrine of multiple heavenly kingdoms in verse 2, or is he saying something else?

What would it mean for the Lord to prepare a place for us? Obviously the language is metaphorical, but of what is this a metaphor?

Verses 4–7: Could the disciples have understood what Jesus said in verse 4 before the Lord's death and resurrection? How might they have understood it when he said it?

In what sense is Jesus "the way," or in other words, the road? The way toward what?

In Psalm 119:30 the way is the way of obedience, of righteous living in conformity with the Torah, the Law. Is what Jesus says here an imitation of that notion in some way?

How is Jesus the truth? How can a person be said to be the truth?

What does Jesus mean when he says that he is the life? Why *the* life rather than just life?

In verse 7 Jesus tells them "from henceforth ye know him [the Father], and have seen him." Why have they known and seen the father "from henceforth"? What has happened that has made that knowing and seeing possible? In other words, does *henceforth* designate the precise moment when Jesus was speaking, or does it have a broader meaning: "the time of my ministry," for example? Or "after the events that begin now and culminate in my resurrection"? Or something else?

Verses 8–14: What does it mean for one person to be *in* another (verses 10–11)? How is Jesus in the Father? How can we be in the Son?

Verses 15–24: Is verse 15 a commandment, or is it a statement of fact: those who love me keep my commandments? Could we love Christ and not keep his commandments?

There are many kinds of love. Some involve strong emotions—for example, the early stages of romance; others do not. Love of one's neighbor doesn't seem to require strong emotional feelings; love of country may not. Some kinds of love involve those emotions sometimes, but not at others, and nevertheless are still love. Marital love may be an example. There are also different kinds of love depending on the relation of those involved: love of a spouse, love of a child, love of a friend, and love for the neighbor are all different, and there are probably other kinds of love as well. What does the word *love* mean in verse 15?

How are verses 15 and 16 connected? Is verse 16 a consequence of verse 15?

The word translated *Comforter* could also be translated *advocate* or *defender*. How is the Holy Ghost a comforter? How is he an advocate or defender?

Note that though we usually use the word *comfort* to mean "solace," it originally meant "assistance" or "aid." (Its roots mean "strength with.") The latter meaning is probably that intended by the King James translators. How does thinking in those terms change your understanding of what the Lord has promised?

Why doesn't the world see or know the Spirit of Truth (verse 17)?

To what time period is Jesus referring in verse 19? To the time after his resurrection, to the second coming, or to some other time?

The other Judas (Jude or Judah) asks a natural question in verse 22: how will we be able to see you if the world cannot? What is Jesus's answer in verse 23? When will the disciples see Jesus? What does that mean to us? When do we or will we see him?

John 15

Verse 1: Are there connections between the tree of life imagery of the Old Testament and the Book of Mormon (Jacob 5) and the analogy that Christ makes here? Are there connections with what we learn from the story of the Garden of Eden?

Verses 2–3: What literal fruit does Jesus have in mind when he gives this analogy? Does that suggest any connection to the sacrament of the Lord's Supper? What else might the fruit of the vine stand for symbolically?

What does it mean for a branch of the vine to be taken away? What does it mean for a branch to be purged? The word we would use today is *prune*, but the word translated *purged* in verse 2 is the same word translated *clean* in verse 3. When you prune branches on a vine, what do you do to them? When were the disciples made clean or purged? Is this related to the foot washing of chapter 13? (See John 13:5.)

How has Christ's word made them clean? What does the word *word* mean in this context?

Verse 4: The word translated *abide* means "to remain with" or "to wait for." Which of those meanings do you think best fits here? Does the analogy of vines and branches suggest one of those over the other? What happens to a branch that is taken from the vine? How do vines and branches abide in each other, and what has that to do with producing fruit? What fruit does Jesus expect from those to whom he is speaking when he gives this analogy?

Verses 5–6: The Greek word translated *without* at the end of verse 5 means literally "separated from." We could probably translate this clause as "severed from me, you can do nothing." How is that true of the branch? How is it true of us?

Why do we burn the branches that have been cut from the tree? Is that symbolic of anything in our own lives?

Verses 7–8: What is the promise of verse 7? Is it a promise that can be fulfilled in this life? (See Helaman 10:5.)

How do we abide in Jesus's words? What does John mean by the word *words* here? Is it the same thing meant by *word* in verse 3? How has he used that word in other places (e.g., John 1:1 and 5:24)?

Compare the promise of these verses to John 14:13. Are the promises the same or different?

How do the disciples' fruits glorify the Father (verse 8)?

How does Christ glorify the Father by doing what we ask in his name?

Verses 9–10: The word *continue* in verse 9 represents the same Greek word that is translated *abide* in verses 4 and 10. So what?

How has the Father loved Christ? What information does scripture give us about how the Father loves the Son? What do passages like John 3:16, which tell how the Father loves us, suggest about how he loves the Son?

Does the Father's love for Christ allow him to escape suffering? Why or why not? What does that mean about the Savior's love for us?

Why do we remain in Christ's love if we keep the commandments? Is it because he withdraws his love from us if we don't keep them? Or is it because we withdraw ourselves from that love?

When Jesus says he has kept his Father's commandments, is he speaking of anything in particular or of the commandments in general? Did he have commandments that we do not have?

Verse 11: Jesus says that he has spoken "these things" so that the disciples' joy might be full. To what does "these things" refer?

How does this verse help us understand 2 Nephi 2:25: "Men are, that they might have joy"?

Verses 12–14: How is this commandment related to the commandments the Lord mentioned in verse 10? Is it an additional commandment or the summary of them?

How is the discussion that we see in verses 10–13 related to Jesus's discussion with the lawyer in Luke 10:25–28?

How has Christ loved them? What does this have to do with the parable of the sheep and the goats in Matthew 25:31–46?

Does verse 14 mean that Christ has laid down his life *only* for those who keep his commandments? If not, what does it mean? If so, how can that be, since no one has kept all of the commandments except Christ?

Verse 15: How are we to understand what Jesus says here in light of what he said about servants in Luke 22:24–27? "I have called you friends" is a reasonable translation, but "I have called you beloved" might be more accurate.

Why does Christ tell them that he now will speak of them differently than he has? What explanation of that change does he give?

Why is important to them to know that he has made known to them everything that he has heard from the Father? If he has taught them everything that the Father has told him, what does that suggest about the things we learn in the New Testament?

Verse 16: As used here, the phrase "I have chosen you" means "I have chosen you for a purpose." The primary meaning of the word translated *ordained* is "to place." How is to be ordained to be placed or put somewhere?

For what purpose does this verse say that the disciples have been chosen? Where have they been placed?

Why is it important for Jesus to remind them that they have not chosen him but he has chosen them? What does that mean to us?

How does Jesus's discussion of election (choice) here fit with the discussion of Doctrine and Covenants 121:34–40?

Here is one way of understanding what this verse says: "I have chosen you and given you authority so that you can bear fruit and so that your fruit can remain (this is the same Greek word translated *abide* and *continue* earlier). And I want your fruit to remain so that the Father can give you whatever you ask for." Is that what it means? If not, what does it mean? In either case, explain what Jesus is teaching in this verse.

How does our election and ordination make it possible for us to bear fruit? How does it make it possible for that fruit to remain? Why do we have to have fruit that remains for the Father to give us what we ask?

Verse 17: Does this verse mean "I command you to love one another," or does it mean "I command you these things *so that* you will love one another?" If the former, why is he repeating this one more time, seemingly out of context. If the latter, how does bearing fruit that lasts make it possible for us to love one another?

Verses 18–25: What does "the world" mean in these verses? (Compare, for example, John 8:12, 23; 4:42; 12:25; 17:6; and 1 John 2:15–16.)

How did the world show its hate for the disciples in the early Church? Does it hate Christians today? How so, if it does? How do we recognize the world's hatred without making ourselves into victims?

What point is Jesus making in verse 20? Why do those who follow Jesus need to know what these verses teach?

Verses 26–27: How are these verses that promise the Comforter related to verses 18–25?

Lesson 24
John 16–17

John 16

Verse 1: Jesus tells the disciples that he taught them "these things" so that they would not be offended. To what does "these things" refer"? Is it just to the teaching in verses 26–27? Does it include verses 18–25? Is it the whole sermon that he gave in response to Thomas's question "We know not whither thou goest; and how can we know the way?" (John 14:5) and Philip's similar request (John 14:9)? Or is it to what he has said about the Comforter? Or something else in the preceding chapters?

A more literal translation of the word translated *offended* might be "caused to stumble." What particular things were they facing that might make them stumble? What things in our lives are like those things?

How would the particular teachings of chapter 15 strengthen them against those difficulties?

Verse 2: How long was it before some people began to think that persecuting Christians was a service to God (verse 2)? (Answering that question may require some historical research, but the Internet should be a sufficient resource.) Are we ever guilty of that kind of thinking? For example, do we ever justify our mistreatment of another person because we believe him to be a sinner? Are there ways in which we do so subtly? Do we have ways of doing so as a society, even if not as individuals?

The phrase "doeth God a service" translates a Greek phrase that literally means "offers worship to God to God," since the verb translated *service* (*latreia*) means "to offer divine service to a god." Why do you think Jesus uses this redundant expression?

Verse 3: What does verse 3 tell us about those who act hatefully toward us? What does that suggest about us when we act that way?

Verses 4–6: Did Jesus think the disciples would understand this sermon when he gave it? What might that tell us about the Gospels themselves?

Does the fact that Jesus gave them teachings that they could return to and remember later tell us anything about the way we learn? about how we should study?

In verse 5 Jesus says that none of them ask where he is going. What about John 13:36 and 14:3? How can he say this? Did they not understand what they were asking?

Do the disciples understand what is about to happen? If not, why are they sorrowing?

Verses 7–11: In verse 7 Jesus doesn't say, "I have to leave you in order to work the atonement." He says, "I have to leave you so that you can have the Comforter." Explain what he says. (The footnote in the LDS edition may be helpful.)

Recall from the questions for lesson 23 that another translation of the Greek word translated *comforter* is *advocate* or *defender*. The idea of the Holy Ghost as our advocate is important to the metaphor that Christ uses in verse 8: though the world will judge you (verses 2–3), the Holy Ghost will defend you and convict the world. Against what does the Spirit defend us?

The word translated *reprove* in verse 8 could also be translated *convict* or *expose*. The King James Version translation, "reprove the world of sin, and of righteousness, and of judgment," is somewhat misleading for modern readers. For us, it sounds as if the Advocate will convict the world of being righteous and having judgment. The phrase might be better translated "reveal the world with regard to sin, and with regard to righteousness, and with regard to judgment." How does the Spirit reprove, convict, expose the world?

What evidence allows the Comforter to convict the world of sin? What evidence is relevant to deciding the world's righteousness (verse 10)? Perhaps a better translation than *righteousness* would be *justice*. A better translation than *judged* in verse 11 is *condemned*.

Who is the prince of this world, and how is he condemned by the Comforter? What do these verses tell us about our need for the Holy Ghost?

Verses 12–15: Why couldn't the disciples bear Jesus's teachings at that time? What does *bear* mean in this context? Is Jesus saying that they cannot understand what he teaches or that, somehow, his teachings would weigh them down? If the latter, how would they weigh them down?

The Spirit of Truth can teach all truth (verse 13), presumably even the things that Jesus cannot teach because it would

275

weigh down his disciples. Why can the Holy Ghost teach them things that Jesus cannot?

Why is "Spirit of Truth" an apt name for the Holy Ghost in this sermon?

What does Jesus mean when he says that the Spirit of Truth will not speak of himself (verse 13)?

What "things to come" does the Comforter reveal? What thing that is to come has Jesus announced in his ministry?

How does the Holy Ghost glorify the Savior? What does it mean to say that he does?

What do verses 14–15 tell us the Comforter will reveal?

Verses 16–22: The disciples ask, "What does he mean that we will not see him in a little while and then in a little while we will?" Does the story of the woman in childbirth answer the disciples' question? If so, how? If not, what question does it answer? Notice that a woman in travail—in childbirth labor—is a common Old Testament metaphor for deep anguish.

The scriptures often use the metaphor of marriage to describe the relationship between God and his people. Is this image of childbirth perhaps connected to that metaphor: ideally the consequence of marriage is childbirth, which requires travail; even so, the relationship between God and his people will result in travail for them? When we speak of our travails, we often say that God will compensate for each of them. Is that what this image suggests?

It may be important to note that the term *man* in verse 21 translates the Greek word *anthrōpos*, which means "human being" rather than "male person."

Verses 23–25: When the disciples see Christ again, why will they have no more questions? Of what are their questions a sign? Asking in Jesus's name and receiving what we ask for has been an important theme of this sermon. (See John 14:13 and 15:7, and the repetition of the teaching in 3 Nephi 18:20.) Why is that such an important teaching? Why is it important to the disciples at this point in their spiritual development? What does it mean to us?

How is what Jesus says in the second sentence of verse 23 related to what he says in the first?

What is the promise of verse 25?

Verses 26–30: Why is verse 26 put in terms of the future rather than the present? Isn't this something that the Savior already does for us?

In verse 27 "have believed" translates a verb that can also be translated "have had faith that" or "have trusted that": the Father loves those who have loved Jesus and had faith or trust in him. Is there a difference between loving Christ and having faith in him?

What point is Jesus making in verse 28?

In verses 29–30 the disciples seem relieved. Paraphrased, they say, "Finally you are speaking plainly rather than in parables! We know you know everything. You don't even need to have someone ask you a question in order to give them the answer. That is why we believe that you came from God." Based on what have they concluded that Jesus knows their answers before they ask the questions? Why would that conclusion lead them to the further conclusion that he came from God? Is what they affirm here the same as what Jesus said in verse 28 or something weaker?

Verses 31–33: In Greek verse 31 is ambiguous. It could be a question, as the King James translators have assumed, or it could be a statement: "Now you believe." Try reading it each way to decide which you think is best.

"To his own" in verse 32 probably means "to his own home." Literally it means something like "to that which belongs to him alone." What contrast is Jesus making in speaking of their being sent back to their homes and his being alone?

What kind of peace does Jesus's teaching bring? What does it mean to have peace *in* him? The preposition *in* is used frequently in the scriptures to speak of relationships: Christ is in the Father, we should be in Christ, we are in the body of Christ, and so on.

The phrase "be of good cheer" sounds to modern ears as if it means "be happy." But Jesus isn't telling his disciples, "You will have afflictions in life, but don't worry; be happy." (Recall that in verse 21 he has just said that we, like the woman in childbirth, will have sorrow.) The Greek here, as well as the corresponding King James English, means "Take courage," "Be brave." Why should the fact that Jesus has overcome or had victory over the world give us courage? Courage in the face of what?

John 17

Many Christians refer to this chapter as "The Great High Priestly Prayer." Why do you think they do so? Latter-day

Saints usually call this prayer "The Great Intercessory Prayer." Why? Are the two names for this prayer related? If so, how?

Though we know that Jesus prayed often, we know the content of only a few of his prayers. Why did John believe it was important to tell us what Jesus said in this prayer?

How does the form of this prayer fit the form given to us in the Lord's Prayer (Matthew 6:9–13; Luke 11:2–4; and 3 Nephi 13:9–13)? If it doesn't, how do you explain the difference?

Verses 1–8: Jesus has often talked about glorifying the Father. (See, for example, John 1:18; 2:11; 9:3; and 15:15.) What do you think he means by the word *glorify*"? How will the Father glorify the Son?

Why does Jesus say that he will give eternal life to those whom the Father has given him (verse 2)? Whom has the Father given him? How has he given them to Jesus? What does it mean to belong to him, to be his possession?

Jesus defines what he means by "eternal life" in verse 3. Does that help answer the last question?

What kind of knowledge is Jesus talking about in verse 3? Compare Genesis 3:22 and Mosiah 4:12. Do they suggest how we should understand the word *know*?

Does Mosiah 4:12 help us understand the glorification of the Father and the Son that Jesus speaks of in verses 1, 4–5?

Does verse 6 explain how Jesus has glorified the Father?

What does he mean when he says, "I have manifested [or "revealed"] thy name unto the men [literally "persons"]"?

How has he revealed the name of the Father? Why is the Father's name so important? What might it stand for?

What does it mean that those whom the Father gave to the Son were given "out of this world" (verse 6)?

How have they kept the Father's word? What is the Father's word?

Does the first clause of verse 7 explain what it means to know the Father (verse 3)? What it means that Jesus has manifested the Father's name (verse 6)?

Verses 9–10: If God loves the world (John 3:16), why doesn't Jesus pray for the world? Does *world* mean the same thing in each case? If not, explain the different meanings.

Why is it important that Jesus speak of the disciples as the common property of him and the Father? What does that tell us?

Verses 11–13: Here we find the request of Jesus's prayer. He prays, "Now that I am leaving them in the world and coming to thee, keep those you've given me in your name so that they can be one in the same way that we are one." Can you think of synonyms for *keep* (verse 11) that help you understand this better?

Why is the unity of the disciples so important now that the Savior is leaving them?

How were they kept up to this point (verse 12)?

The word translated *lost* in verse 12 could also be translated *died*. Why is Jesus using that wording? Is the implicit connection to death important to what he is saying?

Verses 14–16: Why do the disciples need the Father's protection? What protection has been promised? (See John 16:7–8 as well as 15:7, 16.)

Why isn't the Lord asking that the disciples be taken out of the world (verse 15)? If the disciples are not of this world (verse 16), why leave them behind when he knows that the world hates them and will persecute them (John 15:18–21 and 17:14)? Does this tell us anything about our own experience?

Verses 17–19: To sanctify something is to make it holy. What does it mean to be holy? To be *made* holy?

How does the Father make the Lord's disciples holy? What does it mean to say that he does so "through thy truth"?

Jesus sent the disciples into the world, just as the Father sent Jesus into the world. Does that suggest that each has a similar mission? If so, what might it be?

How does Jesus sanctify himself? What does it mean that he does it "for their sakes"? How does his sanctification make their sanctification possible?

Verses 20–23: For whom has Jesus been praying up to this point (verse 20)? Why has he focused on praying for them? Now whom does he pray for?

What does the unity of believers show the world (verse 21)? Why is that important?

Jesus gives a standard for the unity of the Saints: "that they may be one, even as we are one" (verse 22). How are the Father and the Son one? How can we imitate that unity in the Church? Are there destructive ways in which we might

281

merely pretend to imitate that unity? How do we know the difference between real unity and false unity?

The word translated *perfect* (verse 23) can also be translated *complete*. But it means literally "to fulfill the purpose"; that which fulfills its purpose is perfect. Why is unity needed for perfection, for fulfilling our purpose?

Verses 24–26: When Jesus prays "that they also, whom thou hast given me, be with me where I am," what is he asking for? Is he asking for something that only occurs at a future time or for something that can occur now?

What does verse 25 tell us about our relation to the Father?

Why might Jesus use the title "Righteous"—in other words, "Just Father"—here rather than another title?

Do these verses help explain the meaning of Doctrine and Covenants 46:13–14?

What promise does the Lord make when he says, "I have declared unto them thy name, *and will declare it*" (italics added)? What does it mean to declare the name of the Father? How does doing so put the Father's love for the Savior in us?

Why does Jesus say that his declaration of the Father's name will cause "that the love wherewith thou hast loved me may be in them" rather than "that thy love may be in them"?

Verses 26 once again uses the preposition *in* to describe Christ's relationship with those whom he loves. How are your earlier reflections on that preposition relevant here?

Lesson 25

Matthew 26:36–46; Mark 14:32–42; Luke 22:39–46

As important as the events in the Garden of Gethsemane were, they receive very little attention in scripture. Matthew has eleven verses on it, Mark also has eleven, Luke has seven, and John tells us nothing about it at all, though he was as close as anyone to what happened. The Doctrine and Covenants has four verses about it and the Book of Mormon one.

MATTHEW 26:36–46	MARK 14:32–42	LUKE 22:39–46
36 Then cometh Jesus with them unto a place called Gethsemane, and saith unto the disciples, Sit ye here, while I go and pray yonder. 37 And he took with him Peter and the two sons of Zebedee, and began to be sorrowful and very heavy. 38 Then saith he unto them, My	32 And they came to a place which was named Gethsemane: and he saith to his disciples, Sit ye here, while I shall pray. 33 And he taketh with him Peter and James and John, and began to be sore amazed, and to be very heavy; 34 And saith unto them, My soul is	39 And he came out, and went, as he was wont, to the mount of Olives; and his disciples also followed him. 40 And when he was at the place, he said unto them, Pray that ye enter not into temptation. 41 And he was withdrawn from them about a stone's cast, and

283

soul is exceeding sorrowful, even unto death: tarry ye here, and watch with me. 39 And he went a little further, and fell on his face, and prayed, saying, O my Father, if it be possible, let this cup pass from me; nevertheless, not as I will, but as Thou wilt. 40 And he came to the disciples and found them sleeping. And he said to Peter, What, could ye not watch with me one hour? 41 Watch and pray that ye may enter not into temptation: the spirit indeed is willing, but the flesh is weak. 42 He went away again the second time, and prayed,

exceeding sorrowful unto death: tarry ye here, and watch. 35 And he went forward a little, and fell on the ground, and prayed that, if it were possible, the hour might pass from him. 36 And he said, Abba, Father, all things are possible unto thee; take away this cup from me: nevertheless not what I will, but what thou wilt. 37 And he cometh, and findeth them sleeping, and saith unto Peter, Simon, sleepest thou? couldest not thou watch one hour? 38 Watch ye and pray, lest ye enter into temptation. The spirit truly is ready, but

kneeled down, and prayed, 42 Saying, Father, if thou be willing, remove this cup from me: nevertheless not my will, but thine, be done. 43 And there appeared an angel unto him from heaven, strengthening him. 44 And being in an agony he prayed more earnestly: and his sweat was as it were great drops of blood falling down to the ground. 45 And when he rose up from prayer, and was come to his disciples, he found them sleeping for sorrow, 46 And said unto them, Why sleep ye? rise and saying, My Father, if this may not pass away from me, except I drink it, thy will be done. 43 And he cometh unto the disciples, and findeth them asleep again: for their eyes were heavy. 44 And he left them, and went away again, and prayed the third time, saying the same words. 45 Then cometh he to his disciples, and saith unto them, Sleep on now, and take your rest: behold, the hour is at hand, and the Son of man is betrayed into the hands of sinners. 46 Rise, let us be going: behold, he is at hand that doth betray me.

the flesh is weak. 39 And again he went away, and prayed, and spake the same words. 40 And when he returned, he found them asleep again, (for their eyes were heavy,) neither wist they what to answer him. 41 And he cometh the third time, and saith unto them, Sleep on now, and take your rest: it is enough, the hour is come; behold, the Son of man is betrayed into the hands of sinners. 42 Rise up, let us go; lo, he that betrayeth me is at hand.

pray, lest ye enter into temptation.

23 And Jesus answered them, saying, The hour is come, that the Son of man should be glorified. 24 Verily, verily, I say unto you, Except a corn of wheat fall into the ground and die, it abideth alone: but if it die, it bringeth forth much fruit. 25 He that loveth his life shall lose it; and he that hateth his life in this world shall keep it unto life eternal. 26 If any man serve me, let him follow me; and where I am, there shall also my servant be: if any man serve me, him will my Father honour. 27 Now is my soul troubled; and what shall I say? Father, save me from this hour: but for this cause came I unto this hour. 28 Father, glorify thy name. Then came there a voice from heaven, saying, I have both glorified it, and will glorify it again. 29 The people therefore, that stood by, and heard it, said that it thundered: others said, An angel spake to him. 30 Jesus answered and said, This voice came not because of me, but for your sakes. 31 Now is the judgment of this world: now shall the prince of this world be cast out. 32 And I, if I be lifted up from the earth, will draw all men unto me. 33 This he said, signifying what death he should die.

Alma 7:13

13 Now the Spirit knoweth all things; nevertheless the Son of God suffereth according to the flesh that he might take upon him the sins of his people, that he might blot out their transgressions according to the power of his deliverance.

D&C 19:16–19

16 For behold, I, God, have suffered these things for all, that they might not suffer if they would repent; 17 but if they would not repent they must suffer even as I; 18 which suffering caused myself, even God, the greatest of all, to tremble because of pain, and to bleed at every pore, and to suffer both body and spirit—and would that I might not drink the bitter cup, and shrink—19 Nevertheless, glory be to the Father, and I partook and finished my preparations unto the children of men.

Mosiah 3:7

7 And lo, he shall suffer temptations, and pain of body, hunger, thirst, and fatigue, even more than man can suffer, except it be unto death; for behold, blood cometh from every pore, so great shall be his anguish for the wickedness and the abominations of his people.

That is everything or almost everything that the scriptures tell us about Jesus's experience in the Garden of Gethsemane. Why do you think they are relatively silent about such an important event?

Does that tell us anything about how we should understand what scripture is or is not? About how we should understand scripture and its relationship to latter-day revelation?

Matthew 26

Verses 36–46: The word *gethsemane* means "olive press," so the Garden of Gethsemane was an olive grove within which, presumably, there was an olive press. Is there any symbolic connection between the events in this grove and its name?

The first part of verse 38 seems to be a loose paraphrase of Psalm 42:6. Read that psalm and consider how it is related to Jesus's experience in the garden.

As the LDS footnotes point out, the phrase "watch with me" could also be translated "stay awake with me." What is Jesus asking Peter, James, and John to do? Why? Why them and not all of the disciples? How will their staying awake help him?

Can we take their sleep to symbolize anything about our lives?

This is the only record we have of Jesus asking someone to help him. What does this suggest about his experience and what is to come?

In verse 39 Jesus prays, "If it is possible, let this cup pass by me." Why a cup? What metaphor is he using? Is it related to the events of the last supper? What does he wish he could avoid?

What is Jesus's attitude toward what is about to happen to him? Does that tell us anything about our own attitude toward suffering?

What does it mean when he adds, "Nevertheless not as I will, but as thou wilt"? What is the import of *nevertheless*?

Why does Jesus want Peter, James, and John to pray?

The word translated *temptation* in verse 41 doesn't mean here what *temptation* means for us, "to be enticed to do evil." Instead, as in the Lord's Prayer, it means "to encounter a difficulty that cannot be overcome." What is Jesus admonishing the disciples to do? How is it relevant to what is happening to him in the garden?

The Bible does not use the word *spirit* to mean "one's internal psyche," or what we might call "the conscious ego," nor does it use *flesh* to mean simply "the physical body." That usage comes much later. In the Bible the spirit is the force of life. In a Jewish and Christian context, the spirit is something God-given and it has a divine impulse. (See Genesis 2:7.) The flesh, on the other hand, is our concrete existence in the world, including but not limited to the physical body. With that as background, what does "the spirit is willing, but the flesh is weak" mean?

Is it significant that Jesus repeats his prayer three times? What does he mean when he tells the disciples to sleep on, especially when he immediately tells them to get up (verses 45–46)?

Mark 14:32–42

Compare Mark's account with Matthew's. Do you see any meaningful differences?

Luke 22:39–46

What does Luke add that in is neither Matthew nor Mark? What does he leave out? What might those differences tell us?

How do these three accounts compare to John 12:23–33?

Is Alma 7:11–12 about Jesus's experience in the garden?

Does D&C 19:16–19 tell us something that we don't have in other scriptures?

If so, what? If not, why was it revealed?

Does Mosiah 3:7 give us information not found in the Bible?

Lesson 26

Matthew 26:47–27:66; Mark 14:43–15:39; Luke 22:47–23:56; John 18–19

To keep the study materials brief enough to be usable, this chapter will focus on the verses from Matthew.

Matthew 26

Verse 47: This "great multitude" came from the temple priests, so it may have been the temple police rather than a mere mob.

Verses 48–49: Just as it is today for many, a kiss on the cheek seems to have been a standard greeting, but it seems not merely to have been that. Ulrich Luz says that in first-century Palestine the kiss was a sign of solidarity and reconciliation, and so "one would hardly be able to say that the kiss of greeting was a completely normal and thus meaningless ritual in the Jewish society of that day."[1] For two millennia writers have taken this kiss to be *the* symbol of betrayal. The only alternative voice seems to have been that of Origen, who recognized that Judas was neither fully good nor fully evil, and so he probably vacillated in his feelings for the Savior.[2]

Verse 50: Does Jesus mean it when he refers to Judas as "friend"? Is he making a point by using a term of address that contrasts with "brother," the usual form of address between the disciples? Or is he perhaps being ironic? Could he be offering Judas an opportunity to repent?

Is Jesus really asking Judas why he has come? What is the point of Jesus's question? Some translations take this as a statement, "Do what you have come for," rather than a question. Which way of reading what Jesus says makes most sense to you? Why?

Verses 51–54: John tells us that Peter cut off the slave's ear. I once heard a reader say that this sounds like someone who doesn't know how to use a sword in battle has attacked the servant, trying to hit him in the head, but only striking a glancing blow and cutting of the servant's ear. What do you think of that possibility?

Why doesn't Matthew tell us who cut off the ear? In John 18:10 we learn both the name of the swordsman, Peter, and the name of the slave, Malchus.

Why does Jesus reject the use of violence to protect himself? Compare what he says in verse 52 with what he says in the Sermon on the Mount (Matthew 5:39).

In verse 53 we are told that, had he wanted to, Jesus could have summoned almost 70,000 angels to his defense (compare Matthew 4:5–7), but he refuses. What are we who wage war to make of Jesus's pacifism?

Jesus's explanation for why he doesn't call on heavenly defenders seems strange to me: "If I were to do so, scripture would not be fulfilled." For this to be a compelling reason, we also have to assume that all scripture must be fulfilled. However, that assumption doesn't seem to carry very much moral weight. Scripture might prophesy of Judas's betrayal, but if it does, that doesn't absolve Judas of his crime. He can't appear before the Father and say, "I just did what had to be done," can he? Can you explain this puzzle?

Peter, and presumably the other disciples, was willing to use force to defend Jesus. How do you think he responded when Jesus rejected his use of force?

If we put together Peter's response when Jesus washes the feet of the disciples, his insistence that he will go where Jesus goes, and this incident, we have a picture of someone who seems not to understand what is happening, perhaps even someone who is confused. Might that lack of understanding or that confusion help explain why Peter later betrays Jesus? Does that teach us anything about our own lives and situations?

Verses 55–56: Jesus asks why they have taken him at night rather than publicly when they could easily have taken him when he was in the temple. What is the answer to Jesus's question?

Notice that to say Jesus sat in the temple is to say that he was a teacher there. We could translate the last part of verse 55 this way: "I taught daily in the temple—with you there—and you didn't arrest me."

Verses 57–58: To understand what happens in the story of Jesus's arrest and crucifixion, it is necessary to understand something about the political situation among the Jews in Jerusalem. Though the Pharisees had strong opinions about the law, they did not have the authority to enforce religious law. If you will recall, that is because the name *Pharisee* designated a person who was a member of a particular sect and

293

political party, not a person who necessarily had political power. Only the temple priests could enforce religious law. "Scribes and elders" probably refers to the duties of particular temple priests.

Why does Matthew tell us that Peter followed but not tell us Peter's story until later?

Verses 59–68: What does verse 61 mean when it says that many false witnesses came but the officers found none? Remember that the law of Moses required two witnesses for any charge. Finally two witnesses come who say that Jesus has said he will tear down the temple and rebuild it in three days. (Compare Jeremiah 26:1–19.) The threat to destroy the temple would be a serious crime, so this is a serious charge.

Jesus initially doesn't answer their charge, as we can tell by the high priest's question in verse 62: "Don't you have anything to say?" Why is Jesus silent? (Compare Matthew 12:19 and Isaiah 42:2.)

In verse 63 the high priest challenges Jesus to take an oath regarding whether he is the Messiah. In verse 64 Jesus answers the high priest's question: first, he as much as says that he is the Messiah; then he adds a prophecy (using the language of Psalm 110:1 and Daniel 7:13) concerning the Messiah. It doesn't seem to have been blasphemy to claim to be the Messiah. Indeed, a number of previous people had claimed to be the Messiah, and several would do so after Jesus's crucifixion. So how can the high priest accuse Jesus of blasphemy? Tearing one's clothing was prescribed by Jewish law as a judge's sign that he has just witnessed blasphemy.

Verses 69–75: Why does each of the Gospel writers tell this story about Peter, the chief apostle and first president of the early Church? Most interpreters have not seen this as a simple betrayal. Instead, they have seen Peter as an Everyman. Like us, he follows the Lord and shares the Lord's suffering, though at a distance and though he is fearful and sometimes falls. What lesson is there for us in his betrayal?

Matthew 27

We will look at verses 1–2 when we come to verse 11.

Verses 3–10: Matthew deals with two betrayals, one after the other: first Peter's and then Judas's. It looks like he places one against the other so that we can compare them. What is the difference between them?

How sincere do you think Judas's grief was (verses 3–4)? What evidence do you find here for your opinion?

What do you make of the response to Judas of the chief priests and elders (verse 4)? Why do you think they are so cold?

Who do you think is the more responsible party in this crime, Judas or the chief priests and scribes?

Though Acts 1:17–19 deals with Judas's death, Matthew is the only Gospel writer who does. Why does he do so? Why do the other writers ignore it?

What does the chief priests' scrupulousness about how they deal with Judas's silver suggest about them (verse 6)? How is Matthew portraying them?

Though verse 9 says that it is quoting from Jeremiah, it seems to be quoting from Zechariah (11:12–13). So what? Why is a scripture reference important to Matthew, whether it comes from Jeremiah or Zechariah?

Verses 11–14 (and 1–2): What accusation does Pilate seem to be asking about? Is that the same charge that the high priest was dealing with or a new charge? If it is a new charge, what is going on?

What does "You said it" mean in response to Pilate's question?

What accusation do you think the chief priests and elders made in verse 12? Is it the charge of blasphemy or something else? Did it have anything to do with the cleansing of the temple?

Why does Jesus refuse to answer their charges? There is evidence that the high priest was in Pilate's debt. The previous governor of Judea had appointed four high priests during his tenure. (The Romans, like many kings, demanded the right to appoint the religious authority.) Pilate has appointed only one. Does this relation suggest anything about what happened at Jesus's trial?

It is important not to assume that Jesus's trial and execution was something carried out by "the Jews" as we understand that term. Charges were brought against Jesus by some Jewish temple and community leaders of the first century, who appear to have conspired to deliver Jesus into Roman hands as a rebel. Jesus's execution was ordered by the Roman governor, Pilate, and carried out by his soldiers. However, most Jews of the time, even most of those living in Jerusalem, probably knew little about the trial and execution, and few of those who knew about it were involved in bringing it about. A great deal of death and horror has resulted from the charge that "the Jews" crucified Christ. Christians used that charge as an excuse to kill and oppress Jews for centuries, but the charge makes no sense, not only because children are not responsible for the sins of their ancestors (a corollary of Article of Faith 2), but also because few of their ancestors had anything to do with Christ's death.

Verses 15–26: The name Barabbas means "son of the father," and Barabbas's given name was "Jesus": Jesus Barabbas. Why is that name important to this story?

Mark identifies Barabbas as a zealot, someone who believed that Palestine had to be purified of Gentile influence—and, for many, even of Gentile presence—and who believed that the Jews were justified in using violence to do so. Today we would call the zealots terrorists. Is there a parallel between what Barabbas was doing and what Jesus did?

What does Matthew mean when he says that the priests had delivered Jesus to Pilate "for envy" (verse 18)?

Jesus did nothing to prevent the high priest's guards from taking him, knowing that he must be tried and executed in order to fulfill the scriptures and to work the atonement. Why, then, did the Lord give Pilate's wife a dream by which she learned that Jesus was innocent? (I am assuming that the dream came from the Lord.)

How culpable for Jesus's death was Pilate? Did he know that Jesus was innocent? If he did, why did he deliver him to be executed (verse 26)? If he did not, why did he wash his hands (verse 24)?

Notice that Pilate does not really conduct a trial: he hears the accusation, asks Jesus about that accusation, offers to free either Jesus or Barabbas, and delivers Jesus for execution when the crowd chooses Barabbas. He questions no witnesses and delivers no verdict. Scourging (verse 26) was the first step in execution by crucifixion. But if this wasn't a real trial, what was it?

Verses 27–31: Roman soldiers wore a scarlet cloak, so it seems the guards have placed one of their robes on him. Long thorns seem to have been used as kindling for fires; they may have woven those thorns into a wreath to use as a mock crown. Why did the soldiers mock Jesus when it is unlikely that they knew him and probably knew little about him?

Verses 32–34: Roman soldiers had the right to impress anyone into temporary labor. The upright of the cross was permanently installed on the execution site, and the condemned were required to carry the transverse beam to the site.

We are not sure where Golgotha was; there are at least two possible sites. It seems that it was the custom for Jewish women to give condemned prisoners a narcotic drink to lessen their pain. Why does Jesus refuse the drink (verse 34)?

Verses 35–44: Roman citizens were forbidden by law from being executed by crucifixion; it was reserved for slaves, bandits, and rebels. What does that tell us about how Jesus was viewed by the Romans? How is that relevant to our understanding of what he did?

One of the privileges of the execution squad was to divide the garments of the condemned among themselves. Those executed were entirely nude, part of the humiliation of the execution.

Though no charge was specified by Pilate in the trial, some charge had to be made to justify the execution. Matthew tells us that the charge was placed on a placard over Jesus's head (verse 37). What did the title on the placard mean to Pilate and to the executioners? What does the execution of Jesus between two thieves tell us about how they understood the placard? What does the title mean to us?

Those in the crowd who taunt Christ do not hide their reasons for his execution (verses 39–40). What is their charge against him?

How do the priests, scribes, and elders understand what it means to be the king of Israel (verses 42–43).

As we have seen them do before, the priests say more than they know: "he saved others; himself he cannot save" (verse 42). In verse 43 the priests refer to Psalm 22:9.

Verses 45–50: The sixth hour was noon, and the ninth hour was mid-afternoon. Is the darkness referred to in verse 45 literal or figurative? (Compare Luke 22:53.)

The words that Jesus cries out in verse 46 are the first line of Psalm 22. The last words of Jesus mentioned by John (John 19:30) may be from the last line of that psalm (verse 31: "he hath done" can also be translated "it is done"). What do you make of that connection between Jesus's words and the psalm?

A common drink for the poor of Jesus's time was vinegar mixed with water. This is probably what someone from the crowd is offering Jesus. (See Psalm 69:22.) "Yielded up the ghost" or "let go of the spirit" was an idiomatic expression meaning "died."

Verses 51–56: What does tearing the veil of the temple signify?

The dead of Israel recognized Jesus, and the Roman soldiers recognized Jesus. What point is Matthew making by telling us about these people who recognize that Jesus is the Son of God? Whom might he want us to compare them to?

Verses 57–61: Mark tells us that Joseph of Arimathaea was "an honourable counsellor." "A respectable member of the city council" is another possible translation. Besides his concern as one of Jesus's disciples, he probably wished to ensure that the Mosaic law was followed, which forbad allowing the body of one executed to remain on the cross overnight (Deuteronomy 21:23).

Verses 62–66: On what day would the events of verses 62–66 have occurred? What is remarkable about the fact that the priests and Pharisees came to see Pilate on that day?

Mark tells us that they remember that Jesus has prophesied his resurrection. Do the disciples? What does this tell us about the priests and the Pharisees?

Given what the priests say here, how do you think they explained the empty tomb?

Lesson 27
Matthew 28; Luke 24; John 20–21

A detailed comparison of how each of these writers tells the story of Jesus's resurrection would be both interesting and enlightening. There is a great deal to be learned from thinking about the similarities and the differences between the ways these three writers relate those events. But there isn't space enough here for such a comparison. To keep the study materials for this lesson to a reasonable length, this chapter will focus on Matthew 28, Luke 24 (more on the former than the latter), and John 21.

Nevertheless, we can begin with a few questions of comparison: Matthew tells us of an earthquake that no one else mentions. John tells us that Mary Magdalene went to the tomb and then told the disciples, among whom Peter and John returned to see the empty tomb. Mark tells us that Mary and other women saw an angel outside the tomb and a second inside, but Luke and John tell us that they see two angels inside. John and Mark tell us that Jesus appeared to Mary Magdalene outside the tomb, though Matthew tells us that he appeared to Mary Magdalene and the other Mary as they were leaving the tomb.

What do you make of these differences? Is there one story of which each of these is a part? Are we reading separate remembered accounts with the differences that memory often creates? Or are we seeing other things at work in these differences? And what difference do the differences make? How would you answer someone who used these differences to argue that the New Testament is inconsistent and, therefore, not to be relied on?

Matthew 28

Verse 1: Who was the other Mary? (See Matthew 27:57.)

How do you explain the chronology here: how can it be both "the end of the sabbath" and dawn since the Sabbath extends from sunup to sundown?

Verse 2: The verse tells us that there was a great earthquake because the angel descended. That's what *for* means when it begins the second clause: "for the angel of the Lord descended." Why would the descent of an angel cause an earthquake?

"Look!" would be a more colloquial translation of the Greek than "and behold."

The angel rolls back the stone only when the two Marys come to see the tomb. Does Jesus leave the tomb at that time, or has he already left?

Verses 2–5: Why don't the women faint when the guards are so frightened that they do?

Is Matthew using irony when he says that the guards of Jesus's tomb "became as dead men"?

Is it important to what Matthew is saying that the only witnesses are the two Marys, that the guards are unconscious? How so?

The resurrection itself has no witnesses, though there are many witnesses to the resurrected Christ. The Gospels tell us of those who see Jesus after his resurrection, but there appears to have been no human witness of the event of the resurrection. Why do you think that is?

Verse 5: Why does the angel describe Jesus as "which was crucified" rather than "your Master" or "who wrought the atonement" or in some similar way?

Verse 6: "He is risen" translates a Greek clause that can more accurately be translated "He has been raised." What does that passive construction imply?

Why is it important for the angel to remind the two Marys that Jesus had told them he would be resurrected?

How well had those prophecies of resurrection prepared Jesus's followers, like these two, for the event itself? Were they surprised? If so, why? What might that tell us about the nature of prophecy?

The angel invites the women to see the place where Jesus lay, to see that the tomb is empty. Do they take up his invitation? Whichever way you answer, how does your answer affect our understanding of what happened and its meaning for the two Marys?

Verse 7: Why are they told to tell only the disciples? Why weren't they told to tell their message more widely?

In Matthew 26:32 Jesus told the disciples that he would go before them into Galilee. Here the angel tells them he has already gone there. Why do you think he went to Galilee to reunite with his disciples rather than do it where they were, in Jerusalem?

Verse 8: What does it tell us that the women's feelings were of fear and joy at the same time?

Verse 9: The angel told the two Marys to go to the disciples and tell them what they had seen. But as they are on their way, they are met by Jesus himself. Why do you think the events unfold in that way? Why doesn't Jesus either let them take their message to the disciples as his angel instructed, on the one hand, or appear to them at the tomb, on the other?

When Jesus meets the women, he says, literally, "Rejoice," though the Greek word used was a common greeting, used as we would use "Hello." However, in this instance, the literal meaning is also appropriate. What do you make of the women's reaction?

Verse 10: Jesus tells them not to fear, but there is no evidence that they do. Why does he say that to them?

Jesus repeats his instructions that the disciples will meet with him in Galilee, taking us back to the question (verse 7) of why they must go to Galilee to meet with him. This seems to be important to Matthew, since he repeats it. Why is it important to him?

Verses 11–15: What do these verses explain? Why was that important to the early Church? How might it be meaningful to us?

Verses 17–20: Would the last clause of the verse be a surprise to a first-time reader? Why does Matthew tell the story that way?

Why is it important to him to mention that there were doubters among the disciples? What effect might Jesus's words have had on the doubters? Why doesn't he say anything to them about their doubts? Jesus says that they should go and teach *because* he has all power. Can you explain that relation between their call to teach and his omnipotence?

What does Jesus mean when he says, "I am with you, even unto the end of the world [literally, "the end of the age"]"?

Luke 24

Verses 1–11: Why does Luke wait until verse 10 to tell us who came to the tomb?

Notice that the language that each of the evangelists uses to tell the story of the resurrection is simple and straightforward. Why did they choose that kind of language to describe such an important and dramatic event rather than more dramatic language?

What does the word *remember* mean in verses 7–8? Had Jesus's followers actually forgotten that he told them these things would happen?

Why does news of the resurrection first come to women rather than to the presidency of the Church or other priesthood holders? (Compare John 20:11–18.)

Why does the angel's description of what had to be focus on the resurrection rather than on the experience in the Garden of Gethsemane?

The phrase "idle tales" is weaker than the Greek which says, literally, "things said in a delirium." Why don't the apostles believe the women?

305

Verse 12: How does Peter respond to the empty tomb? Does he believe the women's story? If so, why?

Verses 13–35: We don't know where Emmaus was. Since the name means "Hot Spring," it could have been any of a number of places. Wherever it was, it seems to have been about a two-hour walk from Jerusalem.[1]

Verse 13 says "two of them" were on their way to Emmaus. Two of whom? Why doesn't Luke tell us their names or give some other way of identifying them? We later learn the name of one of them, Cleopas (verse 18).

Compare and contrast the experience of these two people with that of the apostles (Matthew 28:17; Luke 24:36–38, 41; John 20:20, 24–25). How quickly does each recognize the Lord?

What is the Lord doing when these two recognize him? How is that significant?

Does each group believe as soon as they recognize him?

In verse 15 the Greek word translated *reasoned* could also be translated *questioned*. Does that alternative translation change the meaning significantly?

In Luke's version of the story, the first words that Jesus is recorded as saying after his resurrection are in verse 17: "What are you talking about as you walk?" Is there any symbolic significance in this for us?

Note that most modern translations differ from the King James in verse 17. The King James Version includes "and are sad" as part of what Jesus said. Most translators, though, take the Greek phrase to be part of the description of those to whom Jesus is speaking; that is, responding to the question, "they stopped, looking sad." Here is a more modern rendering of the verse as a whole: "He said to them 'What are you talking about as you walk?' and they stopped, looking sad." Does that change the meaning of the story at all?

The tradition says that Cleopas (verse 18) was Jesus's paternal uncle, the brother of Joseph. Cleopas's son, Symeon, succeeded James (Jesus's brother) as bishop of Jerusalem. If that tradition reflects the truth, why would Jesus appear to his uncle rather than to someone else?

What does verse 19 show about these disciples' understanding of who Jesus was?

The Greek word translated *trusted* in verse 21 is probably better translated *were hoping*. Does that change your understanding?

Compare verse 30 to Luke 9:16 and to Luke 22:19. What is Jesus doing?

Why doesn't Luke tell us how the two travelers responded to Jesus's sharp rebuke in verse 25? For what does he rebuke them? Is their failure that they haven't recognized him, or is it something else?

What does it mean to be "slow of heart"?

Is there a message for us in this rebuke of these two disciples?

Given what we see in verse 27, how should we read the Hebrew Bible?

After Jesus has expounded the scriptures to Cleopas and his fellow traveler, do they understand what he has said? Why don't they recognize him yet?

307

How does it happen that Jesus, the guest, takes on the duties of the head of the household to bless the bread at this meal (verse 30)?

Is it significant that verse 30 uses exactly the same language as did Luke 22:19a? Why does this thing that Jesus does open their eyes when seeing him in person, speaking with him, and having their hearts burn as he expounded the scriptures did not?

What effect is created by the eleven apostles telling the two of the Lord's appearance to Peter before the latter tell of their experience on the way to Emmaus? Is that significant to the meaning of this story?

Many have seen a chiasmus in these verses:[2]

> A Verses 13–14 Introduction: the disciples are alone
>
>> B Verses 15–19a The narrative frame
>>
>>> C Verses 19b–27 The disciples' dialogue with Jesus, with the angelic announcement of the resurrection (verse 23b) at the center
>>
>> B' Verses 28–32 The narrative frame
>
> A' Verses 33–35 Conclusion: the disciples are alone

There are other parallels within the story, but this gives a good overview of it. It also has many other literary features, which have been noted by many careful readers. Why has Luke (or his source; compare Luke 1:1–3) crafted this particular story so carefully?

Verses 36–49: Notice how the disciples are described: terrified and afraid (verse 37), troubled and doubting (verse

38). Why are the apostles frightened? The two people on the way to Emmaus were not. What are the differences between these two events?

What does Luke mean when he says "they believed not [i.e., disbelieved] for joy" (verse 41)? What does it mean to disbelieve for joy?

In verse 44, to what does "these are the words" refer?

Why does the Lord say to them "while I *was* yet with you" (italics added)? In other words, why does he use the past tense? After all, he is with them when he speaks—or is he suggesting that he is no longer with them in the same way?

To both the people on the way to Emmaus and to the eleven apostles, the risen Lord expounds the scriptures. Why?

To what does "these things" refer in verse 48?

The Greek word from which we get the word *apostle* means "messenger." Does that deepen your understanding of what the scriptures teach? What is the message of these witnesses?

John 21

Verses 1–3: Why do you think the disciples have decided to go fishing? Many have read this as a sign that their faith is weak: they have decided to return to their former occupation, to give up the ministry to which they have been called. Do you think that judgment is correct or too harsh? If it is too harsh, how do you explain what is happening?

In verse 4, why can't the disciples recognize Jesus?

Is it significant that John, "that disciple whom Jesus loved," was the first to recognize Jesus (verse 7)?

Do the events of verses 9 and 12–13 help answer the question about what the disciples were doing?

Do you have any idea why John would tell us the exact number of fish caught? Is it symbolically significant? For example, the early Christian writer Jerome (347–420; the son of the historian Eusebius) tells us that writers of his time believed that there were 153 species of fish in the world.[3] That seems unlikely, but is there perhaps another way of understanding this as symbolic?

This is very odd: "None of the disciples durst ask him, Who art thou? Knowing that it was the Lord" (verse 12). It seems obvious that if I already know who someone is I won't ask, "Who are you?" So what is John saying in those two sentences?

When the Lord asks Peter, "Lovest thou me more than these?" is he asking, "Do you love me more than the other apostles love me?" or "Do you love me more than you love them?"

What would each repetition of the question "Lovest thou me?" (verses 15–17) have done to Peter?

What is the significance of the Lord's request that Peter be a shepherd? How is the figure of the shepherd used in scripture?

On its face, verse 18 looks like a description of what happens to a person as he or she ages: when you are young, you clothe yourself and go wherever you wish, but when you are old someone else must help you dress and take you where he or she wants you to go. How, then, is it a prophecy of Peter's death (verse 19)?

Why does the Lord first humble Peter with his question about love (verses 15–17), then prophesy how Peter will die (verse 18) and conclude by saying, "Follow me" (verse 19). What is the coherence of that sequence of ideas?

If John the Beloved was not to die, as Latter-day Saints teach, then why does he include verse 23b, which says that Jesus didn't say John wouldn't die? For what is verse 23b a corrective? What is the emphasis in the last clause of the verse, the repetition of Jesus's comment to Peter in verse 22?

Lesson 28
Acts 1–5

There are several stories in these chapters: In chapter 1 we learn that Jesus ministered to the apostles for forty days after his resurrection and that Matthias was chosen to fill the vacancy left by Judas. Chapter 2 tells us of the visit of the Holy Ghost on the day of Pentecost, the gift of tongues given to them as a sign of the Holy Ghost, and Peter's sermon admonishing those who hear them to repent and be baptized. Chapters 3–4 tell of Peter and John healing a lame man, which resulted in many people believing their preaching, and the high priest, Caiaphas, and his family demanding that they cease preaching that Jesus was resurrected. Of course, they didn't heed that demand. Chapter 5 begins with the story of Ananias and Sapphira, who withheld part of the money they received for the sale of their property, lying to Peter about how much they had received and dying as a result of their lie. Because many were converted as a result of the preaching of Peter and the other apostles, the high priest had all of the apostles arrested and imprisoned, but they were released by an angel. Called on to account for their refusal to obey the high priest's command not to teach in Jesus's name, they said they would obey God rather than men: as witnesses of Christ, they cannot refrain from preaching him.

We can understand each of these stories not only as historical stories but also as stories that help us understand how to live in the world as Christians. Why do stories do that better than lists of principles for life? Pick one or two of these stories and use them to reflect on what it means to be a Christian.

Acts 1

Verses 1–14: It is important to recognize what verse 1 tells us—that Acts is a continuation of Luke's records. Many scholars refer to the two of them together as one book, Luke-Acts. Does that make any difference in how you approach reading Acts? Does it make any difference in how you understand Luke?

Why do we have nothing in Acts of the teachings of the Lord's forty-day ministry (verse 2)? Why was that ministry important to the apostles?

In verse 3, to what does the word *passion* refer, to the suffering in the Garden of Gethsemane and the Savior's death on the cross, or does it also include the resurrection?

Why does Luke use that word, a word that could also be translated *experience* (Galatians 3:4), *suffering* (Luke 22:15), or *enduring* (Mark 8:31)? Might one of those other translations be equally or more appropriate here? If so, which one and why?

What do the apostles hope that the risen Lord will do (verse 6)?

The *Jerome Bible Commentary* points out that the order of preaching commanded by Jesus in verse 8 corresponds to the parts of Acts:[1]

Jerusalem corresponds to Acts 1–7

Judea and Samaria corresponds to Acts 8–9

The ends of the earth corresponds to Acts 10–28, Rome being the end of the earth

What does that tell us about the book of Acts? What do you make of the angels' response to the eleven apostles in verse 11?

Verses 15–26: Since Mathias never again appears in Luke's account, why was it important that he tell us about his election to the Twelve? Why do you think we do not hear of him again?

Note that the word translated *bishoprick* in verse 20 (*episkopē*) means simply "office." The literal meaning of the Greek word (*episkopē*) is "one who has the duty of watching over others," an overseer. Why did the new apostle have to be chosen from among those who had been disciples from the time of Jesus's baptism until the resurrection (verses 21–22)?

To what is the new member of the Twelve specifically to be ordained (verse 22)?

Does what we learn here about the ordination of Mathias have any relevance to us?

Acts 2

Verses 1–13: The festival of Pentecost (also called the Feast of Weeks) was originally an agricultural feast, but since it coincided with the date when the Israelites arrived at Sinai (Exodus 19:1), it became a feast in which Israel celebrated

315

the covenant of Sinai. That is why, for Qumran Jews, Pentecost was the most important feast of the year. For other Jews, however, it appears to have been a feast of secondary importance. Are there any parallels between the events of Sinai—or the Sinai covenant—and the events portrayed in these verses that would make the day of Pentecost particularly appropriate as the day when the Holy Ghost was given?

What is the significance of speaking in tongues at this time? Does it have symbolic significance? Does it have practical significance? How are the practical and the symbolic related to each other?

Verses 14–36: Verses 23–31 are a long interjection. Read verses 22 and 32–33 together, skipping the verses between. Of what is Peter testifying?

Why is it important that "we all are witnesses"? The Twelve are called as special witnesses (D&C 27:103), but are they the only witnesses of Christ's divinity? If there are others, what is the difference between a special witness and other witnesses?

Acts 3–4

Verses 3:1–11: We have heard about the Seventy doing miracles, but we've not read of any disciples doing them. However, we frequently read about Jesus doing miracles. What role does Peter's miracle play in Luke's story about the development of the early Church?

Verses 3:12–3:26: Why does Peter refer to "the God of Abraham, and of Isaac, and of Jacob" in verse 13? What does that title mean to the Jews? Why is that one of God's names? What does that name mean to us?

In verse 17 Peter says that he assumes that the people of Jerusalem, and their leaders, executed Jesus out of ignorance. Is he giving them the benefit of the doubt here, or does he really think that their ignorance explains what happened? (Compare Luke 22:34.) Does their ignorance explain why preaching is required, namely, to remove their ignorance?

When are "the times of refreshing" (verse 19)?

Jewish tradition seems to have associated the outpouring of the Holy Spirit and the restoration of Israel with the end-time. But they have just seen the former (Acts 3:1–13), and the Lord has made it clear that he will not tell them about the latter (Acts 1:7). Now Peter has suggested that receipt of the Spirit is a fruit of repentance (Acts 2:38) and suggested that the end-time is yet to come (Acts 3:21). Surely Peter's listeners would have found this confusing, given their assumptions. But is there a sense in which they were right? In other words, is there a connection between the reception of the Spirit and restoration? Individually? For the Church?

Why does Peter make an appeal for conversion by referring to the prophets in verses 22–26? Have he and the other Church leaders had a similar recent experience? (See, for example, Luke 24:27 and 24:44–46.)

Verses 4:1–31: Why would the Sadducees, which included the temple priests and the captain of the temple, have been angry about Peter's preaching?

From what Luke tells us in Acts, it appears that the Sadducees and the temple leadership were the primary persecutors of the early Christian Church. Why do you think that was?

Why do the Twelve say they preach (verse 20)? For what do they pray (verse 29)?

Verses 4:32–37: If, as some assume, each member of the Church was required to give his possessions to the Church, why is Barnabas in particular remembered? Why does he stand out if he is doing what everyone did?

Acts 5

Verses 1–11: Verse 4 suggests that Ananias's donation was voluntary rather than a requirement of membership. What, then, was his sin and that of his wife?

Verses 12–16: Why do the Saints meet at the Jerusalem temple? What does verse 13 mean? Why are healings so important to the story that Luke tells?

Verses 17–42: About what is the high priest indignant? Does verse 28 answer that question?

Compare the response here with the Twelve's response to persecution in chapter 4. What differences and similarities are there, and what do we learn from that comparison?

What does Peter mean when he says, "We are his witnesses"? (verse 32).

What does he mean when he says "so is also the Holy Ghost"? To whom does the Holy Ghost bear witness of Jesus Christ?

What does Gamaliel, a Pharisee, suggest about Christianity in verse 39? What is he worried about?

Lesson 29

Acts 6–9

Acts 6

Verses 1–7: Who were the Grecians (verse 1)? We would probably call them "Hellenists." Remember that as yet the gospel has not been preached to the Gentiles, so who might these people have been? Is there anything comparable to this division in today's Church?

Why were the Grecians complaining?

The word *disciples* (verses 1–2) translates a Greek word that means "learners" or "students." Why would Luke use that name to describe the members of the Church?

In verse 2 the phrase "serve tables" is a misleading translation of a Greek idiom meaning "keep accounts." (Just as one of our words for bench, *bank*, can mean either "bench" or "financial institution," the Greeks used *table* to mean both the tables at which they ate and the tables at which they conducted monetary transactions.) The second translation probably fits the context better. What are the Twelve saying is the problem?

What does Peter mean by "leave the word of God" (verse 2)?

How does Peter propose to solve the problem that confronts him?

Why is it important for Luke that "a great company of the priests [i.e., of the Zadokites—Sadducees—the party that controlled the temple] were obedient to the faith"?

Verses 8–15: Stephen's calling is to see to it that the welfare funds are distributed equitably among the members of the Church. However, from here on we see nothing of him carrying out that job. We see only his preaching. Why?

Is there any connection between the story of solving the welfare problem and Stephen's martyrdom other than the fact that Stephen was involved in each?

The description of Stephen in verse 8 is parallel to his description in verse 5. What do you make of that parallel? Why does Luke focus on these aspects of Stephen's character?

In verse 9 we see that several different groups of Jews met in the synagogue. "The Libertines" seems to refer to the descendants of Jews who had been taken as slaves to Rome in 63 BC. The descendants were later given their liberty and returned to Jerusalem. What do you think these groups are disputing with Stephen?

What does verse 10 tell us? In what sense can the members of the synagogue not resist Stephen's wisdom and spirit?

How are "wisdom and spirit" connected with the earlier descriptions of Stephen as "a man full of faith and the Holy Ghost" (verse 5) and as a man "full of faith and power"? What is the connection between wisdom and faith? What is the connection between having the Holy Ghost and having power? What kind of power?

What are the charges against Stephen (verses 11–14)? Is there a parallel between Stephen's experience and Christ's? If so, what does that parallel teach us?

Acts 7

Verses 1–53: How does Stephen's sermon (verses 2–53) answer the high priest's question (verse 1) and the charges made against him (Acts 6:11–14)? If it doesn't, why not?

When Jesus taught the disciples on the road to Emmaus (Luke 24), he did so by teaching them from the history of Israel recorded in scripture. When he next taught the disciples (Luke 24), he did the same thing. When Peter preached (Acts 2–3), he did the same thing. Now Stephen does it. Are they doing the same thing that Ammon did when he preached to King Lamoni: "he began at the creation of the world, and also the creation of Adam, and told him all the things concerning the fall of man, and rehearsed and laid before him the records and the holy scriptures of the people, which had been spoken by the prophets" (Alma 18:36)? Why is this the pattern of preaching for the first Christians? What does this pattern have to do with the audience to whom they are preaching? Does it have anything to do with Peter's assumption that those to whom he is preaching do what they do out of ignorance (Acts 3:17)? What does that ancient pattern suggest about our preaching today?

In verse 51 Stephen tells them that they resist the Holy Ghost just as their fathers did. Does the history of Israel that he has recounted show that they have resisted? How?

Which of the prophets did Israel persecute (verse 52)? (See, for example, 2 Chronicles 36:14–16 and 1 Kings 19:14.) Which did it slay (verse 52)? (See, for example, Jeremiah 26:23 and 2 Chronicles 24:20–21.)

In verse 53 Stephen accuses them of having received the Law but not having kept it. In what sense have they not kept it? Remember that Stephen is speaking not only to Sadducees, for whom the Law means keeping the temple ordinances and the associated purity laws, but also to the Pharisees, for whom the Law means the temple ordinances and purity laws plus their interpretations of those purity laws for everyday life. Both groups have been zealous in keeping the Law as they understand it. Do we have comparable groups in the Church today, those who understand differently what our law means? How might we who are also zealous in keeping the law we have received be like these people to whom Stephen speaks? Is there a sense in which we, too, might receive the law but not keep it, in spite of our zeal for the law?

Verses 54–60: Though the King James Version of verse 54 makes it appear that members of the council starting chewing on Stephen, it probably really means that they gritted their teeth and showed their anger to him by doing so: "they gritted their teeth at him" might be a more literal translation.

What is the significance of Stephen's vision (verses 55–56)?

What does it mean to see "the glory of God"? Is that the same as seeing the Father himself?

Why does the council react to Stephen's vision as they do (verses 57–58)? In verse 57, why do the members of the council shout out loudly and cover their ears in response to the vision?

It appears that the stoning of Stephen was not done in accordance with Jewish law. If that is true, what does it tell us about this event?

"They stoned Stephen" could better be translated "they kept on stoning Stephen." What do we learn from that?

Who was calling out, "Lord Jesus, receive my spirit" (verse 59)? Compare verse 59 to Luke 23:46. What does that comparison suggest?

Acts 8

Verses 1–3: Why does this section begin and end with comments about Saul? How do verses 1 and 3 differ in their depiction of Saul? Why do the apostles remain in Jerusalem even though the other members of the Church flee to the countryside to avoid persecution?

Verses 4–25: What is the consequence of persecution as seen in verse 4? Is the Philip mentioned here (verse 5) one of the apostles, or is he one of the seven men chosen to deal with the welfare problem (Acts 6:5)? How do you know which he is?

What would traditional Jews have thought of Philip preaching to the Samaritans?

Why does Simon join himself to Philip (verses 9–13)? What effect do you think that would have had on Philip's preaching?

Why do Peter and John go to Samaria to see that the people there receive the gift of the Holy Ghost? Why didn't Philip give them that gift (verses 14–17)?

Did Peter and John know of Philip's preaching beforehand?

What was not right about Simon's heart (verse 21)?

In Deuteronomy 29:17 we also see the phrase "gall of bitterness" (verse 23), which has to do with idolatry. Does it have that or a related meaning here?

Had Simon's conversion been genuine? (See verse 13.) What does Simon's response (verse 24) show us?

Verses 26–40: The word translated *eunuch* may not mean a person who has been emasculated but, instead, a government official. Indeed, that was the most common use of the term in ancient literature. Since eunuchs in the former sense were not allowed to convert to Judaism (Deuteronomy 23:1, but see Isaiah 56:3–8 for the Lord's promise to them), it is likely that the latter is the intended sense, especially given the way verse 27 describes him. What would traditional Jews have thought of this man's conversion? (Remember that at this time the Christians were still considered part of Judaism, both by themselves and by the Jews.)

What does Luke intend to show by telling this story and the story of Philip's preaching in Samaria, one right after the other?

If the eunuch has gone to worship in Jerusalem (verse 27), what do we know about him? Note that he was almost certainly reading out loud (verse 28). It appears to have been rare in the ancient world for a person to be able to read silently.

What problem is the eunuch having with Isaiah 53:7–8 ("Esaias"; see Acts 8:30–31)?

Note that though the meaning of verse 37 is consonant with the story in which it appears, that verse was probably not part of the original manuscript. It seems to be a later addition. Why might someone have later added that verse?

Why do you think that the Spirit carried Philip off after he baptized the eunuch (verse 39)?

Acts 9

Verses 1–2: It is probably helpful to know that the Roman government had given the council of Jerusalem (the Sanhedrin) authority over Jews living in cities outside the boundaries of Judea. Why do you think Paul would have chosen Damascus as a place to root out Christianity?

Verses 3–9: How is Saul persecuting Christ (verse 4)?

Jesus uses a Greek proverb: It is difficult to kick against the goads (verse 5). What is the point of that proverb? What happens to an ox that kicks when it is goaded by its master?

Is Christ warning Saul? If so, of what?

Why doesn't the Lord tell Saul what he wants him to do (verse 6)? Why does he send him to Damascus to find out? Why do you think that Saul was struck blind?

Verses 10–22: A saint is someone dedicated or consecrated to God (verse 13). What does it mean to be consecrated to a god? What does it mean to say that we are consecrated to our Christ?

How are verses 15 and 16 parallel? Why and in what sense or senses must those who bear Christ's name to unbelievers suffer for his sake?

Given what we have seen before about the early Christian method of preaching, how do you suppose that Saul went about proving that Jesus was the Messiah (verse 22)?

Verses 23–31: Why do the Jews want to kill Saul?

How does the Jerusalem Church's response compare to that of those in Damascus (compare verse 26 to verses 19–22)?

Why does Barnabas take Saul to see the apostles (verse 27)?

Why might Saul have particularly preached to the Grecians in Jerusalem (verse 29)? Are these the same Grecians referred to in Acts 6:1?

Why would the Grecians want to kill Saul (verse 29)?

What does it mean to say "then had the churches rest" (verse 31)?

Verses 32–43: Why is it important for Luke to tell this story? Presumably there were other miracles stories that he does not tell. Why tell this one?

Note on the names Saul and Paul

Though it is common to say that the name is Saul before his conversion and Paul afterward, that appears not to be the case. For one thing, the book of Acts refers to him as Saul after his conversion (Acts 13:1). For another, the scriptures give us no reason for the two names.

Roman citizens generally had three names, a personal name, a clan name, and a family name. Many people also had a nickname. Paulus (Paul in English) was a common Roman family name and never occurs as a personal name in any documents outside the New Testament, so it is unlikely that it is a personal name there either. However, Saul was a common personal name among Jews. So the name Saul appears to have been his personal name while the name Paul was probably his family name as it was for his first convert, Sergius Paulus, though there is no evidence that they were related. (The name Paul occurs frequently in Roman documents as a family name, but it never occurs as a personal name.) Of course, a person then, just as now, could be known by his family name. It is not uncommon for someone to refer to me as Faulconer, for example, rather than by my given name. We don't know what Paul's clan name might have been.

Lesson 30

Acts 10–14; 15:1–35

This part of Acts tells the story of the beginning of the mission beyond the area immediately surrounding Jerusalem to "the uttermost part of the world" (Acts 1:8).

As you read these stories, notice how important the Twelve are in that work. Why do you think that they didn't delegate more of the missionary work? Is there any connection between the extreme dependence of the early Church on the Twelve and the later apostasy?

Notice also that the members of the Church come into greater conflict with traditional Judaism because of this missionary work. For most of the first century and perhaps even into the second, Christians did not think of themselves as a different religion from Judaism. Why did missionary work eventually change that? Does that perhaps suggest something about our relation to contemporary Christianity?

To try to keep these study materials to a reasonable length, I will concentrate on chapters 10 and 15, with some questions on the intermediate chapters.

Acts 10

Verses 1–8: Where was Caesarea, and what was its importance to Palestine?

Italian was the name of the infantry cohort to which Cornelius belonged. The phrase translated "feared God" is a

329

technical phrase that tells us that Cornelius was a person who believed in the God of Israel and attended services in the synagogue but did not keep the whole law of Moses and was probably not circumcised. Another term used to describe such people (and there seem to have been many of them) was "proselyte of the gate," in other words, people who had been converted but had not come all the way in. What do we know about Cornelius, and why does Luke think it important to tell us these things about him?

Why does Luke tell us the time of day when this occurred?

What does the angel mean when he says that Cornelius's prayers have come up to God as a memorial? (Compare Exodus 17:14 and Leviticus 2:2, 9, 16.)

Verses 9–18: For the origin of the differentiation between those animals that could be eaten and those that could not, see Leviticus 11:2–23 and Deuteronomy 14:3–20.

What does verse 17 mean in saying that "Peter doubted in himself what this vision . . . should mean"? *Doubted* is a good translation; *was perplexed* would be another.

Verses 19–33: Given the content of his vision, how did Peter come to the conclusion that he had been told not to consider any person unclean? The vision was about food, so it could easily have been understood to be a revocation of the laws concerning what could be eaten and what not. How might Peter have gotten from that understanding to the understanding he expresses in verse 28?

As for food, how do we square the Word of Wisdom with this vision? Does the Word of Wisdom declare some foods unclean? If not, how do we explain its prohibitions?

In verses 6 and 32 we learn that Peter was staying with a man who was a tanner. Because it deals in the hides of dead animals, tanning was one of the unclean professions; the Pharisees called all of those who had such unclean professions "sinners" (something to keep in mind whenever we read about Jesus dealing with sinners). How does knowing that Peter was staying with a tanner, by definition a sinner, give this story nuance?

Verses 34–48: Had Peter previously believed that God was a respecter of persons, in other words, a person who showed favoritism to some (verse 34)?

Verses 36–39 give a résumé of Jesus's ministry, presumably focusing on its most important parts. How is the gospel an announcement of peace? Peace between whom (verse 36)?

How could Peter expect Cornelius already to know the word that was preached (verse 37)?

Why was it important that Jesus's ministry was throughout Judea?

Peter speaks of the Father anointing Jesus with the Holy Ghost and with power (verse 38). Why might he use that word, *anointing*?

Why was it important for Peter to testify that Christ went about doing good and healing? What does each of those two things have to do with preaching the gospel? Is it possible to preach the gospel without them?

Why does Peter characterize those healed as having been "oppressed of the devil" (verse 38)? Is he just speaking in their terms, or could we also reasonably say that those who are ill are oppressed by the devil? If so, how? If not, why not?

Why is it important that Peter and the other members of the Twelve be witnesses of what Jesus did during his lifetime? That he was crucified (verse 39)?

Verse 40 is Peter's testimony of Christ. Why does he speak of the resurrection rather than the atonement?

What does Peter mean when he says that the witnesses were chosen *before* (verse 41)?

The Twelve are witnesses of Christ. Here Peter says that they are witnesses that Christ was ordained to judge the living and the dead (verse 42). Why is that the important point to make?

Of what have all the prophets been witnesses (verse 43)?

How is the remission of sins related to the rest of Peter's testimony?

What do those who are with Peter find astonishing (verse 45)?

Why didn't the Lord just tell Peter that he wanted the Church to baptize non-Israelites from now on? Why have him go through this experience to learn?

Why does the conversion and baptism of Cornelius bring about a change in Christian practice when the baptism of the Ethiopian eunuch did not?

Acts 11

Verses 1–18: Why does Luke describe those who disagree with Peter as "they that were of the circumcision" rather than "the Jews"?

What is Peter's proof that what he did was of God (verses 15–17)?

Verses 19–30: Does *Grecians* in verse 20 mean the same as it meant in Acts 6:1?

Why did Barnabas go to Antioch (verse 22; compare Acts 8:14)? Why did Barnabas go fetch Saul (verse 25)?

Does the fact that *Christian* is a Latin rather than a Greek word shed any light on the end of verse 26?

One scholar (Erik Peterson) suggests that the passive voice in verse 26 ("were called") suggests that this is a name the Romans gave to the early Church. Hans Conzelmann agrees, but he argues that the name wasn't an official designation. What do you think of Peterson's proposal?[1] How does it compare to us being called Mormons?

Why did the brethren raise money for the Saints in and around Jerusalem (verses 27–30)? Historical records give evidence that a famine occurred during the year AD 46/47 and that, on top of the famine, the year was a Sabbath year.[2] What does it mean that it was a Sabbath year, and how might that make the famine worse?

Acts 12

Verse 1: Luke has already mentioned the persecution of the Church that began with Stephen. How does this persecution differ from that?

Verses 1–19: Why would this story have been important to the early Church? How might it be important to us?

Acts 13

Verses 1–3: Previously we have seen everything in the Church coming out of Jerusalem. What does it mean that now we see it coming also from Antioch?

As mentioned in last week's materials, tradition says that Saul changed his name from Saul to Paul after he was baptized. However, notice that verse 1 speaks of him as Saul after his baptism. Notice, too, that verse 9 says he was *also* called Paul: he was called both Saul and Paul. Refer to the materials for lesson 29 for more discussion of Paul's name.

Verse 5: Who is this John whom Barnabas and Paul have as their minister or assistant? (See verse 25 as well as Colossians 4:10.)

Verse 31: Does Paul claim to be one of the special witnesses? Why or why not?

Verses 42–43: What kind of response did Paul get to his preaching? Why should I care about these events?

Verse 46: What is Paul's message to the Jews of Antioch who will not accept his message?

Acts 14

This is an interesting story, but what has it to do with us today?

Acts 15

This chapter tells us of what was perhaps the most important general conference of the early Church.

Verses 1–5: What is the problem that Paul and Barnabas must deal with? Which members of the Church seem to have been the problem? Who are on the two sides of the dissension? Hadn't they already heard Peter declare that the gospel should be preached to Gentiles? How might they have answered him? What lesson might there be in this for us?

How does Luke explain the decision that Barnabas and Paul should go to Jerusalem (verse 2)? How does Paul explain it (Galatians 2:2)? What do you make of that difference?

Verses 6–21: What yoke is it that neither the fathers of those at this council nor those at the council could themselves bear (verse 10)?

Is it relevant that the view Peter expresses in verses 7–11 was probably not the view of Jews at his time?

Why is it important for Paul and Barnabas to report on the miracles they have wrought among the Gentiles (verse 12)?

In verse 13, who is James and why does he seem to have such authority in this group? (He cannot be James the brother of John, for that James is already dead; see Acts 12:2.)

Who do you think Simeon (verse 14) is? Consider the spelling of his name. What person whom we have already frequently seen goes by a name that is spelled much like that? This name is just a version of that name.

Why does James propose to require only the four things that he mentions in verse 20? (Compare Leviticus 17–18, particularly 17:8–12, 15 and 18:6–18.)

Verses 22–30: Note that the name Silas in verse 22 is the Aramaic equivalent of Saul.

How many were sent to Antioch, including Paul and Barnabas?

How have those who demanded circumcision subverted the souls of others (verse 24)?

Verses 30–35: Compare Galatians 2:11–14. Is this the same or a different disagreement?

In these confrontations with other Church leaders, could Paul expect to win? Why or why not?

What do you make of these disagreements that, from all we can tell, were quite strong? Do we learn anything about being a leader or being a follower from these stories?

Lesson 31
Acts 15:36–18:22; 1 & 2 Thessalonians

Almost all of our Sunday School lessons must cover an incredible amount of material in order to get through the book in question in one year. However, this lesson covers even more material than usual: three chapters of Acts, five chapters of 1 Thessalonians, and three chapters of 2 Thessalonians. To try to make the material more manageable, these questions will focus on 1 Thessalonians 4–5.

First Thessalonians is the oldest New Testament document we have, written before any of the Gospels or other letters. Thessalonica was a Greek city, the capital of the Roman province of Macedonia. You can see its location on your Bible maps. Acts 17:1–14 tells of Paul's missionary work in Thessalonica. A review of those verses would be good background for reading this letter.

Some of Paul's letters are letters of correction, responding to doctrinal and other problems in congregations that he has left behind. First Thessalonians, however, is a letter of exhortation. Paul wishes to strengthen the congregation by reminding them of his preaching. Because it is a letter of exhortation to an early branch of the Church, 1 Thessalonians is also a good example of how Paul taught the gospel.

See the Bible Dictionary for more information about and an outline of 1 Thessalonians. The outline shows that there are two major parts to Paul's letter, a section in which he reminds them of his work among them and of his integrity in doing that work (chapters 1–3) and a section in which he exhorts them to live expecting Christ's return at any moment (chapters 4–5). These notes will focus on the second section.

1 Thessalonians 4

Verses 1–2: Clearly the early Christian leaders taught their converts how to live: "as you have received of us how ye ought to walk and please God." Paul speaks of the Thessalonians receiving instruction for how to live in verse 1, and he reminds them in verse 2 that they know the things they have been taught.

Being a Christian meant more than confessing belief that Jesus was the Messiah. It meant adopting certain rules and conventions of behavior, and the essence of those seems to have been "Live as Jesus lived." (See 1 John 2:6.) Can you paraphrase as closely as possible what Paul is saying in verse 1?

Paul uses a Hebraism: the word *walk* to mean "behave." In other words, he uses a Greek word in a way that reflects Hebrew usage. (This Hebraism is common in Paul. For examples of the Hebrew usage, see Genesis 17:1; Exodus 16:4; Leviticus 18:3 and 26:3; and Deuteronomy 8:6.) How do you imagine that walking became the metaphor for behaving? Why is walking a good metaphor for behavior?

What does it mean to "abound more and more"?

To what authority does Paul appeal in both verses 1 and 2? Why does he state that authority explicitly and repeat it? (Compare 1 Thessalonians 2:13.)

Verses 3–8: Italicized words in the King James Version (KJV) are words inserted by the editors, words they believed were required to make the English more readable. However, how does verse 3 read if you remove the word *even*: "For this is the will of God, your sanctification, that ye should abstain from fornication"? Now try also placing a colon after the word *sanctification.* (The Greek text had no punctuation, so the punctuation has all been supplied by the editors.)

Here's the result of making those changes: "For this is the will of God, your sanctification: ye should abstain from fornication." Does that make the verse more intelligible? Does it change what Paul is teaching? If so, is that change for the good or the worse? Are there other possible ways to read the verse that make sense?

When the KJV was translated, the word *fornication* had a broader meaning than it has today; it referred to sexual impurity in general. It translates a Greek word that also often has that broader meaning of the King James English. Does that change your understanding of what Paul teaches?

The word translated *sanctification* in verses 3 and 4 could also be translated "consecration." Would doing so make a difference to the meaning?

In verse 4, to what do you think the word *vessel* refers? (The Greek word—*skeuos*—means "pot" and is one of the root words for our word "casserole.") The two most common interpretations are that it means (1) one's own body or (2) a wife. Which do you think most likely? Why? Are there any scriptures that might provide evidence for one of these rather than the other?

Given your interpretation of *vessel*, what does it mean to possess one's "vessel in sanctification and honor"?

Another translation has "lustful passion" instead of "lust of concupiscence" in verse 5. Does that change the meaning of the verse?

Paul says that the will of God is that the Saints refrain from sexual impurity and that they not defraud their brothers (verse 6). Some understand verse 6 to refer to adultery rather than to business fraud. What do you think of that proposal?

If you understand verse 6 to be about fraud in its usual sense, why do you think he singles out avoiding lust (verse 5) and being honest (verse 6) to summarize God's expectations of those who accept him?

What warning does Paul give in the last half of verse 6? What motivation for obedience does Paul give in verse 7? How does that motivate obedience? What does it mean to be *called* to holiness?

Paul is preaching sexual purity to people who live in a society that has little concept of it. For a man in Roman society, sexual relations outside of marriage were seldom frowned on. Sometimes some were encouraged. It was not unusual, for example, for wealthy men to marry in order to establish business and political ties and to provide an appropriate mother for their children and, at the same time, to have a mistress for intellectual companionship, friendship, and most of the other things we associate with a good marriage today. Greek and Roman philosophers taught moderation, but moderation did not preclude marital infidelity. Preaching the gospel in this society required that one emphasize the completely different standard required of Christians (the same standard, by the way, for which Jews were already known). It probably helped that many in the audiences to which the early Christians preached were Jews or proselytes of the gate who had similar moral expectations. (See the study materials for Acts 10 in lesson 30.) How would they have made their case to those in the wider community?

Remember also that even Jesus's disciples found his teaching about marital fidelity hard. In Matthew 19:9 he teaches his disciples that only adultery justifies divorce, and his disciples respond, "If that is how it is with a man and his wife [i.e., if those are the only grounds for divorce], then it is better not to marry" (Matthew 19:10). What do we take from these observations? Do they say anything to us about teaching morality, for example?

In verse 8, what is the object of the first use of *despiseth*? Is it another person, or is it Paul's message in the preceding verses?

How is it relevant that God has given us his Holy Spirit? Does it have something to do with being called to holiness? What does it mean to be called to holiness? How would we put that in contemporary terms?

Verses 9–12: How does Paul know that God has taught the Thessalonians to love one another (verses 9–10)?

What is Paul asking them to increase at the end of verse 10?

Though verse 11 begins with *and*, perhaps a better translation would be *namely*. How would that link the previous and the following admonitions? Would that clarify anything for readers?

In verse 11, what does "study to be quiet" mean? The verb translated there, *hēsuchazō,* means "to relax from normal activity." How does one do that? What is Paul advising them in verse 11? Related words are used in Luke 23:56 and in Luke 14:4. Is he telling them to observe the Sabbath, or is he saying something else? Do the phrases that follow in verses 11–12 help define what Paul means here? What would it mean for us to take Paul's advice to study to be quiet?

In verse 12 the Greek word translated *honestly* might better be translated *appropriately.* Does that change the meaning of the verse?

In the same verse, who are those who are "without," in other words, outside? Outside of what?

How does loving those in the Church and living appropriately toward those outside make it so that we lack for nothing (verse 12)? In practical terms, what does "lack for nothing" mean? What is the difference between *lack* and *want*? Is it related to the difference between *want* and *need*? Why do you think Paul sent this particular message to those in Thessalonica? What might have prompted this part of his message?

Verses 13–18: Why might this message about the resurrection of the dead have been important to the Thessalonians?

What kind of sorrow is Paul trying to deal with (verse 13)? What kind of people would have had no hope for the dead? How is that relevant to our own situation today? When do we have that kind of sorrow?

What words is Paul referring to when he says "comfort one another with these words" (verse 18)?

What connection does Paul assume between Jesus's resurrection and the resurrection of the dead in verses 14–18?

1 Thessalonians 5

Verses 1–5: Why does Paul feel it necessary to remind them that they do not know when the second coming will occur?

"The Day of the Lord" is a phrase from the Old Testament. See Amos 5:18, Joel 2:31, and Malachi 4:5, for example. What does it mean in the Old Testament? Is that the same thing that it means here?

Verses 6–11: In verses 2 and 4 Paul said that the Saints know the Lord will come as a thief. Then in verse 6 he draws his conclusion about how we should live if we don't know when the Lord is coming: "watch and be sober." How does what he says in verse 6 follow from what he said in verses 2 and 4?

Sober is a literal translation of the Greek word. What does sobriety connote? How do verses 8–9 answer that question? (Compare what Peter has to say about sobriety: 1 Peter 1:13; 4:7–8; 5:8–9.) Other translations use *well-balanced* or *self-controlled.* Are those helpful?

How is Peter's advice in 1 Peter 4:7–8 related to Paul's advice here?

How does verse 11 tie together the earlier discussion of love, the discussion of the resurrection, and this discussion of the second coming?

What does verse 10 tell us about the purpose of the atonement?

When we speak of the atonement, we often focus on Christ's suffering in the garden rather than on his death. Why might Paul and other early Christians have focused, instead, on his death?

Verse 11 says that we ought to edify one another, and it recognizes that the Thessalonians are doing so. How do we edify one another? (Compare 1 Corinthians 3:9–17 and Ephesians 2:20–23.)

Verses 12–13: What does it mean to comfort another?

What problem do these verses suggest the Thessalonians have been having? Another translation of the word translated *know* (verse 12) is *recognize*. What does it mean to know or recognize those who labor over us?

Why does Paul say "labour among you, and are over you" rather than just "are over you"? Why do you think he phrases this as he does?

What does it mean to be over someone "in the Lord"?

Why should we love those who lead us (verse 13)?

What does it mean to be at peace among ourselves? Surely it doesn't mean that we must agree on everything, so what does it mean?

Verses 14–22: Are verses 14–15 addressed to the leaders who were spoken of in verses 12–13 or to the members of the Thessalonica branch of the Church in general?

How does the substance of verses 16–18 differ from that of verses 12–15?

Verse 18 says "this is the will of God . . . concerning you." To what does the word *this* refer?

What do verses 19–20 recommend?

How is verse 21 related to verses 19–20?

Would it make sense to begin verse 21 with *nevertheless*?

I believe that a better translation of the word *appearance* in verse 22 is probably *form*, making verse 22 a kind of synopsis of the previous verses. Do you agree or disagree? Give reasons for your response.

Verses 23–24: Paul often refers to God as "the God of peace." Why?

Verses 22 and the first half of 23 (to the semicolon) might be one sentence rather than two. If they are one sentence, what does it mean?

Why is it important to remind the Saints in Thessalonica that God is faithful (verse 24)? What does it mean to say that he is?

Paul speaks of the members here as called. He uses similar language in Romans 1:6 and elsewhere. What does it mean to be *called* to be a member? Isn't being a member something we have chosen to do rather than something we have been called to do? Does the name of the contemporary Church, The Church of Jesus Christ of Latter-day Saints, tell us anything about what we are called to?

What does Paul promise that God will do (verse 24)?

Lesson 32
Acts 18:23–20:38; Galatians

The readings from Acts tell of Paul's third missionary journey, to Galatia, Ephesus, Macedonia, and Greece. (See the maps in your LDS Bible.) Most of the questions for this assignment will be on Galatians.

Acts 20

Verse 28: To whom is Paul preaching in these verses? (See verse 17 and the LDS footnotes for verse 28.)

The Greek word translated *overseer* is *episkopos*, the root word for the English word *episcopal*. It is often translated *bishop*, but *overseer* is a good (and very literal) translation because it shows what the *episkopos* does: he watches over others to see that they do their jobs properly. Over whom should the elders first keep watch? Why?

What does it mean to say that Jesus has purchased the Church with his blood? What metaphor is Paul using?

Verse 29: How soon does Paul expect the wolves to enter the flock? Who might these wolves be?

He is leaving Ephesus to return to Jerusalem. Is that the departure he is talking about, or is he talking about his death?

Notice that the word translated *grievous* could also have been translated *savage* or *cruel*. Whom is Paul concerned about, and how are they cruel?

Verse 30: Does this verse say something different from verse 29, or does it repeat what verse 29 says in a different way?

Another good translation for *perverse things* is *distorted things.* As you read Paul's letters, ask yourself, "Against what distortions of the gospel is he preaching?" Is the false doctrine itself a problem, or is the problem that these people draw disciples to themselves, creating divisions in the Church?

Verse 31: How long does Paul say he taught at Ephesus? Against what did he warn them?

Verse 32: What does Paul tell them will strengthen them, presumably against the distorted teachings that are to come?

What does Paul mean when he says, "I commend you to God"?

What does he mean when he says, "I commend you . . . to the word of his grace"? What does "word of his grace" mean? Some possibilities are the Old Testament (the scriptures of Paul's day), Jesus's teaching (had, at the time, primarily as something taught orally), or Paul's teaching about grace. Are there other possibilities?

What does it mean to have "an inheritance among all them which are sanctified"?

Compare what Paul says here with Deuteronomy 33:1–4. Are they related? Is this, perhaps, what Paul had in mind?

Galatians 1

Verse 1: Why do you think Paul begins by emphasizing that he was made an apostle by God?

Verses 1–5: Why does Paul have such a long introduction? Letters often began "So-and-so to So-and-so, grace (or peace) . . ." Paul is using that standard format, but he has lengthened it considerably.

Why is it important for Paul to deny that his apostleship has a human origin?

Why is the fact that the Father raised Jesus Christ from the dead the description of him that Paul thinks most appropriate to use in this letter? How is Paul's apostleship related to Jesus's resurrection?

In verse 4 the phrase "present evil world" is a translation of a Greek phrase that means simply "present evil." Does that change of the translation, dropping the word *world*, change the meaning of the verse?

Verses 5–8: What problem are the churches in Galatia faced with?

Galatians 1:13–2:14

Why is it important for Paul to explain his relation to the other apostles? What might people have been saying about him that would require this history of his work? Compare his claim to apostolic office with the requirements for that office when Matthias was chosen (Acts 1:21–22).

Galatians 2

Verse 4: Of what bondage is Paul speaking?

Verse 6: "To be somewhat" could also be translated "to be somebody." So what?

Verses 7–10: What is Paul's point here?

Verses 11–13: What is Paul's criticism of Peter? Why does Paul feel it necessary to deal with Peter's problem publicly? Did Paul confront Peter publicly immediately, or did he do so only later?

Verses 15–16: Is what Paul says in these verses addressed to Peter alone or also to a wider audience?

Perhaps a better translation of *by nature* (verse 15) is *by birth*. What's Paul's point?

What does *justified* mean? Another translation has *upright* instead of *justified*. *Made righteous* is another way to translate the Greek. What does it mean to say that we are "not justified by the works of the law"? What does it mean to be justified "by faith of [in] Jesus Christ"?

What does "works [or "deeds"] of the law" mean? (Compare Galatians 3:2, 5, 10 and Romans 3:20, 28.) Compare the end of verse 16 with Psalm 143:2.

Why is Paul so emphatic about this teaching about works and faith? To what false teaching is he responding?

Verses 17–21: In verse 17 Paul seems to be responding to a hypothetical objection. What would that objection be? Do we encounter anything like that position today? Do we ever *take* a similar position?

What is he referring to when he speaks of something being built again after the person who built it destroyed it (verse 18)? What does verse 18 imply about the Judaizers?

To understand verse 19, compare Romans 6:11 and 2 Corinthians 5:15. How has the Christian become "dead to the law" (verse 19)? Does Paul have a particular law in mind, or is he speaking of law in general? What difference does it make which law he is speaking of?

How did the law bring death about? What does it mean to "live unto God"? We know that baptism is a symbol of our death, burial, and resurrection with Jesus Christ. What does that have to do with our death to the law (verse 20)?

What does Paul mean when he says (verse 20) that he is no longer alive but that Christ lives in him?

Against whom is verse 21 directed? Are there any contemporary positions like that against which it is directed?

Why has Christ died in vain if we can be made righteous by the law? Are we ever guilty of assuming that we can be made righteous by the law?

What does the word *grace* mean? To think about that, think about the many ways in which it can be used in English: in its scriptural context, as here; to describe a person ("He carried out his duties with grace"); as the name of a prayer of thanks ("She said grace before the meal"). What do these usages have in common that might help us understand its use in the scriptures?

Galatians 3

As you read this chapter, ask yourself how the things that Paul reminds the Galatians of in this chapter support his claim at the end of chapter 2 that if the law brings righteousness, then Christ died in vain.

Verse 1: "Translate" this verse into contemporary English for yourself. You can do that by paraphrasing its meaning, but be sure that your paraphrase leaves nothing out. Does doing that allow you to see how insulting verse 1 is?

What must Paul's relation to the Galatians have been like for him to get away with this insult?

Verse 3: What does verse 3 tell us about the preaching of those who have corrupted the Church in Galatia?

Verses 1–5: In the first five verses, Paul appeals to the experience of his hearers. What does he imply about that experience?

Verse 6: Why does Paul turn to scripture in verse 6, in particular to the example of Abraham? Of what is Abraham an example in the context of this letter?

Verse 7: What is the teaching of verse 7?

Verse 10: What does verse 10 tell us about the law?

Verses 10–12: Paul quotes from Habakkuk 2:4. Why does he quote this from the Old Testament? What is he teaching about the law in the verses?

Verse 13: What has verse 13 to do with verse 10?

Verses 15–18: The word translated *covenant* has two meanings, and Paul is playing on those meanings. It means "last will and testament" as well as "covenant" as we use it in understanding Israel's relation to God. How does that wordplay work? Is it important to what Paul is teaching?

Paul explains scripture in verse 16, pointing out that in Genesis 15:18 and similar scriptures the word *seed* is singular, not plural—in other words, *descendant*, not *descendants*. What descendant does Paul have in mind?

What point is Paul making about the covenant and the law in verse 17?

How does verse 18 show that the Judaizers are wrong?

Verse 19: According to verse 19, what is the purpose of the law? Why was it given? (See Romans 4:15; 5:13–14, 20 and 7:7–13.)

Verses 24–29: How does verse 24 explain the law?

Does verse 25 mean that we no longer need to be obedient? If not, why not?

What is the point of verse 28?

What is the promise of verse 29?

Galatians 4

Verse 1: The beginning of chapter 4 might be better translated as "This is what I am saying."

Verses 1–3: As you read this chapter, it is important to remember what Paul reminds his hearers of in verse 1: children in a household had no more rights than did slaves. The father of the family had the right to do with them as he wished. Technically that right included killing his children, though few did so and doing so was strongly disapproved of—but it was not illegal. It may also be helpful to remember that tutors and governors (verse 2) were almost always themselves slaves.

Verses 4–5: What is the point of saying "made of a woman, made under the law" (verse 4)? Another translation could be "born of a woman; subjected to the law." What is Paul saying about the Savior?

What does it mean to redeem something or someone? How is that the right word for Paul to use when speaking of Christ's atonement for us? From whom or what have we been redeemed?

Why is the teaching of adoption important? Aren't we already sons and daughters of God? If so, why do we need to be adopted?

Why is adoption something that we receive? The word that Paul uses here (*apolambanō*) means "to receive," as the King James Version has it. But it can also mean "to receive back something." Is that a relevant meaning?

Further, the word can mean "to welcome." Is that relevant to interpreting what Paul says?

Verses 6–7: Paul gives an overview of what it means to be a Christian: Christ's redemption makes it possible for us to be children of God. If we receive that adoption, then we can have his Spirit. As a result, we are no longer servants of God, but his children and, being children, we receive an inheritance from the Father, which comes to us because of what the Son has done. How does what Paul says here map onto our usual way of talking about the plan of salvation?

Verses 8–11: In these verses Paul asks a rhetorical question—"Having become a child of God, how can you now have become, once again, slaves to the weak, poor things of the world" (verse 9)—and he expresses his concern: "I'm worried that the work I did for you was useless" (verse 11).

This backsliding has happened even though "ye have known God, or rather are known of God" (verse 9). Why does he make that change from *known* to *known of*? What difference is he underlining?

In verse 10 Paul gives a general description of ritual observance. This is what religions often do: they order what they do by the calendar, with feast days and Sabbaths, and so on. He uses this as his evidence that the Galatians are on the verge of apostasy. But what is wrong with such calendars? We have a less full religious calendar than most, but we nevertheless order our lives by the Sabbath and by holidays like Easter and Christmas. Can you explain Paul's criticism?

Verse 12: Why does Paul tell them not to worry about having injured him? What is he thinking of?

Verses 12–16: What is the point of these verses? Could you paraphrase them using your own language?

Verses 17–18: To whom does *they* refer in verse 17? Has Paul said who these opponents were?

Verse 17 is difficult to translate, and the King James Version is likely to leave most readers baffled. Here's an alternative translation: "They court your favor, but not for the good; rather, they want to shut you out so that you will court their favor." The overall meaning is clearer in that translation, but a problem remains: from what do these enemies want to shut the Galatians out? Is it the Church? Fellow believers? Christ? Paul? What do you think Paul intends?

What is the good thing that he describes in verse 18?

Verse 19: How does Paul's image of giving birth to the Galatians fit with the images of the sermon he has been preaching? What do you make of the additional image, that of the Galatians gestating Christ in themselves? Can you explain each of these images and their relevance to Paul's sermon?

Verse 20: One commentator says that "change my voice" means "exchange my voice for this letter," in other words, speak to them in person.[1] Do you think that is a good interpretation? What are the other possibilities?

Galatians 5

From 5:1 to 6:10, Paul offers a series of exhortations to the Galatians. This is not a sustained argument on one topic, but a series of exhortations that he thinks they need. There is general agreement that the King James Version of the first verse of this chapter is weak. Here is the translation of the New American Bible, a Catholic translation: "For freedom Christ set us free; so stand firm and do not submit again to the yoke of slavery." Does that translation help you understand anything that you didn't understand with the King James Version? What liberty (freedom) has Christ given us (verse 1)? How do we receive that freedom? What bondage is he admonishing us to avoid?

Verse 15: Explain what Paul is saying.

Verses 15–16: How do the verses explain the difficult teaching of chapter 3?

Verse 16: What does it mean to walk in the Spirit?

Verse 24: What does it mean to crucify the flesh? What did it mean for Christ, and is that helpful in understanding what it means here? Is the resurrection relevant to understanding the crucifixion of Christ? If so, is it relevant to understanding what it means for us to crucify the flesh?

Galatians 6

Verses 1–10: How can Paul give these admonitions, having just argued that the law cannot save us?

Verses 12–13: To whom do these verses refer? How do they help us understand the problem that Paul is facing?

Verse 15: What does it mean to say that "a new creature" is required of those who are in Christ Jesus?

Verse 16: What rule is Paul referring to here?

Verse 17: What might Paul mean? How are the marks he bears related to the trouble that some have given him?

Warriors sometimes showed their scars as a way of proving their courage. Is that the metaphor that Paul is using?

Some have understood this to mean that Paul received the stigmata, the marks on the hands, feet, and sides that are said to have appeared mystically in some saintly people. Is that what he means?

Paul has described himself as a slave (servant) of Christ. Might he be referring, metaphorically, to the brand often given to slaves? After all, the word translated *marks* is the Greek word meaning "brand."

What about the wounds that some of his enemies may have inflicted?

Or is he thinking of his imitation of Christ: Jesus suffered and was wounded; Paul imitates Christ.

Can you think of other explanations?

Verse 18: What does it mean for Christ's grace to be with a person's spirit? When Paul says this, does he mean "with the individual spirit of each of you," or does he mean "with the spirit of the congregation of the Galatians"?

Lesson 33

1 Corinthians 1–6

Some background on 1 Corinthians (in addition to that given in the Bible Dictionary): The Church at Corinth was founded by Paul in AD 51, and this letter was probably written in the early spring of 57. Corinth had a reputation for debauchery in the ancient world, and it had that reputation in a world that was tolerant of sexual promiscuity of all kinds. Paul is responding to two things. He first takes up (1 Corinthians 1–6) reports from Chloe, a prominent sister in the congregation, about what is happening in Corinth. Then in 1 Corinthians 7–15 he responds to a letter that the Corinthian members have written and sent to him with Stephanas (1 Corinthians 16:17), asking him questions about marriage, eating meat that had been sacrificed to idols, how women should conduct themselves in Church, and so on.

Paul has learned that three, or perhaps four, factions have arisen among the members of the Corinthian Church:

> (1) One of the factions has made a hero of Apollos, a Jew from Alexandria (and, therefore, a Hellenized Jewish convert). He is well educated and eloquent and seems to have impressed a significant number, though a minority, in the Corinthian congregation. (But he is with Paul at Ephesus when Paul writes this epistle to the Corinthians; the scriptures do not portray him as

a usurper or competitor with Paul. See Acts 18:24–28; 1 Corinthians 3:4–6; 4:6; 16:12.) In fact, some believe that Apollos rather than Paul was the author of Hebrews, perhaps writing what he had heard Paul teach.

(2) There appear also to be Jewish Christians from Jerusalem who have created a faction by questioning Paul's authority and arguing, once again, for the necessity of keeping the Mosaic law.

(3) A third faction, apparently the majority and probably made up mostly of poor freedmen and slaves, have rejected the other two factions and boast that they follow Paul.

(4) It is disputed, but there may have been yet a fourth faction, those who claimed a special relation to or special knowledge of Christ. (The end of 1 Corinthians 1:12 suggests this possibility.)

With that background in mind, ask yourself whether we see anything like this in the Church today. What causes *our* divisions? Why aren't those divisions relatively harmless? (Compare Doctrine and Covenants 98:76–101.) Is it relevant that the word *heresy* comes from a Greek word that means "division"?

If we don't have such divisions, must we all be exactly alike? What is the difference between a difference between us and a division among us?

Since the concept of Christian wisdom is central to both parts of the letter, these questions will focus on Paul's explicit discussion of that topic (1:17–31) but will also include discussion of other verses.

1 Corinthians 1

Verse 4: The word *grace* translates the Greek word *charis,* which means "favor" or "gift." For what is Paul expressing thanks in this verse? Is that relevant to understanding what he means when, in various places, he teaches that we are saved by grace?

Verses 5–7: Is this something else for which Paul is thankful ("I am thankful for the grace that God has given you through Jesus Christ, *and* I am thankful that your utterance and your knowledge are enriched by him"), or is this how God has given the Corinthian Saints a gift through Jesus Christ?

Do verses 6–7 help answer that question?

Verse 17: Why might Paul have said that he wasn't called to baptize? Remembering that the Greek word translated *sent* is closely related to the Greek word translated *apostle* may give you an idea.

What does it mean to preach the gospel? What is one preaching when one preaches that?

What does he mean when he says that he was sent "to preach the gospel: not with wisdom of words [or speaking]"? What is the wisdom of words? What other wisdom can there be?

What does Paul mean by "the cross of Christ"?

Why would the cross be of "no effect" if Paul were to teach by the wisdom of words? Does it help to know that "should be made of no effect" translates a phrase that means "might not be emptied"?

Verse 18: Whom is Paul speaking of when he refers to "them that perish"?

What does it mean to preach the cross? Why do you think Paul puts such focus on the cross rather than on the resurrection or on the suffering in the Garden of Gethsemane?

Why is the cross foolishness to some? To whom in Paul's world? To whom is it foolishness today? Do we ever make it foolishness?

How is the cross the power of God to those who are saved?

Verse 19: Paul quotes the Greek version of Isaiah 29:14, which is slightly different from the version we use: "the wisdom of their wise men shall perish, and the understanding [or prudence] of their prudent men shall be hid." Look at the Isaiah passage to see its context. Does that context tell us anything about what Paul is saying here?

Is Isaiah speaking of two groups, the wise on the one hand and the prudent on the other, or is he using a parallelism to speak of one group, those who are wise or prudent? Does Paul use this to speak of two different groups, the wise and those who need a sign (verse 22)?

Verse 20: Compare Isaiah 33:18. What does Paul mean when he asks, rhetorically, whether God hasn't made the wisdom of the world into foolishness?

What might those in Corinth who laud Apollos have thought wisdom to be? What did the Judaizers understand to be wisdom? How has the wisdom exhibited through the cross turned each of those kinds of wisdom into foolishness?

Could "the wise" refer to Greek philosophy (the word *philosophy* means "love of wisdom") and "the scribes" refer to Jewish wisdom?

The Greek word translated *disputer* can also be translated "debater." What could "disputer of this world" or "this world's debater" mean?

The word translated *world* is also often translated *age*. It usually refers to a segment of time. It less often refers to a spatial world. To what age might Paul be referring?

Verse 21: The first part of this verse is difficult to read. Here is the translation of the *New Jerusalem Bible*, which may help you understand what Paul is saying: "Since in the wisdom of God the world was unable to recognize God through wisdom," though that is also not easy to understand. Put what Paul is saying into your own words, or figure out how you might explain that clause to someone else.

In that difficult clause, what does "in the wisdom of God" mean? Does it mean that the world had been given God's wisdom but didn't use it to recognize God? Or does it mean something like "surrounded by God's wisdom, the world didn't recognize him"? Perhaps it means "God wisely made it so that the world could not recognize him through its own wisdom." Which of these makes the most sense, or is there another alternative?

What does "the foolishness of preaching" mean? How does God preach to us? How can preaching be salvific?

What does Paul say is the problem with the wisdom of the world? What is the wisdom of the world in our day? If, as the First Presidency has said, God has inspired many thinkers and religious leaders, then not everything said by someone outside of scripture or the prophets is "the wisdom of the world." A significant portion of what is said by those outside the Church is inspired (just as, we assume, a significant portion of what is said by those inside the Church is not inspired). In that case, how do we recognize the wisdom of the world as such?

What does God do in response to the problem of the wisdom of the world? Is Paul condemning worldly knowledge? If not, what is he doing?

Who are "those who believe"? Believe what?

Verses 22–25: What sign or signs did the Jews seek? (Compare Matthew 12:38 and John 4:48; 6:30–31.) What wisdom did the Greeks seek? How does the preaching of the gospel compare to signs and wisdom?

How was Christ's crucifixion a stumbling block to the Jews? What made it foolishness to the Greeks? Seeking a sign on the one hand and wisdom on the other, what do they both require that God refuses to give?

Is Paul criticizing the Jews and the Greeks, or is he simply describing the world as it is?

Create a paraphrase of verses 23–24. Explain what Paul is saying.

Verse 24 tells us what Christ crucified means to those who have been called. How do the power of God and the wisdom of God compare to the signs and wisdom sought (verse 24)?

If God doesn't have foolishness or weakness, how can Paul say what he does in verse 25?

Verses 26–29: Compare Doctrine and Covenants 1:19. Why does God seldom call "wise men after the flesh," or powerful (mighty) people or well-born (noble) people as his leaders?

Why do the wise and the mighty need to be confounded?

What do you make of the fact that Paul begins verse 26 with a phrase that means essentially "Think about your own calling, brethren, and you will see"? What is he saying to those in Corinth? Is that an insult or a criticism? If we think about our callings, do we see the same thing?

Notice that verses 27–28 correlate the groups in verse 26 that he introduces:

Wise — Foolish

Mighty — Weak

Noble — Base and despised (i.e., low born)

The word *base* translates a Greek word that literally means "unborn," in other words, those whose status at birth means nothing. Those on the left of that list are what Paul refers to when he speaks of "things that are" (verse 28), while those on the right are the "things that are not" (verse 28).

Whom might Paul have had in mind as the weak? Who would have been despised by the Jews (verse 28)? By the

Greeks? In other words, who are these "things that are not"—supposedly nonentities (see Romans 9:24–26)—who Paul says will overcome "things that [supposedly] are," in other words the wise, mighty, and wellborn?

The term *glory* that appears in verses 29 and 31 could also be translated *boast* or *brag*. How has the criticism of bragging become part of the discussion? What has it to do with the wisdom of the world?

How does the Lord's way of working, using those who are supposedly nothing to do his work, make it impossible for anyone to boast?

Why is boasting in the presence of God something he wishes to prevent? (See Doctrine and Covenants 29:36 and Moses 4:1.)

Verses 30–31: I would translate the first part of verse 30 as "But through him you are in Christ Jesus."

John reports that Jesus used the preposition *in* to describe the relationship of the Son to the Father (John 14:10–11). Like Paul, he also used it to describe our relationship to the Son (John 2:24). Peter uses it (1 Peter 5:14) and so does Alma (Alma 5:44), though Alma's usage may have a slightly different meaning than the other instances. We see *in* used both to describe the Son's relationship to the Father and our relationship to the Son in modern scripture, for example in Doctrine and Covenants 50:43. Clearly those uses of the word *in* aren't unique to Paul, though that isn't a way of speaking common to contemporary Latter-day Saints. But Paul describes our relationship to Jesus that way more than anyone else, by my count thirty-nine times! The phrase is obviously an important one to him, the person responsible for more of the New Testament than any other.

Obviously Paul is not speaking in spatial terms. *In* doesn't mean "inside" as Paul is using it. So what does it mean to be "in Christ Jesus"?

Verse 30 says that Christ is made wisdom, righteousness (in other words, his justice), sanctification, and redemption to us. What does that mean? Paul says that a *person*, Jesus Christ, is wisdom, righteousness, and so on, though we usually think of these things as principles rather than people. What does his usage mean?

How does that confound the Jews of his time? The Greeks? When we understand it, does it confound the wisdom of the contemporary world?

In verse 31 Paul quotes Jeremiah 9:24 (the Greek version) to tell us that if we glory or boast we should glory in God.

By *God*, does he mean "the Father"? Does it matter?

1 Corinthians 3

Finally consider a frequently quoted scripture from this letter, 1 Corinthians 3:16–17: "Ye are the temple of God." The Greek word translated *ye* in these verses is plural rather than singular. What does that suggest about what he is saying? What is he comparing to the temple of God?

How does 1 Corinthians 6:19 fit with this verse? (*Ye* is also plural in that verse.)

How is that image of the temple of God a response to the problems that Paul is dealing with?

Lesson 34
1 Corinthians 11–16

Recall that in this part of his letter Paul is responding to questions that the Corinthians have asked him by letter. (See the questions for lesson 33.) Chapters 7–15 comprise his response to their questions, and one problem we have interpreting his response is knowing when he is quoting their letter and when he is speaking as himself. For example, in chapter 10, verse 23 (and also in 6:12), Paul says, "All things are lawful for me, but not all things are expedient." Many scholars have argued that when he says "all things are lawful for me," he is not saying something that he believes. Instead, he is quoting from things that some in Corinth have said and to which he must respond. Some at Corinth have reasoned, "I am made free from the law by Christ's sacrifice, so I can do anything I want." In that case, the second part of the verse, "not all things are expedient [or profitable, something we should do]," is Paul's response to their misunderstanding. (Notice how the JST recognizes the problem and makes sense of the passage.)

The Corinthians seem to have asked four major questions: (1) Given their expectation that the second coming was imminent, what was Paul's advice about marriage (dealt with in chapter 7)? (2) Could a member of the Church eat meat that had previously been offered to idols, something forbidden by the Mosaic law (chapters 8–10 and

11:1)? (3) How should they conduct their worship services (11:2–14:40)? (4) How were Christians to understand the doctrine of resurrection (chapter 15)?

Once again, the study questions will focus on some themes from these chapters but will not cover all of the assigned material.

1 Corinthians 11

Verse 2: As the footnote in the LDS Bible indicates, the word translated *ordinances* in this verse could also have been translated *traditions.* That is almost certainly a better translation. How might the alternative translation help explain some of the oddities that follow in chapter 11? (Notice that Paul uses a related term, *custom,* at the end of the discussion of women wearing veils, 11:16.) The Greek word translated *ordinance* in verse 2 means "something handed down." The word translated *custom* in verse 16 means "something shared," "something that has become standard."

Verses 4–7: As you can imagine, these verses have long been controversial. It isn't easy to know what to make of them, so the temptation is to skip over them. Let's consider them anyway, though we ought not to be surprised when after doing so we remain perplexed.

It is important to remember how little we know about customs in first-century eastern Mediterranean culture. We make inferences from some later documents. Because of the ravages of time, we try to see the whole through the very small keyhole provided by the documents that remain. But anything we say has with it a degree of unknowability, and some things are quite uncertain. We are reasonably sure that Jewish custom of the day was for women to cover their hair when in public, but we are less sure what the Greek and Roman custom was.[1] As a result, it is difficult to know what controversy Paul was responding to. Without knowing that, it is difficult to know how to understand his response. As we read these verses, we mustn't forget that uncertainty.

Verse 7 teaches something that we don't find in the Hebrew Bible, so we don't know whether Paul is introducing a new teaching, whether he is telling people to abide by local custom, or something else. Do you have a guess as to which it is? Why do you think as you do?

Explain in your own words what verse 7 says. Is that something you believe? If so, how do you square that teaching with the 2 Nephi 26:33: "He [the Lord] doeth nothing save it be plain unto the children of men; and he inviteth them all to come unto him and partake of his goodness; and he denieth none that come unto him, black and white, bond and free, male and female"? How can it be that the woman's relationship to God is mediated by the man's (as verse 7 appears to teach) yet the Lord invites men and women both to come to him?

Verses 8–10: In these verses Paul takes up a biblical argument. In verses 8–9 he tells us that the woman was made from the man, but not the reverse. Obviously he is thinking of the creation story in Genesis 2. So he concludes in verse 10 that the woman ought "to have power on her head because of the angels."

Is Paul arguing that women deserve protection of some kind?

What does he mean when he says "because of the angels"?

How might Paul's argument have been different had he referred to the creation of man and woman in Genesis 1:27 instead?

Verses 11–12: With what does the word *nevertheless* contrast? Is he now saying something like "You have believed X (which we saw in the preceding verses); nevertheless, I teach Y"? What would justify such a conclusion? What would undermine it?

The Greek word translated *without* means "outside of" or "separate from," just as the English word can. What does it mean to say "neither is the man without the woman"? What would it mean to say the reverse, "the man is without the woman"?

What does "in the Lord" add to the meaning of verse 11? Does it explain what it means for man and woman to be together?

The end of verse 12 suggests that Paul is speaking of the creation: "all things of [i.e., created by] God." Verse 8 used *of* that way when it said "man is not of the woman; but the woman of the man." So verse 12 seems to say "as woman is created from man, even so is man also created by the woman, but all things are created by God." What is Paul thinking when he says "man is also created by the woman"? Is it relevant that he says that woman is created *from* man and that man is created *by* woman? The different prepositions accurately represent differences in the Greek.

Verses 17–19: It appears that some early Christians celebrated the ordinance of the sacrament by having a meal together in commemoration of the Passover meal that Jesus at with his disciples when he instituted the ordinance of the sacrament. Evidently this was the practice in Corinth. When Paul speaks of them "coming together," he is speaking of them coming together to share that meal.

What is Paul's complaint in verse 17? Do we ever come together at church "for the worse" rather than "for the better"? If we do, what causes that?

The words translated *divisions* (verse 18) and *heresies* (verse 19) are synonyms, and *heresies* is not a good translation. *Factions* would be better. How is the Corinthians' problem with the sacrament related to the problem that Paul addressed in the beginning of this letter (1 Corinthians 1:10–13)? If there are factions, how can one avoid being part of them?

In verse 19 Paul seems to think that there is at least one good thing that comes from these factions. What is it? How would having factions do what Paul says it does? Could the factions in our midst have a similar effect? Would that mean that it would turn out that one faction would be the righteous faction and that the others would be proved wrong, or would factionalism somehow allow "they which are approved (in other words, shown to be genuine)" to be revealed apart from the factions?

Verses 20–22: They are coming together and they are eating, but why does Paul say in verse 20 they are nevertheless *not* partaking of the Lord's Supper (the sacrament)?

What does he mean when he says "every one taketh before other his own supper" (verse 21)? What would a person have to be doing in order to become drunk at the Lord's Supper?

What contrast is Paul creating when he says "*his own* supper"?

How is it relevant that they have "houses to eat and to drink in" (verse 22)?

Do you think that Paul's instruction here leads the Corinthians away from celebrating the Lord's Supper as a communal meal and toward the more ritualistic celebration that, whatever the denominational differences, we would recognize as an ordinance?

Verses 23–25: Why does Paul feel that he needs to tell them how the ordinance of the sacrament began? How will recalling this history help solve the problem in Corinth?

Scholars believe that in the material from the last half of verse 23 through verse 25 Paul is quoting from another source, one that he seems to have given the Corinthians earlier. Since 1 Corinthians is probably the oldest New Testament document that we have, Paul is quoting from some very early Christian text. So what?

What does Paul mean when he says, "I have received of the Lord that which also I delivered unto you" (verse 23)? Don't we assume that he probably learned the ordinance when he was taught by Christians in Arabia, Damascus, and Tarsus before he began his work as an apostle (Acts 9:19, 30)?

Is the name Paul uses here, "the Lord Jesus," significant? He could have chosen other names, so why this particular one? The Greek word translated *Lord* is *kurios,* one who is in charge because he possess something or someone, a master. Is that relevant? Does Paul's testimony in Galatians 2:20 explain his use of *Master*?

Why is it important to the story of the sacrament that Jesus instituted it "the same night in which he was betrayed" (verse 23)? Another translation of the word translated *betrayed* is *handed over.*

Mark and Matthew tell us that Jesus blessed the bread; Paul says he gave thanks. Is that difference significant? If it is, what does it tell us about how each is thinking about the event?

In Greek nouns and pronouns have gender. As a result, one way to tell which pronouns refer to which nouns is to see which ones correspond in gender. Masculine nouns are referred to with masculine pronouns. In verse 24 the pronoun translated *this* in the phrase "this is my body" is neuter. In English the pronoun seems to refer to the word *bread,* but that Greek word is masculine, so it isn't the referent. The closest neuter noun is *body,* which follows almost immediately. Is that the referent, or does the pronoun refer to something else?

The basic sense of the word translated *do* in verse 24 (*poie*) is "to produce something." *Do* is a good translation, but what kind of deeper meaning might the broader sense add?

If we are to eat the sacramental meal "in remembrance" of the Savior (verse 24), what is it that we should remember? How do we remember? The phrase "in remembrance" seems

375

to be a repetition of an Old Testament phrase, as in Leviticus 24:7, where it is translated "be a memorial." Does that shed light on what we are asked to do at the sacrament table?

In verses 25, why does Jesus say that the cup is the new covenant ("new testament" in the King James Version)? He didn't say that about the bread. Is that significant?

Was Jesus referring to Jeremiah 31:31–34 when he spoke of a new covenant? Does that reference answer some of the questions that the Corinthians have?

What significance do you see in Jesus saying, "This cup is the testament covenant *in* my blood" (italics added)? Is that an implicit reference to Exodus 24:8? Is Leviticus 17:14 relevant?

Verse 26: The word translated *shew* means "proclaim." When we take the sacrament, how are we proclaiming the Lord's death? Is Paul's point related to the fact that he preaches "the cross" (1 Corinthians 1:18)?

Why does Paul add "till he come"? Does he mean that the sacrament will no longer be needed after Christ returns? If so, why not? If not, what else can he mean?

Verses 27–28: The Greek word translated *unworthily* is the negative form of a word meaning "worthy," just as is our English word. The Greek word meaning "worthy" originally meant "weighty" or "valuable," which suggests that to be unworthy is not to be weighty or not to be concerned with weighty things. Given that, how might we understand what it means to take the sacrament unworthily? How do we take it worthily?

Does this way of thinking about worthiness offer a different perspective on what it means to be a worthy person, something other than thinking of that in terms of keeping rules?

What have the Corinthians been doing that made them unworthy?

If we take the sacrament unworthily, why are we "guilty of the body and blood of the Lord"? We will be held responsible for the death of Jesus Christ! What does that mean? Is Paul being hyperbolic?

Verse 28 enjoins those who take the sacrament to examine themselves, to put themselves to the test, to take stock and determine their genuineness. Self-deception is so easy. How do we avoid self-deception when we perform this self-examination?

Verses 33–34: Is Paul merely correcting the way that the Corinthian Saints had practiced the sacramental meal or is he abolishing the practice?

1 Corinthians 13

This is perhaps the most famous chapter in the New Testament. There are good reasons for that, but one consequence is that we often read it as if on automatic pilot, understanding the chapter through the things we've heard said about it rather than directly from itself. So to understand this chapter better, ask yourself why Paul writes this in response to the Corinthians' question about gifts of the Spirit. In other words, how is chapter 13 related to chapter 12, particularly to 12:31: "But covet earnestly the best gifts:

and yet shew I unto you a more excellent way"? And how is what he teaches in chapter 13 related to what he says at the beginning of chapter 14: "Follow after [i.e., seek] charity, and desire spiritual gifts, but rather that ye may prophesy"? (Don't forget what Paul said about prophecy in 13:2, 8.) Asking the same question another way: why does Paul interrupt his discussion of spiritual gifts (chapters 12 and 14) with this independent discourse on Christian love?

Some have referred to this as a hymn or psalm. Though it is highly structured rhetorically, a beautifully written passage, it is nevertheless prose rather than poetry.

The Wisdom of Solomon, one of the deuterocanonical books of the Bible (one of those books that Protestants refer to as "the Apocrypha") has a similar list of the attributes of wisdom. If you have access to that work (it is available online), compare Wisdom 7:22–8:1 (especially Wisdom 7:22–23) with this chapter. Assume that Paul's listeners were familiar with that passage from Wisdom. What would Paul's list of the virtues of charity teach in that comparison?

Verses 1–3: Paul is using hyperbole when he says, "Though I speak with the tongue of men and of angels," but what point is he making with that hyperbole? How would you paraphrase what he says in that clause?

Why is each of the actions named here nothing without charity? How is charity different from giving to the poor (verse 3)?

"Though I give my body to be burned" is another Pauline text that is mysterious to us. Some assume that Paul is perhaps talking about martyrdom by fire. In any case, Paul is talking about extreme self-sacrifice.

Verses 4–7: What does it mean to be long-suffering (verse 4)? We use the word *patient* as a synonym, which means "passive" or "waiting." What does *long-suffering* connote? (Remember that in King James English, *suffering* didn't necessarily mean that one felt pain; it meant that one endured or allowed something.)

What is envy or jealousy, and why is it inimical to love?

How do we vaunt ourselves (brag)? What is wrong with doing so? Why is it incompatible with love?

What is the problem with being puffed up? Does Paul's teaching about Christian wisdom help us see why bragging and pride are forbidden by love? (Compare 1 Corinthians 1:29–31.)

What is unseemly behavior (verse 5)? (See the footnote in the LDS scriptures.) Why would unseemly behavior make one unloving?

What does it mean to seek one's own, in other words, to seek one's own advantage? Can you give examples? What's wrong with seeking the advantage? Isn't that what our social and economic systems require? If it does, how can we avoid doing what is contrary to charity?

We could replace *thinketh* in "thinketh no evil" with the word *calculates* and we would improve the translation. When would a person calculate evil?

In verses 6, what does it mean to rejoice in iniquity?

When do *we* do that? Here is another translation of verse 7: "It keeps all confidences, maintains all faithfulness, all hope, all steadfastness." What do you think of saying "keeps all confidences" instead of "bears all things"? Which fits Paul's teaching better? Another, fairly literal translation is "covers all things." What do you think of that translation? If you think that the King James Version makes more sense, can you explain what it means to bear all things? Think about Paul's teaching and try to make your own "translation" of verse 7.

Verses 8–11: Why is charity eternal when the gifts of the Spirit are not?

What is perfect or complete (verse 10; the two words mean the same thing in Paul)? What is incomplete?

Verse 12: What promise does Paul make in this verse? Could that promise also be a warning?

Verse 13: What word could you substitute for *abideth* without changing the meaning of this verse?

Why is charity greater than either faith or hope? Can you explain how that teaching accords with Paul's insistence that he preaches Christ crucified?

Lesson 35

2 Corinthians

As with other assignments, because of the amount of material these notes and study questions will focus on a few verses from the assignment rather than the whole chapter.

Background

1 and 2 Corinthians are two of perhaps four letters that Paul wrote to the Saints in Corinth. The first letter (referred to in 1 Corinthians 5:9–13) has not been preserved. First Corinthians is the second letter, written partly in response to reports of problems in Corinth and partly in response to questions that the Corinthians had written to ask Paul. As we can see in 1 Corinthians 16:3–6, when Paul wrote 1 Corinthians, he intended to visit Corinth later, and he promised to send Timothy to Corinth. Timothy may have been the messenger who carried 1 Corinthians to Corinth.

After writing and sending 1 Corinthians, Paul made a second trip to Corinth, but that visit was a difficult one, with bad feelings between Paul and the Corinthians. (First Corinthians 2:1 refers to that visit.) After that tense visit, it seems that Paul wrote a third letter (no longer in existence) from Ephesus rather than from Corinth again. (See 2 Corinthians 1:15 and 23.) This lost letter would have been quite critical of the Corinthians but written in Paul's anguish (2 Corinthians 2:4).

After writing the third (hypothetical and missing) letter, Paul left Ephesus for Troas and continued on to Macedonia, where he met Titus. Titus brought news that the Corinthians had repented and were reconciled to Paul (2 Corinthians 7:5–13), and Paul wrote 2 Corinthians in response. Thus, 2 Corinthians seems to be the fourth letter in the series, written after Paul learned of the Corinthians' repentance.

Paul sent Titus back to Corinth with the letter that we call 2 Corinthians, a letter that included instructions for raising money to aid the Jewish Christians in Jerusalem (2 Corinthians 8:16–20).

There are three main parts to 2 Corinthians:

> 1. 2 Corinthians 1:12–7:16
>
> Paul defends his relation to the Corinthians, explaining his anger, tears, and joy
>
> 2. 2 Corinthians 8:1–9:15
>
> He discusses the welfare collection being made for the Saints in Jerusalem
>
> 3. 2 Corinthians 10:1–13:10

Paul confronts apostates within the Corinthian church, in particular some who think of themselves as what we might call "super apostles" ("chief apostles" in the King James Version—11:5) teaching a new, supposedly superior version of the gospel.

These supposed super apostles seem to have been a new kind of Judaizer: wealthy Palestinian Jewish converts, they insisted on reading the Old Testament only allegorically, they claimed special spiritual knowledge, they seem to have argued that Christ's death made no difference to him because he was just as heavenly before as afterward, and they believed that wealth is proof of righteousness (and so denied that we must suffer and sacrifice).

Are there those today who are comparable to these super apostles? If so, how do we deal with their teachings? How do we avoid them? More important, how do we avoid becoming one of them?

2 Corinthians 1

Verses 3–4: Given the circumstances in which the letter was written, why is it appropriate that Paul begin by praising Jesus as "the Father of mercies, and the God of all comfort" (verse 3)?

What does it mean to say that the Father is "the Father of mercies"?

What does the word *comfort* mean? According to the *Oxford English Dictionary*, when the Bible was being translated into English, the word meant "to strengthen (morally or spiritually); to encourage, hearten, inspire, incite." Does that change the meaning of the verse for you?[1]

How are mercy and comfort related?

What reason does verse 4 give for Paul's gratitude? What kind of comfort does Paul offer those who need comfort? How was Paul comforted by God?

The words *comfort* and *consolation* in verses 3–7 all translate variations of the same word, *parakaleō*. Christ has used the noun form of the word to describe both himself and the Holy Spirit, "the paraclete." (See John 14:16; see also 1 John 2:1.) The word means not just "comforter," though that translation is meaningful and important, but "one who stands beside another," "an advocate for another." Does that understanding of the word change your understanding of these verses? What does the promise of a comforter mean to us when we are suffering?

Verses 5–7: What does Paul mean when he says "the sufferings of Christ abound in us" (verse 5)? Might we reasonably understand this to mean "the sufferings *for* Christ"? We live in a time that is relatively free from persecution. What might it mean to suffer for Christ today? Can we do so in our personal relations, such as those with our family, ward, or community members?

Here is another translation of verse 6: "If we suffer, it is for your help and salvation; if we are helped, then you too are helped and given the strength to endure with patience the same sufferings that we also endure." What is Paul saying when he says that if he suffers it is to help the Corinthians? What does he mean when he says that if he is helped then they too are helped? Do we see anything like this in our own relations?

In verse 7 Paul tells the Corinthians that he has a steadfast hope for them because he knows something. What does he know? How does that knowledge yield hope? Hope for what?

2 Corinthians 4

Verses 1–2: In verse 1 Paul says that he has received his ministry, his calling, through God's mercy. What does he mean by that? Are *our* callings given to us by divine mercy? How does having received his calling by God's mercy make it possible for him to be strong?

What might the "hidden things of dishonesty [or shame]" (verse 2) be? *Craftiness* is the same word translated *beguiled* in 2 Corinthians 11:3. What is Paul talking about?

What does it mean to use the word of God deceitfully, in other words, to falsify it? How might we do so? Do we ever do so without thinking that we are?

What does it mean to commend oneself to the conscience or awareness of men in the sight of God?

Verses 3–6: Who are "them that are lost" (verse 3)? Why is the gospel hidden from them? Does it mean that they should not be proselytized?

How does Paul explain their loss (verse 4)?

Why does Paul think that he must remind the Corinthians that he is not preaching himself (verse 5)? What does he mean when he says that he preaches himself a servant for Jesus's sake?

Paul begins verse 6 with a reference to the creation. Why does he use that reference to speak of his conversion? What does the creation have to do with his conversion?

In whose face did the Jews see the glory of God (Exodus 39:29–33)? In whose face did Paul, like other Christians, see that glory?

Verses 7–12: Who is the earthen vessel, the clay pot, in which a revelation of Jesus Christ has occurred?

How does that revelation show "the excellency of the power of God, and not of us" (verse 7)?

The word translated *troubled* (verse 8) means "confined, narrowed." Is that a good description of what it means to be troubled? The word translated *distressed* means "cramped" and so, also, "afflicted." Paul is hemmed in on every side, but he is not cramped. What does he mean by that? One translation of the first clause is "being afflicted in everything, but not being anguished." Do you think that captures well what Paul is saying? Why or why not?

The word translated *perplexed* means "to be uncertain." What does *despair* mean to you? Why might perplexity lead to despair? Why doesn't Paul despair? Does that say anything about our despair? Other translations of the word translated *despair* are "at a loss psychologically," "in great difficulty," "in great doubt," and "embarrassed." Do you think one of those would make a better translation? If so, why?

Why is it important for Paul to remind the Corinthians that he has been persecuted (verse 9)? Are any of those he is writing to, perhaps, among the people he thinks of as his persecutors? What does it mean to be cast down (struck down)?

In verse 10 Paul says that he always carries the death of Jesus in his own body. What does that mean? How is Jesus's death revealed in Paul's body?

The word *for* at the beginning of verse 11 tells us that this verse explains what Paul has just said. What is the explanation?

"Delivered unto" might be translated as "are in danger of." Does that help you understand the verse?

How was the life of Jesus revealed in Paul's body? How is it revealed in ours?

Given what Paul has just said in verses 10–11, can you explain what he means in verse 12? In what sense or senses is death something at work in Paul's life? How is life at work in the lives at those in Corinth?

Verses 13–15: In verse 13 Paul quotes from the Septuagint, the Greek translation of the Old Testament (the version that he and most of those to whom he wrote would have used). He quotes Psalm 116:10: "I believed, and therefore have I spoken." What point is Paul making by quoting that scripture?

In verse 14 Paul tells what he believes, in other words, what he was referring to in verse 13. What does he believe, and how is that relevant to the discussion?

How would you describe the topic that Paul has been discussing? Is it announced in verses 1–2? In verses 8–11?

Somewhere else? Are the topics of those two passages different or the same?

What is Paul saying in this verse? To what does "these things" refer? There is no verb in the Greek text. In Greek one could omit the *to be* verb, leaving it understood. Do you think that the King James translators have assumed the correct verb, *are*? Or should it be in either the past or the future tense: "were" or "will be"?

Paul does what he does so that many will thank God and, through those thanks, glorify him. Is that what motivates us when we fulfill our callings? What other motives are there? How do we know whether our motives are good or bad?

Verses 16–18: Paul says this is why he doesn't lose strength. Explain what he says in these verses. What keeps him going?

In verse 16, what does "outward man" refer to? How about "inward man"? The word *perished* might literally be translated "is being corrupted," and the word *renewed* might literally be translated "is being renewed or reinvigorated." What causes the outward person to perish? What reinvigorates the inward person?

In verse 17 Paul says that though he is afflicted now, he will receive "a far more exceeding and eternal weight of glory." He just said that he is motivated by the desire that people will praise God. Now he says that he is buoyed up by the promise of a great reward. Is there a contradiction between those things? If not, explain why not. If so, explain the contradiction and see whether you can explain how Paul could have made the mistake.

In 2 Corinthians 11: 23–27 Paul describes some of the afflictions that he suffered: beatings and stonings, imprisonment, shipwreck and being lost at sea, the many great dangers of travel in those days, weariness, pain, sleeplessness, hunger and thirst, cold and nakedness. How can he describe his affliction as *light* (verse 17)?

Elder Neal Maxwell said: "When we take Jesus's yoke upon us, this admits us eventually to what Paul called 'the fellowship of [Christ's] sufferings' (Philippians 3:10). Whether illness or aloneness, injustice or rejection, . . . our comparatively small-scale sufferings, if we are meek, will sink into the very marrow of the soul. We then better appreciate not only Jesus's sufferings for us, but also His matchless character, moving us to greater adoration and even emulation."[2]

What does it mean to take Jesus's yoke on ourselves? How is suffering related to doing so? According to Elder Maxwell, what is the effect of suffering meekly? Why is adoration important? What would suffering bring us to emulate?

Why does Paul describe eternal glory as a weight?

In verse 18, what are "the things which are seen" and "the things which are not seen"? What does this verse have to do with the previous discussion?

Lesson 36
Romans

For much of Christian history, especially since the Reformation, the book of Romans has been one of the most frequently read and discussed books of the New Testament. But this letter from Paul to the Saints in Rome is less familiar to Latter-day Saints. Perhaps that is because some who talk about salvation by faith do so in ways that are incompatible with the restored gospel. In any case, our neglect of the book of Romans is unfortunate because so much of what Paul teaches is also taught in the Book of Mormon.

Romans, indeed all of Paul's writings, has a reputation for being difficult to understand, a reputation that began with Peter, who says:

> And account that the longsuffering of our Lord is salvation; even as our beloved brother Paul also according to the wisdom given unto him hath written unto you; as also in all his epistles, speaking in them of these things; in which are some things hard to be understood, which they that are unlearned and unstable wrest, as they do also the other scriptures, unto their own destruction. (2 Peter 3:15–16)

Part of the problem is our unfamiliarity with King James English and, to add difficulty, the fact that the King James Version is sometimes too literal. Anyone who speaks a foreign language knows that a literal translation is not always the most easily understood. Peter's point in those verses is itself not easy to understand in King James English. Here's an alternative translation:

> Regard the steadfast endurance of our Lord as salvation, just as our beloved brother Paul wrote to you in all of his letters by the wisdom that was given to him—as he does in all of his letters, speaking in them about these things [the things Peter is discussing: that we should await the second coming by being clean, without fault, and at peace with God (2 Peter 3:14)]. In those letters are some things that are hard to understand, which the ignorant and the unstable twist to their own destruction, as they also do the rest of the scriptures.

Peter goes on to describe those who twist Paul's letters and other scriptures as "wicked" (2 Peter 3:17). The Greek word is *athesmos*, literally "without law," "without principle."

Notice a couple of things: first, Peter says that some things in Paul are difficult to understand, not everything. Presumably things that are difficult to understand are not impossible to understand, and we may be well rewarded by taking the time to understand difficult things. Second, Peter says that ignorant, unstable, and unprincipled people twist those difficult things in Paul's writings, just as they do the rest of scripture. Those points suggest that most things that Paul teaches are not difficult to understand and that we should beware of those who may be using some of Paul's teaching for their own purposes.

It would be unfair to suggest that today any who disagree with us about Paul's teachings are ignorant, unstable, and unprincipled. Besides, Peter may have been using hyperbole when he described those who twisted Paul's teachings in his day. But the larger point remains: we should understand what Paul teaches within the wider teachings of the rest of the scriptures. If a particular interpretation of something Paul said is not in accord with the other teachings of scripture, then there are two possibilities. One is that Paul was wrong. The other is that the interpretation that puts him at odds with the rest of scripture is wrong.

Not all who have taught the gospel over the centuries have agreed with each other on every point. Some things that we understand today were not revealed in previous dispensations. Some have taught things that we have later learned were mistaken. So it is possible to read something taught by Paul and say, "On this point he's wrong." But we must be careful that when we do so we are sure we understand what he taught. It is always a good working hypothesis to begin by assuming that an interpretation that puts what he (or any other prophet) says at odds with the rest of scripture is mistaken. Give Paul the benefit of the doubt.

These study notes cannot cover everything in Romans, so they begin with an overview of the book as a whole and then take up questions concerning a few particular passages.

There are many ways to outline the book of Romans, but here is one that may be helpful. It shows that the book contains three interrelated discussions: first faith, then life, and finally covenant.[1]

I. Faith in its relation to justice and mercy (Romans 1–8)

A. God's righteousness (justice) assures the faithful of salvation (Romans 1:18–4:25)

1. All are under condemnation because of sin (Romans 1:18– 3:20)

2. The atonement applies to all equally (Romans 3:21–4:25)

II. God's love (mercy) assures the faithful of eternal life and glory (Romans 5–8)

A. Christ's death puts an end to the reign of death and gives us peace with God (Romans 5)

B. I cannot loose myself from the spiritual hold of death (Romans 6–7)

C. The Holy Ghost gives life to all who exercise faith (Romans 8)

1. To live by the Holy Ghost is to be a child of God, to inherit jointly with Christ (Romans 8:13–18)

2. To live by the Holy Ghost is to be one of God's chosen people (Romans 8:28–33)

III. The covenant and the faithful life of the chosen people (9:1–15:12)

A. God's fidelity to his covenant with the chosen people, Israel: the enactment of God's justice and mercy (Romans 9–11)

1. Israel must have faith, must be faithful (Romans 9–10)

2. Salvation by faith does not undo God's covenant with Israel (Romans 11)

B. God's relation to the Church; the Christian's obligations to obedience, our "reasonable service": the enactment of human faith and justice in fidelity to our covenant (Romans 12:1–15:12)

IV. Personal messages (Romans 15:13–16:27)

All three of the major parts of this letter are equally important. Paul isn't preaching only salvation by faith, though he is preaching that, as do all of our scriptures. He is also explaining what it means to live by faith and explicitly teaches that life by faith requires obedience. Faith saves, not obedience. But to be disobedient is to be unfaithful because faithful life is life in covenant with God and to disobey is to break that covenant.

Why do you think that Paul took these three topics—faith, eternal life, and covenant—to be so important for his audience of believing Christians in Rome? What was he trying to explain that they might not have understood?

Given this outline of the book, how would you explain the relation between faith and the law?

How might you outline the book differently, and what would that outline emphasize?

Romans 1

Verse 7: Why does Paul describe the Saints in Rome as "beloved of God"? Doesn't God love everyone? If he does, why describe any particular group as beloved?

In verse 1 Paul said that he was called to be an apostle. In verse 6 he tells the Saints in Rome that they too have been called, and in this verse he tells them to what they have been called: to be Saints. What does the word *saint* mean? What does it mean to be called to be a saint? When do we receive that calling? How do we fulfill it?

Romans 3

Verses 9–10: What does it mean to say that both the Jews and the Gentiles are "under sin"?

In verse 10 Paul quotes Psalms 14:1 and 53:1. How can Paul (or the Psalmist) be serious when he says that *no one* is righteous? For example, isn't the living prophet righteous?

Compare these verses to verse 23. What is Paul's point?

Verses 19–20: This is the Joseph Smith revision of verse 20: "For by the law is the knowledge of sin; therefore by the deeds of the law shall no flesh be justified." Does that revision change the meaning of the verse or does it clarify it? Explain in your own words what the verse means.

According to these two verses, what does the law teach us? What does it mean to be justified? Justified before whom? Why can't the law justify us?

Verse 28: *Without* in this verse means "separated from," "outside of," or "apart from." (Compare the use of the word *without* in the hymn "There Is a Green Hill Far Away.") The word translated *deeds* could also have been translated *works*. Using that information, put this verse in your own words. Can you explain what Paul is saying?

Compare this verse to 2 Nephi 25:23. Are Paul and Nephi saying different things? If so, explain how. If not, explain why not. (See also Luke 17:7–10 and Mosiah 2:21, as well as 2 Nephi 31:19.)

Romans 4

Verses 1–3: Paul's argument in these verses is that in Genesis 15:6 we see that Abraham's faith counted as righteousness *before* God gave him a law to obey: the Lord declared Abraham righteous before he could have declared him obedient. Therefore, obedience to law is not what makes one righteous. Do you think that argument holds? If not, where does Paul go wrong?

Verses 4–5: What does verse 4 tell us about those who work for a wage? How is that relevant to Paul's discussion of our relationship to the law?

In verse 5, who is Paul speaking of when he mentions the ungodly? Who justifies the ungodly? See also Romans 5:6. Does that verse help make sense of what Paul is teaching here?

Verses 6–9: Paul cites scripture to back up his claim, Psalm 32:1–2. Does that scripture support Paul's argument, or does it say something else?

Romans 5

Verses 1–2: What kind of peace with or in relation to God do we have? How has Christ given us peace with God?

What is grace? The Greek word here, *charis*, denotes attractiveness and favor. It can also mean "gift."

What does it mean to say that we stand *in* grace (verse 2)?

Paul says that we "rejoice in hope of the glory of God." What does that mean? Does it have anything to do with eternal progression?

Romans 6

Verses 1–2, 11–15: Paul doesn't believe that the doctrine of salvation by grace and not by works means that we can do whatever we please if we are saved by faith. Explain why not.

When we argue with others about the relationship between works and faith, how much of our argument is a misunderstanding of the other person's position? Of course, that will vary from case to case, but think about any particular experience of that argument you've found yourself in and use it to think about this question.

Romans 8

Verses 1–2, 4: If I don't have to obey a set of rules, what do I have to obey? How is that different from obeying the law, the rules?

Verse 13: What does *mortify* mean? *Webster's American Dictionary of the English Language* (1828) gives these definitions:

1. To destroy the organic texture and vital functions of some part of a living animal

2. To subdue or bring into subjection

3. To subdue; to abase; to humble; to reduce; to restrain

4. To humble; to depress; to affect with slight vexation

5. To destroy active powers or essential qualities.

The Greek word means "to put to death." Which of the meanings from Webster seems the most accurate translation of the Greek meaning? What does Paul's metaphor mean?

How is Paul using the word *flesh*? (See the first clause of verse 9 for help answering that.) What does Paul mean when he speaks of killing the flesh? Is he speaking of asceticism or self-torture? How do you justify your answer?

Verses 15–17: What is the promise to those who, through faith in Christ, live by the Spirit?

What does it mean to say that this promise is conditional, that to receive it we must "suffer with him"? How do we do that?

Romans 12

Verse 1: What mercies of God has Paul just described (chapters 9–11)?

What does it mean to present our bodies a living sacrifice? (Compare Omni 1:26.) Why is doing so our "reasonable service"? Christ made his body a living sacrifice. Is Paul asking us to imitate him? How would we do so since, presumably, we are not expected to suffer as he did in Gethsemane or be crucified?

Do the things that follow in this chapter and the next chapters tell us what it means to make ourselves a living sacrifice?

What does that suggest about "good works"? Why do we do them, for example?

What would the difference be between doing good works as a reasonable sacrifice and doing them in order to obtain salvation?

Verse 2: What does it mean to be "conformed to this world"? How would we avoid that? (See Alma 5, especially verse 14.)

What can transform us?

As used here, the word translated *mind* has a different meaning than we usually associate with that word. It refers to how we orient ourselves in the world, whether that orientation is explicitly conscious or not. What difference does that make to the meaning of the verse?

What does the word *prove* mean as it is used here?

Why do our minds (in Paul's sense of the word) have to be renewed in order for us to know what is good, pleasing, and perfect according to the will of God? Does that help us understand why the law cannot save us?

Given what you have read of Paul, how would you explain the relation between works, grace, and salvation to an LDS teenage or young adult Sunday School class? To a child of primary school age? To a non-LDS colleague who is not a Christian?

If a non-LDS Christian challenged you, saying that Latter-day Saints don't believe in salvation by grace, could you explain why he or she is wrong?

Lesson 37

Hebrews 1–5; 6:20; 7–11

The book of Hebrews may be what scholars call a "homiletic midrash" on Psalm 110, meaning that it may be a sermon that uses Psalm 110 as its inspiration. Whether or not that thesis is correct, the themes are certainly similar. It might be useful to read that psalm before reading Hebrews and to keep it in mind as you read the book.

Most contemporary scholars, including some LDS scholars, do not believe that Paul wrote this book. It is last among the letters of Paul because those compiling the New Testament (in the early third century AD) were not sure that Paul had written it. There are a variety of reasons for these doubts, but the most significant is that the language of Hebrews is quite different from that of the rest of Paul's letters. (However, the content and occasion of the letter are also different, and that might account for the difference in language.)

Notice also that, though the title traditionally given to this book is "Letter to the Hebrews," it doesn't have the form of a letter. Some who do not believe that Paul wrote Hebrews believe it may have been written by Apollos, one of Paul's followers. In the end, however, it doesn't matter whether Paul, Apollos, or someone else wrote the book of Hebrews. The message of Hebrews is Pauline, even if Paul didn't write it. Christians have accepted this book as scripture for 2,000 years and modern-day prophets have confirmed that it is scripture.

These notes will refer to Paul as the writer of Hebrews because it is conventional to do so, not because I am taking a position one way or the other on the question of who wrote the book. As with other lessons, the study notes will not cover everything assigned.

The Bible Dictionary has a good outline of Hebrews. Here is another.[1] These may help you better understand what you read by giving it a context.

I. God's contemporary revelation in Jesus Christ: the Son is in the image of the Father and, having purged our sins, sits at the right hand of God (Hebrews 1:4–2:18).

II. The Son is higher than the angels, though he condescended to take human form (Hebrews 1:4–2:18).

III. The Son is higher than Moses, for three reasons:

A. He is a Son rather than a servant.

B. Unlike Moses, he will lead his people into their rest.

C. He is the Great High Priest (Hebrews 3:1–4:16).

IV. What it means to say that Jesus is the High Priest (Hebrews 5:1–10:39).

A. He was appointed by God and perfected in obedience (Hebrews 5:1–10).

B. We must teach first principles first, and we must continue to reiterate those principles (Hebrews 5:11–6:12).

C. God's promises; the Abrahamic covenant (Hebrews 6:12–20).

D. Melchizedek was superior to Levi; the Melchizedek priesthood is superior to the Levitical (Hebrews 7:1–28).

    1. The perfect priest, Jesus Christ (Hebrews 7:20–28).

E. The old and the new worship (Hebrews 8:1–9:28).

    1. Old worship: Christ's earthly ministry, the first covenant, and the temple (Hebrews 8:1–9:10).

    2. New worship: Christ's sacrifice, the covenant of blood, the heavenly ministry (Hebrews 9:11–28).

F. The superiority of the new worship: the atonement can only be effective in the second (Hebrews 10:1–18).

G. Since these things are true, we must be faithful (Hebrews 10:19–39).

    1. If we are not, then the atonement has no effect in our lives (Hebrews 10:26–31).

    2. We must remember what Christ has done for us (Hebrews 10:32–35).

Hebrews 1

Verses 1–4: What does it mean to say that, prior to Jesus's incarnation among human beings as the Son of God, the Father had spoken "at sundry times and in divers manners"? Were those different from the way that he spoke at those times through his Son, Jehovah?

Why is it important for us to know that the world was created through the Son?

Why is it important that we know that Christ has "the brightness of [the Father's] glory" and that he is in "the express image of his person"?

What does it mean to say that the Son upholds all things by the word of his power? The Greek word translated *upholding* means "carrying," "bearing," "bringing forth, "causing to continue." Does one of those make the passage more meaningful than the others?

Verses 4–14: Why is it important that we know that the Son is higher than the angels?

In verses 7–8, what is the difference between God's angels and ministers on the one hand and his Son on the other?

Hebrews 2

Verses 1–4: What are "the things that we have heard" (verse 1)? What is Paul afraid will happen if we don't pay heed to the things he has pointed out in chapter 1?

The word *them* in verse 1 is in italics because the translators inserted it in the text. There is nothing in the Greek original corresponding to that word, but they thought it was needed in order for the translation to make sense in English. Try ignoring that word. If you do, what does it mean to say "lest at any time we should let slip." (The Greek word translated "let slip" means "glide by.")

These verses warn against apostasy, and that warning occurs regularly in Hebrews. Are these warnings against individual apostasy or against the apostasy of the Church as a whole? What kind of apostasy does Paul have in mind?

How are those warnings related to the main theme of Hebrews, namely, the nature of Christ and his work?

What witnesses does Paul say the early Christians have of the gospel (verses 3–4)? What witnesses do we have?

What is the significance of "according to his will" at the end of verse 4?

Verses 9–11: What is the overall point of these verses?

Christ has said, "Follow me" (e.g., Matthew 16:24), and we have seen that Paul teaches that we are to imitate Christ (e.g., Romans 12:1–2). What do these verses teach us about what it means to follow or imitate Christ? For example, why did he suffer death, and what does that suggest about our obligation as Christians?

Why does Paul remind us that dying made Jesus a little lower than the angels (verse 9)? Why did it? How are his dying and his glorification connected? Does that teach us anything about our own possibility of being glorified?

What does it mean to say that Jesus is the captain, in other words the leader, of our salvation?

Verse 15: Of what bondage is Paul speaking? (See verse 14.)

Whom is he speaking of in this verse?

He seems to be saying that the fear of death puts us into bondage. What does he mean?

Hebrews 3

Verses 1–6: What makes us holy (verse 1)?

What makes us brothers and sisters to Christ, as implied by verse 1? Is it our spirit birth before mortality, or is it something that happens in virtue of his sacrifice?

In verse 1, what is "our profession"? Another translation is *confession.* The Greek word means "assurance," "promise," "admission," and "concession." Which of those fits the context best?

What makes Christ the Apostle of our profession or confession? What makes him its High Priest?

Why does Paul compare Jesus to Moses in verse 2?

What is Paul saying when he describes Christ as "a son over his own house" (verse 6)?

Verses 7–19: In these verses Paul is speaking to the Israelites. How did ancient Israel err?

Why would these verses have been important to the early Christians? Why are they important to us?

Hebrews 4

Verses 1–2: Do these verses give an answer to the previous question? Explain Paul's warning in your own words.

Why did the Israelites refuse to enter the promised land? (See Numbers 14:1–38.) What parallel to this is there in our own lives?

Paul is using the promised land as a figure of God's rest. What does "God's rest" mean to us?

Verses 9–10: What does it mean to say that those who have entered God's rest have ceased from *their own* works? Do they do someone else's works? If so, whose? Is this an answer to the hoary faith vs. works problem? If so, explain how.

How do we labor in order to enter into rest (verse 10)?

Does this chapter have implications for how we understand the Sabbath?

Verses 14–16: Why do we need a Great High Priest (verse 14)?

What does it mean to say that because we have that High Priest we should "hold fast our profession" (verse 14)? (*Profession* translates the same word we saw in Hebrews 3:1.)

Jesus taught that to look on a woman with lust in one's heart is to sin (Matthew 5:28; 3 Nephi 12:28). That seems to mean that if we desire to do something we ought not, we sin. If that is true, how can it also be true that Jesus "was in all points tempted like as we are, yet without sin"? What must it mean to be tempted? What must it *not* mean?

The Greek word translated *tempted* here is the same one used in the Greek version of the Old Testament at Genesis 22:1 and Deuteronomy 8:2; 20:20. Do those verses help explain what it means to be tempted?

Hebrews 5

Verses 1–3: Can you put the point of verse 1 in your own words?

In verse 2, on whom does the human high priest have compassion? Why is he able to deal gently with them? "Those that are out of the way" should be understood literally: those who are no longer on the path.

To what does "by reason hereof" refer? Why is it that the high priest ought to offer sacrifices for the sins of the people and himself?

Verses 4–10: What would it mean to take the office of high priest on oneself?

What does it mean to be "called of God, as was Aaron" (verse 4)?

Verse 5 quotes Psalm 2:7 and verse 6 quotes Psalm 110:4. Psalm 110:1 is often quoted in reference to Jesus, but verse 4 is quoted only here. Why do you think that is?

Verse 7 explains why Jesus was able to have compassion on sinners. How is the motivation for his compassion different from that of the merely human high priest (verse 2)?

In verse 8 the word translated *suffered* is *paschō*. It means "to experience," but almost always has a negative sense. How did the Lord learn obedience through negative experience? Wasn't he already obedient to the Father?

Verse 9 tells us that the Son was *made* perfect. Wasn't he always perfect? In what sense was he made perfect? The word *perfect* translates a Greek word (*teleioō*) that means "to be complete," "to be finished." Does that give meaning to the teaching of this verse?

What is the connection between Jesus's suffering and his being made perfect?

Why did Jesus have to endure suffering in order to save us?

Verses 11–14: What is Paul telling us about the teaching of Hebrews?

Hebrews 6

Verses 17–20: Who are "the heirs of promise" (verse 17)?

In verse 17 the phrase "the immutability of his counsel" might be better translated "the irrevocability of his plan." To what plan is Paul referring here?

What are the "two immutable things" (verse 18)?

From what do we seek refuge (verse 18)?

What hope has been set before us (verse 18)?

Paul uses a mixed metaphor in verse 19: hope is an anchor to the soul, and it takes us into the holy of holies in the temple. Explain each of those metaphors.

When did Jesus enter the holy of holies on our behalf (verse 20)? In what sense did he do so as a forerunner for us?

Hebrews 10

Verses 1–2: We have here an explanation of why the law cannot perfect us. Can you explain that explanation? (A better translation than "very image" in verse 1 might be "actual form.")

Verses 3–4: Paul's argument seems to be this: the fact that we are reminded of our sinfulness every year when the sacrifices are made proves that they don't perfect us. If they did, we would only have to offer them once. So it isn't possible for blood sacrifice to take away our sins. What might a non-Christian Jew of Paul's time have said in response?

Is there any relevance of what Paul says about sacrifice to our own lives today? We don't offer blood sacrifice. What might have a similar standing in our lives as Latter-day Saints?

Verses 16–18: In verses 16–17 Paul quotes scripture again, Jeremiah 31:33–34. Then in verse 18 he concludes that sacrifices for sin no longer need to be offered. What justifies that conclusion?

Verses 19–25: Verses 19–21 rehearse the conditions that have been given us: we have confidence (*boldness* in the King James Version) that it is possible to enter into God's presence, a way has been consecrated for us to do that, and we have a High Priest, namely Jesus Christ. Verses 22–25 tell us three things that follow from those three conditions. In your own words, what are they?

Verses 26–27: What is Paul's warning to those who sin after learning the truth of Christ? Since we are all human beings and continue to be subject to the vicissitudes of human weakness (as Paul recognizes quite vividly in Romans 7), what does this warning mean in practical terms? Is this about ongoing judgment or about how our lives will be measured in the judgment at the end of time?

Is it relevant that there are no sacrifices in the Hebrew Bible to atone for sins committed knowingly, only for those committed in ignorance?[2] Does that help answer the previous question? What kinds of sins do these verses have in mind?

Verses 32–39: Verses 32–34 describe the suffering that those reading this sermon have experienced. What is the advice and promise in verses 35–36?

In verses 37–38 Paul quotes from the prophet Habakkuk (Habakkuk 2:3–4). What were Habakkuk's circumstances when he wrote those verses? What was happening to Israel when he wrote? What is Habakkuk's admonition is verse 38, an admonition that is central to Paul's understanding of the gospel?

Hebrews 11

Verses 1–2: Having introduced the idea that the righteous ("the just") must live by faith, Paul tells us what faith is. What does the word *substance* mean here? (See the footnote in the LDS edition of the scriptures.) The Greek word used (*hypostasis*) is complicated. It can mean "essence" or "underlying structure of reality." It can also mean one's plan of action as well as "realization" and "assurance." Which of those meanings seems best to fit the context?

How is faith the substance of/underlying structure of/plan of action for/realization of/assurance of the things we hope for?

The word translated *evidence* could also be translated *proof.* How is faith in God, in other words trust in him, a proof of things that we can't see, that we can't know?

What does it mean to say that the elders (those of ancient times) "obtained a good report"? A good report from or approval from whom?

Verses 3–39: The long list of examples of faith are followed by verse 39: "Even though these were all approved because of their faith, they did not receive the promise." What promise?

Verse 40: Those who came before, "the elders," showed great faith in their lives and in the difficulties of those lives. But God had provided something better for us, so that they could not be perfected without us. Why would he have postponed their blessing? Why is our perfection necessary to theirs?

Hebrews 12

Verse 1: What witnesses was Paul referring to? (Don't forget what we just saw in Hebrews 11.)

Why does he refer to them as a cloud? What does that metaphor convey?

What are the weights he wishes us to lay aside?

Another translation of *easily beset* is *cling*. How does sin easily beset or cling to us? What might Paul have meant by saying that sin clings to us?

Explain the metaphor of the race.

Verse 2: Another translation of the Greek word translated *author* is *leader*. Two others are *originator* and *first one*. This is the same word translated *captain* in 2:10. If we translate the first sentence of the verse with *leader* instead of *author*, then Paul is continuing the metaphor of the race. How do the other translations affect its meaning? How is Christ the leader in the race we find ourselves in? If, instead, we translate the word as the King James translators have done, *author*, how is Christ the author—creator—of our faith? Is Paul continuing the metaphor according to that translation?

What does it mean to say that Christ is the finisher, the one who brings the race to a successful conclusion?

Lesson 38
Acts 21–22; 26–28

These notes focus on Acts 21–22 and 26, the parts of the assignment having to do with Paul's call and testimony.

Verses 10–14: Who is Agabus? What does it mean to say that he is "a certain prophet"? Another translation would be "some prophet," without the negative connotations that phrase often has in English. Is this a prophecy from God? If so, what is the status of the person who delivers it?

Why would his friends' weeping break Paul's heart?

Why does Paul's testimony of his readiness to die calm his friends' weeping and pleading?

Verses 17–26: Is "thousands of Jews" in verse 20 an exaggeration?

The Pharisees were "zealous of the law" (verse 20). They believed that the Levitical law—the purity rules for priests offering sacrifice in the temple—should be followed by not only the priests but everyone. And they believed that they were the best interpreters of that law. How do they understand what it means to be a convert to Christianity, and what do they think Paul is doing?

Is Paul guilty of what the rumors say he is doing? Paul could take one of at least three possible positions: he could agree with the Pharisees both about the need for everyone

415

to live the Levitical laws of purity and about their interpretations of those laws, he could reject the need to follow the law of Moses, or he could agree that converts should follow the law of Moses but disagree with its Pharisaic interpretation and the need for everyone to live the Levitical laws. What position do you think he held? Why do you think that? See Romans 3:13 for Paul's attitude toward the law of Moses.

Do the elders ask Paul to make a public, hypocritical show (verses 22–26)? If not, why not? Why does it matter what the "many thousands of Jews" (verse 20) think of Paul and his mission?

For the requirements of the Nazirite vow, see Numbers 6:1–21. How heavy a requirement has been laid on Paul? Why would the elders have asked Paul to take such a vow with the four brothers who were taking it? What does his attitude seem to be?

Verses 27–40: The Nazirite vow was usually for thirty days. Has Luke made a mistake in verse 27?

Are the people who are raising their concerns the same people whom the elders in Jerusalem were concerned about?

What are their charges against Paul (verses 28–29)? What do you think the mob would have given as its reason for killing Paul?

The translation *castle* (verse 37) is odd. The Greek term simple means "military camp," "military headquarters," or "barracks."

What does verse 38 suggest about why the Roman guards have taken Paul prisoner?

Why is it important to the story that Paul speaks Hebrew (verse 40; see also Acts 22:2)?

Acts 22

Compare this account of Paul's conversion (verses 3–15) with the account in Acts 9:1–22. How do they differ? For example, in Acts 22:9 Paul says that his companions saw the light but didn't hear the voice that spoke to him, though Acts 9:7 says that they heard the voice. Both of these were written by the same person, Luke, so what do you make of that discrepancy? What about other differences?

Verse 3: The Greek word translated *exactness* could also be translated *sharpness*. It means "strict." Paul emphasizes his strict interpretation of the law and says nothing about now rejecting that interpretation. But compare Philippians 3:5–11, where he gives another account of his life and, speaking of his zealousness for the law, says: "But whatever things were profitable to me, these things I have regarded as forfeit to me because of Christ" (Philippians 3:7). How do you explain this difference?

Verse 4: Why does Paul refer to Christianity as a *way*, a path or road? Why doesn't he call it a teaching, a belief, or a faith instead?

Verse 12: In this context why is it important that Paul was sent to a man who was devout with regard to the Mosaic law and well regarded by the other Jews of Damascus? Why might it have been important to Paul himself?

Verse 17: Why is it significant that upon Paul's return to Jerusalem, probably three years after his conversion, he is praying in the courts of the temple?

The Lord seems not to have appeared to Paul in his first vision. He reports a blinding light, but not a vision of the Savior. Why does the Lord wait until now to appear to him?

Verse 22: What has Paul said that makes his audience so angry?

Verse 24: What does the Roman commander want to learn that he thinks he may find out if he flogs Paul?

Verse 30: Why does the commander call the Jewish council to explain their complaint against Paul?

Acts 26

Paul's legal process eventually brings him before Agrippa, king of Judea, grandson of Herod the Great, and himself a Jew. What do we learn in this chapter that we don't know from chapters 9 and 22?

Verse 3: How is Agrippa "expert in all customs and questions which are among the Jews"?

Verses 6–8: According to Paul, he is being accused of hoping for what was promised to Israel. Can you explain specifically what Paul is saying? What event was Israel promised that Paul has hope in?

Verse 11: In contemporary English *foreign* is a better translation than *strange.*

Verse 14: A prick is a goad, a sharp-pointed stick used for herding cattle. When has Paul kicked against the goads? Has he been resisting influences that would have had him follow the way of the gospel? Was he obeying the law when that happened or fighting against it?

Perhaps, instead, the goad influencing Paul was the blinding light and Christ's voice speaking to him. If so, what sense to you make of the proverb that the Lord quotes? What point is he making with it?

What are the goads in our lives, and when do we kick against them?

Verses 15–18: Paul gives a great deal more detail of what he heard in his vision than he has given before. Why do you think he does that before Agrippa?

In verse 16 the Lord says that Paul is to be "a minister and a witness," or in another translation "a servant and witness." The Greek word translated *minister* means "one who helps or assists another." The helper is usually subordinate to the person that he or she helps. The word is used, for example, of priests' helpers. With what does Paul assist the Lord? Is it in the Lord's function as the Great High Priest? Is it by preaching the gospel? Something else?

Verse 17: The Lord promises to deliver Paul from the people he is sent to. But we know, and Luke knew as he was writing his history, that Paul would be taken prisoner in

Jerusalem and sent to Rome where he would eventually be executed. What, then, is the Lord promising?

Verse 19: How is Paul's life and training as a Pharisee reflected in his obedience to this vision?

Verse 20: Is it significant that Paul first taught "throughout all the coasts of Judea" and only afterward taught the Gentiles?

Verses 22–23: Where did Moses say that Christ should come, suffer, and be the first to be resurrected? Paul speaks as if these are things that any dispassionate observer would recognize: Jesus of Nazareth has been resurrected in fulfillment of Old Testament prophecy. If Agrippa knows Judaism well, as he presumably does, how can Paul make this claim?

Verse 27: In the context of Luke's account, what is the force of Paul's question?

Verse 28: What are we to make of Agrippa's answer? Some translators take Agrippa to be asking a question rather than making a statement: "Do you think you will make me a Christian in a short time?" How do you imagine the tone of Agrippa's response? Is he being ironic or serious?

Verse 32: What is the irony of Paul's situation? What would probably have happened had he not taken advantage of his right to appeal to Rome?

Lesson 39

Ephesians 1:9–10; 2:12–22; 4:1–16, 21–32; 5:22–29;
6:1–4, 10–18

Many scholars doubt that the Apostle Paul was the author of this letter. The reasons for those doubts need not concern us here, and rather than deciding the question, the materials that follow will refer to Paul as its author for convenience's sake.

Ephesians 1

Verses 3–6: These verses are one long sentence. Consider parsing that sentence to see how its parts relate to one another.

What makes a blessing spiritual (verse 3)? Is it that it has to do with our individual spirits (as opposed to our body or our body plus our spirit, our soul) or that it has to do with the Spirit? What does it mean to say that those blessings are given "in heavenly places"?

What does "in Christ" mean? When someone says, "We are brothers and sisters in Christ," what does the phrase mean? Does it mean the same thing here or something different? The phrase occurs very often in Paul's letter to the Ephesians, more often than elsewhere. Why do you think that might be?

What does it mean that believers were chosen "before the foundation of the world" (verse 4)? When was that foundation? Does this verse support the teaching of preexistence?

What does it mean that we were "chosen . . . in him"?

What does it mean to be chosen by God? Does Abraham's blessing give any clues to an answer? For what does verse 4 say we were chosen? Are chosen people chosen *because* they are holy and without blame?

Verse 5 may be confusing because the grammar of the Greek has been translated so literally. Here's an alternative translation: "Having decided in advance that we should be adopted as children to him [i.e., to the Father] through Jesus Christ, according to the good pleasure of his will." The verb translated *predestinated* in the King James Version and *decided in advance* in the alternative translation literally means "have placed boundaries." What kinds of boundaries are set for us in advance of our birth? Does this verse teach that those who are members of the Church were chosen to be so in the preexistence? Does that mean that there are people in the world who were not so chosen? If they were not, why not?

Verses 9–10: These verses are part of another long sentence. It begins in verse 7 and goes through verse 12. Read the sentence as a whole before trying to understand these two verses. Consider parsing the sentence as a whole to see how its parts are related to one another and, particularly, to see how verses 9–10 are related to the rest of the sentence.

When is or was "the dispensation of the fulness of times"? How do you know? What does it mean to say that a time is full or complete?

The Greek word for *dispensation* is *oikonomia*, the root of our word *economy*. It can mean the act of administering, what is administered (such as a plan), or a person's stewardship.[1]

According to these verses, what is the mystery—the secret—of God's will? Why is that said to be a secret or a secret teaching? From whom is this secret kept? Is Romans 3:7 relevant to thinking about what the mysteries of God are? How about Ephesians 6:19?

What does it mean to "gather together in one all things in Christ" (verse 10)? The verb translated "gather together in one" is most often translated "sum up." It is the same verb used in Romans 13:9. What can it mean to sum up all things, both in heaven and in earth, in Christ? How does he bring all things together in a unity?

Ephesians 2

Verses 1–3: Whom is Paul addressing in these verses?

The King James translators have added the italicized words "hath he quickened," even though the sentence makes sense without them. It is not a complete sentence, but we can understand it: "And you who were dead in trespasses and sins." (Another translation might be "And you, being dead in trespasses and sins.") Why do you think the King James translators added those words?

What is Paul's point if we leave out the added words? Which of the following verses would naturally come next if those words were left out?

How would you put these three verses in your own words?

Verses 4–7: Paraphrase this sentence. What point is Paul making by juxtaposing it and the previous sentence?

Verse 5 begins, "Even when we were dead in sins, . . ." taking us back to verse 1. Why did Paul interrupt the thought that began in verse 1 to give us what he says in verses 2–3?

What does it mean to say that we were quickened ("made alive") with Christ (verse 5)? What does it mean, concretely, to be made alive in Christ?

In Romans 8:11 Paul uses the same verb to speak of the future resurrection. Is that what he is referring to here? If not, explain why he uses the same word.

Why does Paul feel it necessary to interject "By grace ye are saved" in verse 5? How is that interjection related conceptually to what has come before and what comes afterward?

Verses 8–9: What would it mean to be saved by works? What teaching is Paul rejecting here? Why is he rejecting it?

Here is a paraphrase of verse 8: You are saved by God's gift through your trust in him; this doesn't come from you because it is a gift of God. Does the word *this* in that paraphrase refer to *trust*, or does it refer back to verse 7, making the two parts of verse 8 parallel to each other in meaning?

Verse 10: When Paul says that we are the work of God, "created in Christ Jesus," is he speaking of our creation as human beings or our creation as Christians?

What does it mean to say that we were "created . . . unto good works"?

When did God ordain that we should *walk* in good works? What does *before* mean here?

Verses 11–13: From what point of view does Paul ask the Roman members of his audience to see themselves when he refers to them as "Gentiles in the flesh" (verse 11)? After all, they would not have referred to themselves as *Gentiles.*

Why does Paul add "in the flesh"? What point is he making by adding that phrase? It may help to know that among Jews the term *uncircumcision* was a derogatory term for those who were not of Israel.

What does it mean to say that those he addresses had been "aliens from the commonwealth of Israel" (verse 12)? *Commonwealth* translates the Greek term *politeia*, "a sociopolitical unit or body of citizens, *state, people, body politic.*"[2] Is "strangers of [i.e., alien to] the covenants of promise" parallel to "aliens from the commonwealth of Israel"? (*Strangers to* and *aliens from* translate different Greek words, the first meaning "separated or estranged from" and the second meaning, literally, "alien.")

What does it mean to be "without Christ"? Why are those who are outside Israel "without Christ," in other words apart from him?

Why would those who are outside of Israel have "no hope" and be "without God in the world" (verse 12)? Hope for what?

How does the promise of verse 13 respond to the problem set up in verses 11–12? Is Paul speaking of the promise of Isaiah 2:2–4?

What blood brought ancient Israel nearer to God? How is that relevant to understanding verse 13?

Verses 14–17: What does it mean to speak of a person as peace (verse 14)? "He is our peace" is an unusual usage. What does it mean? Is it merely metaphorical, or is there more to this than metaphor?

What has Christ made one (verse 14)? What wall had separated those who are now one? Is this also a reference to the wall that separated the Court of the Gentiles from the rest of the temple? Or is it a reference to the law of Moses, the wall or fence protecting Israel?

Another translation of "the law of commandments contained in ordinances" is "the law of commandments expressed in rules" (verse 15). What does that mean? What other kind of law is there?

Why does Paul describe that law as *enmity*, "hatred"? Hatred of whom? By whom? How did Jesus Christ abolish that enmity "in his flesh"?

Can you explain the clause "for to make in himself of twain one new man, so making peace" (verse 15)? The phrase "one new man" could also be translated "one new humanity." Which do you prefer and why?

What kind of peace does Jesus Christ create? Jews among Paul's readers could hardly have avoided thinking of the *shalom* of the Old Testament when they heard Paul speak of the peace that God brings. What kind of peace does the Old Testament anticipate?

Paul speaks of the peace or reconciliation between Gentile and Jew with God (verse 16). What element has he added that is new to his discussion?

He says that peace with God happens "in one body" (verse 16). Why this emphasis on Jesus's body as that which brings peace between Gentile and Jew and between Gentile and Jew, on one hand, and God, on the other? Does this have anything to do with the sacrament—or vice versa?

Why is the cross so important to Paul when he recognizes that the resurrection is central to the proclamation of Jesus as Messiah? (See, for example, Romans 1:4.)

How did the cross, according to Paul, accomplish the reconciliation of human beings to God (verse 16)?

Verse 17 seems to be a reference to Isaiah 57:19: "Peace, peace to him that is far off, and to him that is near, saith the Lord; and I will heal him." If that is right, then Paul is proof-texting since the original was addressed to groups within Israel, those in exile and those still in the land, rather than to Israel and those outside it. How might Paul have justified that use of the Isaiah verse in this context?

Verses 18–22: Verse 18 begins with *for.* It gives an explanation. Of what? Does it tell us what reconciliation of all people with the Father means?

What does "access by one Spirit" mean? What is Paul talking about here?

How might that access to the Father through the Spirit unify us?

Verse 19 begins with an illative, a word that tells us that what follows is a conclusion. As you read verses 19–22, ask yourself how what they say follows from the earlier discussion of this chapter.

To whom is Paul speaking when he says, "Ye are no more strangers and foreigners" (verse 19)? To Gentiles? To Jews? To both? Justify your answer based on what he has said in this chapter.

The word *citizens* is a variation on the word in verse 12 that was translated *commonwealth*. The phrase "members of the household" translates one Greek word, *oikeios*. That word refers to any closely knit group, usually those who are in a close kinship relation, though it can also refer to a temple.[3] What does this tell us about our relationship with God? Paul has been using political imagery. Why does he switch to familial imagery?

We often say that the Church is built on the foundation of apostles and prophets, but verse 20 literally says that the Saints are. *Ye* in verse 19 is the subject of "are built." What does that suggest about how Paul means *church* here (though he doesn't use the word itself)? How is that thinking related to the earlier discussion about being outside and inside and about being unified?

What do you make of the fact that Paul doesn't say the apostles and prophets lay the foundation of this building, but that they are that foundation?

Jesus Christ is the cornerstone of the foundation (verse 20). Is it relevant that the building of this edifice has already been begun? When would Paul think it began?

Does verse 20 help answer the earlier question about why Paul says that the Saints are built on the foundation of the apostles and prophets?

What does the image of the Church as God's temple teach (verse 21)?

What does it mean to say that this temple grows into a temple *in* the Lord?

Paul says, "You also are builded" (verses 22), but didn't he say that in verses 19–20 by saying, "Ye . . . are built upon the foundations"?

In this chapter Paul has emphasized two things about the unity of Christians: it is made possible through the body of Jesus Christ and it happens "through the Spirit" (verse 22). How ought we to think about our relationships with one another, given those emphases?

Ephesians 5

Many people, especially many women, have difficulty with this reading. Does it merely reflect the culture of Paul's time and the first-century Palestinian understanding of the relationship of husband and wife, or does it teach doctrine? Ephesians 6:5, for example, part of the same set of admonitions that begins in verse 21, tells slaves to obey their masters as if they were Christ, but we no longer believe that to be doctrinal. If that part of Paul's teaching about personal relationships is incorrect or out-of-date, how do we know which parts of the rest of his teaching remain binding on us?

Is there perhaps a mixture of ancient culture and unchanging doctrine in what Paul teaches? If so, how do we sift the doctrinal from the cultural? If the assigned verses or some aspect of them is doctrinal in a relatively straightforward way, what does it mean in contemporary society? These are issues that any careful reader will have to wrestle with. The study questions, however, will focus on Paul's meaning, assuming that readers will take up those larger questions on their own.

Before you focus on the assigned verses, read the chapter as a whole. Then ask yourself, "Why does Paul decide to address this topic? What motivates these verses?"

Verse 21: What does it mean for one person to be submissive or subordinate to another? What does it mean for two people to be submissive or subordinate to each other? How would that be possible?

Does this verse give us a clue to understanding the set of admonitions about personal relationships that it introduces? If so, how does the mutual submission demanded here lead to the relationships described in verses 22–23?

The literal meaning of the word translated *reverence* is *fear*, but *reverence* is a good translation in this context, the "fear of the Lord" of the Hebrew Bible.

For help understanding this verse, see also Galatians 5:13 (the second part of the verse) and Philippians 2:3–4.

Verses 22–24: Paul doesn't see any difficulty between what he said in verse 21 and what he says in verse 22. How do you think he could have believed both even though to us verse 21 suggests an equality of all believers and verse 23 clearly says that women are not on an equal footing in the relationship with their husbands?

What kind of subjection ought a Christian have toward the Lord? Is it coerced or willing, for example? What does the comparison of the woman's subjection to her husband and her subjection to the Lord tell us about what Paul expects of the marital relationship? We can ask the same questions of verse 24, which repeats the point: how does the Church submit to Christ?

Verse 23 gives us the reason for wives' subjection with an analogy: as Christ is to the Church, so the husband is to the wife. What is Christ's relationship to the Church?

Why does Paul add "and he is the saviour of the body" to the analogy? In chapter 2 (Ephesians 2:1–10) we saw a description of what it means to say that Christ is our Savior. Does that help explain what Paul is saying with this part of the analogy?

Is there some sense in which the parallel of the husband to Christ suggests that the husband is to be the savior of the woman's body?

Are *head* and *saviour* intended to be parallel, so that this is a repetition of the previous phrase?

Perhaps the phrase isn't intended to be part of the analogy. If not, why is it included at all?

Verses 25–27: What does verse 25 tell us about how Paul understands what it means for the husband to be the head of the wife? Is there anything in the verse about command or authority?

Compare Ephesians 5:1–2. What does it mean to love another as Christ does? Those verses are the thesis statement of chapter 5 and chapter 6, verses 1–20. What do they tell us about how to interpret each part of these admonitions, including those admonitions to wives and husbands?

How does the description in verses 26–27 of what Christ has done for the Church provide an example for how husbands ought to love their wives? Can a husband cleanse his wife? If not, how is the example relevant? If he can, what does that mean?

Is the imagery of Ezekiel 16:1–14 relevant to understanding what the Lord has done for the Church? Is it relevant to this analogy between the relationship of the Church and Christ and the wife and husband? How far did Paul intend us to take the analogy?

Verses 28–29: What does Genesis 2:24 (cited in verse 31) have to do with what Paul says in verses 28–29?

Ephesians 6

Verses 1–4: Compare Paul's admonitions here (and in Ephesians 5) with Colossians 3:18–4:1. Does that shorter version of the same admonitions help give this longer version focus?

What does it mean to obey parents "in the Lord" (verse 1)? Does what Paul says to slaves (verses 5–6) help explain what Paul means here? It may be important to remember that children held a social status similar to slaves in Paul's day. If that is a legitimate way of understanding Paul's admonition for children to obey their parents "in the Lord," what does that tell us about children's place in Paul's understanding of the Christian community? Were they able to have a relationship of their own to the Lord?

Do verses 2–3 say anything that wasn't said in verse 1?

What does Paul mean that this, the fifth commandment, is the first commandment with promise (verse 2)? Presumably he has the Ten Commandments in mind, and the second commandment, not to make graven images (Exodus 2:4–6) seems to contain a promise: "Shewing mercy unto thousands of them that love me, and keep my commandments" (Exodus 20:6). Is the latter a promise associated with not making graven images? Might *first* mean something other than "chronologically first"?

What kinds of behaviors might Paul have in mind when he counsels fathers not to make their children angry? Is Colossians 3:21 relevant to answering that question? Does Ephesians 4:26, where Paul also speaks of anger, use the same Greek word, *help*?

What is the second half of verse 4 commending to fathers? Is "nurture and admonition" a hendiadys (the use of two words connected by *and* to say the same thing)? The word *nurture* translates a word that means "education" or "training." The word *admonition* translates a word that means "counsel about avoiding improper conduct."[4]

Verses 10–11: These verses introduce one of the most well-known passages in Paul's writings. As you read the

433

passage as a whole, try to find ways of reading it anew, as if for the first time.

Why does Paul begin this pericope by reminding his readers of the source of their strength (verse 10)?

Why is the "armour of God" needed (verse 11)? Against whom is this armor designed to protect us?

Sometimes we read this and try to create a one-for-one association with Roman armor. There may or may not be such a correlation, but Paul is more focused on Old Testament images of God as a warrior than he is on contemporary Roman soldiers, even if he uses the latter as his metaphor.[5] See, for example, Isaiah 11:4–5 and especially Isaiah 59:17. Compare those scriptures to Paul's in the following verses. Where are the similarities? The differences? Is Isaiah 52:7 relevant? Who is the audience in Isaiah, and what is the context? How is that the same as or different from the audience and context for Ephesians?

Verses 12–13: Here is another translation of verse 12: "Because our struggle is not against flesh and blood, but against the rulers, against those in control, against the world-rulers of this darkness, against the spiritual wickedness in heavenly places." Given that translation, how would you explain what Paul means by *principalities, powers, the rulers of the darkness of this world*, and *spiritual wickedness in high places*? Are there comparable threats today?

Many scholars believe that "thrones, principalities, powers," and so on were the names for categories of invisible beings who work evil in the world, in other words, names for different categories of evil spirits. Paul's use of the terms in

Colossians 1:16 suggests that he is using them in that way. How would that assumption change your understanding of this verse? If that assumption is correct, could you explain Paul's meaning in a way that makes it applicable today?

The audience of the letter to the Ephesians doesn't appear to have been under persecution when the letter was written. How, then, do you explain Paul's concern that they prepare for spiritual battle against evil?

The King James translators have captured a play on words in verse 13: "Ye may be able to withstand in the evil day, and having done all, to stand." How would you explain what Paul is saying through that play on words?

When is "the evil day" for which we must be prepared?

Verse 14: Why is the metaphor of standing fast so important to Paul's thought? (See, for example, Romans 1:28; 4:1; and 5:2; 1 Corinthians 10:12; 15:1; and 16:14; 2 Corinthians 1:24; Galatians 5:1; 1 Thessalonians 3:8; 2 Thessalonians 2:15.)

How do other scriptures use the phrase "gird your loins"? What does that act signify? How does girding one's loins with truth prepare a person to do that?

What does *righteousness* mean here? Do the earlier Isaiah references help answer that question?

Verse 15: What is "the preparation of the gospel of peace" or "the equipment of the good news of peace"? What peace is Paul talking about? How is the proclamation of that good news preparation or equipment for our battle with evil?

Verse 16: In the Old Testament, God is often said to be a shield, as in Psalm 18:2, 30, and 35. This letter says that faith in God, trust in him, is that shield. Is that a significant difference?

Verse 17: The King James Version of this verse says "take the helmet," but "receive the helmet" is a better translation. From whom do we receive that helmet?

Of course, that also means that Paul tells us to receive the sword of the Spirit. In what sense is the Spirit a sword?

What does it mean to say that the Spirit is the word of God?

Verse 18: Having told us what we need to defend ourselves, Paul now tells us what we need for our offense: constant prayer and supplication. Are those two different things?

Being alert is a better translation than *watching*. Luke 21:36 uses the same verb, and the admonition is the same: be alert and pray always. Why does prayer require alertness on our part? Alertness to what?

Why does prayer require perseverance?

Verses 19–20: What does Paul want his audience to pray for on his behalf?

Why does he ask to be able to speak boldly twice?

What is oxymoronic about Paul describing himself as an "ambassador in bonds," in other words, in chains?

Lesson 40
Philippians; Colossians; Philemon

Our lesson will concentrate on Philippians 2:5–15, Colossians 3:1–17, and Philemon. The last of these is particularly interesting because it is so short and, at least at first glance, appears to have no gospel content.

Philippians

Verse 5: The word *you* is plural rather than singular. Does this mean "each of you should have the mind that Christ had," or does it mean "as a church you should have the mind that he had"?

In either case, what does it mean to have the same mind or attitude that Christ had?

Verses 6–11: This is another instance where many scholars believe that Paul is quoting from an early Christian hymn. Here are the verses arranged as part of a hymn. Of course, the rhythm of the original doesn't come through in translation:

> 6 Who, being in the form of God,
> thought it not robbery
> to be equal with God:

> 7 But made himself of no reputation,
> and took upon him the form of a servant,
> and was made in the likeness of men:

8 And being found in fashion as a man,
he humbled himself,
and became obedient unto death,
[even the death of the cross.]

9 Wherefore God also hath highly exalted
him, and given him a name
which is above every name:

10 That at the name of Jesus every
knee should bow,
of things in heaven, and things in earth, and things
under the earth;

11 And that every tongue should confess
that Jesus Christ is Lord,
to the glory of God the Father.

To understand the hymn better, try writing it in your own words using modern English or look at a modern translation of these verses.

Verses 6–8: The Greek word used for *form* (verse 6) is only used to refer to outward appearance, not to refer to things such as a mind. In what sense was Christ in the form of God before his incarnation?

"Thought it not robbery" is an odd translation. Literally the verse says that, having the form of the Father, Jesus "thought it not something to be clutched at [or "clung to"]." In other words, he was equal to God, but he didn't cling to that equality. What does Paul have in mind here? What would it have meant for Christ to have clung to his equality with God?

The beginning of verse 7 is also translated oddly: "emptied himself" is the literal meaning. Of what did Christ empty himself by becoming a human being?

The phrases "took upon him the form of a servant [literally "a slave"]" and "was made in the likeness of men" are parallel. Hebrew poetry uses parallelism to show that two things are the same. (Though the hymn was written in Greek, the heavy Jewish influence in the early Church resulted in many Hebraisms, such as this, in early hymns.) What do these two phrases tell us about human beings, and why is that important for us to know?

For Christ, why was taking death on himself humbling himself (verse 8)? Assuming that Paul inserted the last line of verse 8 into the hymn as he used it for his letter, why do you think he added it? Why does the line begin with *even*?

Verse 5 told us that we should have the same mind or attitude as did Christ. Then verses 6–8 describe that mind. How do these verses about Christ tell us how we should live our lives?

Do we have the form of God? Are there any ways in which we cling to that form?

What would it mean for us to empty ourselves in imitation of the Savior?

Do we understand that to be a human being is to be a servant of God? If so, how do we show that understanding?

What does Jesus's death on the cross teach us about our own lives? Does it teach us anything about what genuine humility requires?

Verses 9–11: The word *wherefore* (verse 9) is the same as the modern word *therefore*. It tells us that what came before explains what follows. So what is the hymn saying about how verses 6–8 explain verses 9–11?

Verse 8 spoke of the Savior's humiliation. How is that related to his exaltation?

What does it mean to say that Jesus's name is above every other name?

What is the significance of bowing the knee (verse 10)? Is there anything in particular about bowing or knees that gives this act significance?

What does the phrase "of *things* in heaven, and *things* in earth, and *things* under the earth" refer to?

The word translated *profess* in verse 11 can also be translated *acknowledge* or *consent*. How might each of these translations help us understand what this hymn says?

What does the word *lord* mean? What does it mean to acknowledge that Jesus is Lord? How do we acknowledge that?

"To the glory of the Father" tells us why every knee will bow to Christ and every tongue will confess him. So what does it mean that they will do those things to the Father's glory?

Verses 12–13: We could paraphrase what Paul says in verse 12 this way: "So, since you have always obeyed, whether I was there or not, work out your salvation in fear and trembling." What do the parts of this sentence have to do with each other? In particular, why does he say "*since* you have obeyed, work our your salvation"?

Paul is going to use the contents of the hymn to preach obedience. What in the hymn gives him the material he needs to do that?

"Fear and trembling" is an Old Testament phrase. (For example, see Exodus 15:16, Isaiah 19:16, and Psalm 2:11.) Does this phrase mean that we should dread God's presence? That we should be afraid that he will treat us unjustly, change his plan, or go back on his promises? As we work out our salvation, what should we fear?

The Greek word translated *work out* could also be translated *accomplish* or *move in the direction of*. Do those alternative translations give you any ideas about what Paul might mean?

What does it mean to say that God is at work in us (verse 13)?

Do you think that in the phrase "it is God which worketh in you" the word *you* means "you individuals" or "you, the Church"?

Note that the Greek word translated *good pleasure* means "a state of being kindly disposed" or "contentment." Does that shed any light on the meaning of verse 13?

Verses 14–15: What does verse 14 mean about how we should act? Verse 15 tells us *why* we should act that way. How does doing what we do without grumbling make us blameless and harmless (*sincere* may be a better translation)?

Paul makes "sons of God" parallel to "blameless and harmless." Why?

Does the beginning of verse 15 have anything to do with having the same attitude or mind in us that Christ had?

441

Without blemish is a better translation than *without rebuke*. Paul seems to be explicitly comparing us to Christ. What permits that comparison? What does it mean for us to be lights or lamps in the world?

Colossians 3

Verses 1–4: Verse 1 continues the line of thinking that Paul began in Colossians 2:20: "Since you have died with Christ as to the spirits that control the world, why are you subject to their rules as if you lived in the world?"

What does it mean to "be risen with Christ"? Is that only a metaphor, or is there also something literal about its meaning? If there is, what is it?

"Seek upward" might be a good translation to replace "seek the things which are above" (verse 1). What contrast with Colossians 2:20 is intended here?

Is it significant that Paul doesn't contrast the rules of the world with the rules of heaven, but the rules of the world with Christ, who sits on the right hand of God?

In verse 2 *mind* or *attention* or, perhaps best, *intentions* is a better translation that *affections*. If our intentions or attention is on "the above," what will determine our interests? How is what Paul says here related to what he said in Philippians 2:5? Can you say anything about what that might mean in practical terms?

Verse 3 tells Paul's readers that they are dead. What does he mean?

What does it mean to say that the lives of the Saints are "hid with Christ in God"? From whom are their lives hidden? How are they hidden?

When will Christ be revealed (verse 4)? Why won't our lives be revealed until then?

Verses 5–11: Another translation of the first part of verse 5: "So put to death that in you which is of the earth." Why are the sins that follow that admonition "of the earth"? Is everything that is "of the earth" sinful? What about eating a ripe peach, for example? If Paul is not saying that everything of the earth is sinful, how should we understand his use of that phrase?

Why are these sins idolatry (verse 5)? Is all sin idolatry? Is there something about these sins in particular that makes the label of idolatry appropriate? Explain.

What reason do verses 5 and 10 give for why we should not sin?

Look at Paul's command in Romans 13:14 and compare Galatians 3:27 with verse 10. What do those verses suggest Paul means by "the new man"?

How might we go about putting on Christ, as if we were putting on clothing? In verse 8 he has spoken of putting off the old man with the same metaphor? What is the significance of that metaphor? When does a Christian put on Christ? What language do we use that means the same?

The Greek of verse 10 says only "put on the new." If you were making the translation of the Greek, what other word might you insert after *new* to make sense of the clause? Obviously *person* would work, but what about *life*? Does that capture Paul's meaning, or does it change it? Are there other words that we could insert?

To what does *where* refer in verse 11? What location has Paul mentioned recently? If he hasn't mentioned one, why does he use a relative pronoun denoting space?

Does what Paul says in verse 11 mean that all cultural differences between Greeks, Jews, Scythians, and others have disappeared? If not, in what sense is there no difference between them? What does Paul's teaching suggest about contemporary life in the Church?

Why is there no distinction between Greek and Jew and so on (verse 11)? What has Paul taught that explains the impossibility of making such distinctions?

Bond means "slave" (verse 11). In Paul's world, a slave was not a person but a piece of property. Owners were expected to treat them humanely—to take good care of their property—but there was no penalty for not doing so. What does it mean for Paul to include this difference, "bond nor free," among the differences that he says do not exist for the Christian? Does it suggest anything for our own times, or is it merely an artifact from the ancient world?

Verses 12–15: Why are Christians described as "the elect of God"? What does it mean to be elect or chosen?

What does it mean to forebear one another? When do we find ourselves doing that? When do we fail to live up to this requirement? Can you think of times when you've not forborne someone whom you ought to have? What made that difficult, and why was it necessary?

Does verse 14 add an additional virtue, charity, or does it sum up the virtues required in verses 12–13? If it sums them up, can we use verses 12–13 as a kind of provisional definition of charity?

The word translated *bond* in verse 14 means "fastener" or "clasp" and is used to denote a bond that creates unity. What is the bond of perfection or, in other words, completeness?

Verses 15–17: How does the peace of God differ from other kinds of peace (verse 15)? What does it mean to have peace rule in one's heart? If peace doesn't rule, what rules in its place? Compare 2 Thessalonians 3:16 and Ephesians 2:14.

What does it mean to say that we are "called in one body" to the peace of God?

For what is it that Paul wants us to be thankful? Is this a general admonition, "Be thankful," or is he saying, "Be thankful that you are called to the peace of God"?

If we are grateful for having been given the gospel and being members of Christ's Church, how do we express that gratitude?

In verse 16, does "word of Christ" mean "the word which proclaims Christ" or "the word that Christ speaks"?

What does Paul mean by *wisdom*? Is Colossians 1:28 relevant to answering that question?

How does the word of Christ dwell in us? What does that metaphor, of a word dwelling in persons, mean? Can you think of synonyms for the word *dwell* that might help you think about Paul's meaning here?

Here is an alternative translation of verse 16: "Let the word of Christ dwell richly in you, teaching and admonishing one another with all wisdom by means of psalms, hymns, and spiritual songs, singing with thankfulness to God in your hearts." How does that mean differently than does the King James Version?

The last phrase of verse 16 can be translated in several ways. One is in the alternative translation above. But the King James Version is quite reasonable in contemporary English—"singing with grace in your hearts to the Lord." What does that mean?

Who is to do the teaching in the congregation? What makes that teaching possible?

How do we teach wisdom with music? When do we do so? Is this something we might be lax in doing?

Can you say, in practical terms, what it means to "do all in the name of the Lord Jesus" (verse 17)?

Philemon

This letter is 335 words in Greek. It was probably written early in Paul's imprisonment in Rome. Since it is so infrequently read or discussed, I will provide some commentary on it in addition to questions.

Why is this book part of the scriptural canon? A man named Onesimus was later made bishop of Ephesus. Might that be relevant? If this is the Onesimus of the book of Philemon, what does it tell us about Onesimus's life?

Why does Paul include Timothy's name on the letter?

What does it suggest that Paul calls Philemon a "fellow labourer" (verse 1)? A modern translation might be *coworker*.

Apphia is a woman's name. Most assume she is Philemon's wife. We don't know who Archippus was, but he might have been Philemon's son. Otherwise it would be odd to include him in a personal letter like this. What does Paul's description of Archippus as his "fellowsoldier" (verse 2) suggest?

What do verses 4–7 tell us about Philemon? The Greek word *pistis,* translated *faith* in verse 5, could also be translated *faithfulness* or *reliability*.

Many have interpreted verse 5 and the first part of verse 6 as a chiasmus. Can you see the chiastic structure that some impute to this verse? Does that structure reveal anything about how we should read the verse, or is it simply how the clauses are organized?

Verse 6 is notoriously difficult to translate since it is equally difficult to understand its meaning in Greek. How might you "translate" or paraphrase the verse into ordinary contemporary English?

Everything up through verse 7 has been introductory. The body of the letter begins in verse 8. Why do you think Paul has such long introductions to many of his letters, even a short one like this?

What does it mean to say that Paul has enough confidence or boldness to order Philemon to do what he wants (verse

8)? Does Paul remind Philemon of his confidence, boldness, and authority in order to intimidate him to do what Paul wants him to? Does verse 14 help answer this question? What does it mean to say that Paul appeals to Philemon "for love's sake" (verse 9)? Paul has already mentioned love twice. Is that relevant to understanding how and why he refers to it here?

In verse 9 the King James Version translates the word *presbytēs* as *the aged*, but the word can also mean "the ambassador" (just as *elder* can mean both "an old person" and "one holding a particular priesthood office"). Which translation do you think makes the most sense in context?

Onesimus has been converted by Paul (verse 10). Why does Paul call Onesimus his child?

In verse 11 the Greek words for *useful* (*profitable* in the King James Version) and for *useless* (*unprofitable* in the King James Version) are a pun. Paul may also be playing on Onesimus's name since most translators understand it to be another word for *useful*. It was a common name for slaves. Is there a point to that play on words?

Paul assumes that Philemon himself would have been willing to do the work for Paul that Onesimus is doing (verse 13). What does that tell us about the kind of work Onesimus is probably performing? What does it say about the kind of relationship that Paul and Philemon have?

Onesimus is a runaway slave; Philemon is his master, a Christian. Onesimus offended Philemon in some way and then ran away. Based on verse 18, we usually assume that Onesimus stole Philemon's money. But what he owes Philemon (which Paul says he will repay) may be merely the work he should have done. We cannot be sure what the original offense was.

Paul wanted to keep Onesimus as *his* slave (verse 13), but it would have been illegal for him to keep him—as well as a breach of his friendship with Philemon. The law required someone who had given a runaway slave refuge either to return the slave to his or her master or to sell the slave in the market and give the master the money earned from that sale. However, Deuteronomic law, which Paul knew well, forbade returning a runaway slave (Deuteronomy 23:15–16). Is that contradiction a problem for Paul? Why or why not?

Paul has great affection for Onesimus: "my very heart" or, in the very literal King James Version, "mine own bowels" (verse 12), and Onesimus has been helping him (verse 11). What reason does Paul give for returning Onesimus (verse 14)? The Greek word that the King James Version translates *benefit* (*agathos*) is probably better translated *good* or *favor*: "that the favor you give would not, in effect, be by compulsion, but by your willingness." Does that change the meaning of the verse?

How is the explanation of verses 15–16 related to what Paul says in verse 14?

Paul says he has a request of Philemon in verse 10. He makes his request—receive the slave as he would receive Paul, that is, as a beloved brother—considerably later than he first mentions it (verse 17). Why does he wait?

Paul does not command Philemon (verse 14). He doesn't ask that Onesimus be freed, but that he be treated as a brother, both as a brother in the flesh and as one in the Lord (verse 16). What would it mean for a person to remain a slave but to be treated as a brother or sister?

Why doesn't Paul ask Philemon to free Onesimus?

Why does Paul make the offer to pay Philemon if Onesimus owes him money (verses 18–19)?

Verse 20 puns on Onesimus's name: the Greek word translated *benefit* is *oninēmi*, the root of Onesimus's name. Paul isn't making a joke, so why do you think he makes that play on words?

Paul says he knows that Philemon will obey the will of God and will do even more than Paul has suggested (verse 21). Why does Paul speak of obedience here when he has been speaking of willingness in response to love before? Is this "even more" the thing that Paul wished for in the first place, that Onesimus might remain with him as his servant? Or is it that Philemon will free Onesimus on his return?

Has Paul asserted his apostolic authority over Philemon indirectly even if not directly?

Do you think Philemon acceded to Paul's request?

What does this letter teach us about relationships between Christians who have civil or social authority over one another, for example, teachers and students or bosses and employees?

Lesson 41
1 Timothy 4; 2 Timothy 1–4; Titus

These study questions will focus on 1 Timothy 4 and selections from 2 Timothy and Titus. Before looking at 1 Timothy 4, read the last two verses of 1 Timothy 3 to give the next chapter more context.

1 Timothy 3:15–16

When he speaks of "the house of God" (verse 15), does Paul mean the Church as a whole or individual congregations?

How is the Church "the pillar and ground of truth"? What metaphor is Paul using? How does that metaphor help us understand what the Church does?

What does Paul mean when he says "without controversy" (verse 16)?

To what is Paul referring with the word *mystery* (verse 16)? Why is that the right word? (Verse 16 seems to be another quotation from a hymn.)

What is Paul talking about when he says that Christ was seen by angels?

1 Timothy 4

Verses 1–5: Paul has just finished speaking in chapter 3 of the qualifications of bishops and deacons. How is that topic related to the one that he takes up now, apostasy?

451

When did Paul and Timothy think the "latter times" would be (verse 1)?

What does it mean to give heed to seducing spirits or doctrines of devils? Can you think of specific examples of doing so? Why is it tempting to do so? Do we ever do so?

The practice of the time was to brand criminals and fugitive slaves. How is that practice related to what Paul says in verse 2?

In verse 3 the Greek word translated *meat* means "food." *Meat* was a general term for food in King James English. How do you square Paul's teaching here with the Word of Wisdom?

Compare these verses to passages such as Matthew 24:10–12, Acts 20:29–30, 2 Thessalonians 2:3–12, 1 John 2:18 and 4:1–3, and 2 John 7. Why is apostasy an important New Testament theme? Why does that theme matter to us today?

Verses 6–7: What is Paul telling his readers to remember (verse 6), everything he has said in this chapter or just what he has said in the verses about food?

However you answer the previous question, how does remembering "these things" make a person "a good minister of Jesus Christ" (verse 6)?

Is Paul making a distinction when he says "the words of faith and of good doctrine" (verse 6)? Are those two different things, or is this a case of hendiadys?

To what might Paul be referring when he speaks of myths and "old wives' fables"? Is the second of these an instance of the sexism of first-century Palestine?

Verses 8–11: Another translation of the first part of verse 8 is "Bodily exercise is somewhat valuable, but godliness is of value in all things." How does this verse fit with Paul's point in these four verses?

Is verse 9 a reflection on verse 8 or an introduction to verse 10? Are verses 9 and 11 intended to be parallel or almost parallel in meaning?

Verses 12–16: Some have estimated Timothy to have been about thirty-five at the time of this letter and the personal advice of these verses.[1] Compare 1 Corinthians 16:10–11. What kind of person was Timothy? His weaknesses? His strengths?

In verse 12 the Greek word translated *conversation* means "behavior," which was also the meaning of *conversation* in King James English. We might say "in speech and behavior" rather than "in word, in conversation." How does understanding that translation change the meaning of the verse?

Paul speaks often of love and faith, but what does he mean by *purity* (verse 12)? Is he speaking here of sexual purity or of something else?

In verse 13, is Paul reminding Timothy to read his scriptures regularly, or is he admonishing him to take part in the Church's worship, which had adopted the synagogue's practice of reading and commenting on scripture as the focus of worship? The word *doctrine* (verse 13) translates a Greek word, *didaskalia*, which means "teaching." So we could translate the verse as Paul exhorting Timothy "to reading, to exhortation, to teaching." Does that translation suggest an answer to the question about reading? Which kind of reading would be most parallel to exhortation and teaching? Does the fact that almost no one in this time period knew how to read silently help you understand what Paul means here?

What gift do you think Timothy is not to neglect (verse 14)? (The word *presbytery* means "council of elders.") Is it his calling as bishop or some other calling?

Rather than "meditate upon these things" (verse 15) the clause might also be translated "work on these things" or "pay attention to these things." Which translation do you think best fits the context?

What do you think Paul means by *profiting* (verse 15)? Is it progress? Usefulness? Something else? What is it that Paul wants the congregation to see in Timothy? Why?

Paul says "pay attention to yourself and to your teaching" (verse 16). How is that a good summary of what he has said to Timothy?

2 Timothy 2

Verses 23–26: What does Paul mean by "unlearned questions" (verse 22)? Can you give examples of "foolish and unlearned questions" that we take up today?

What is wrong with dealing with questions that start quarrels? Notice that the word *strifes* in verse 23 and the word *strive* in verse 24 are variations of the same root, both in English and in Paul's Greek.

What does it mean to say that the Lord's servant must be gentle to everyone (verse 24)? How do we preach gently? How can we rebuke gently or exhort gently?

Verse 25 will make more sense if you understand *instructing* to mean "correction" and you put "to him" after the phrase "oppose themselves."

What does it mean to say that repentance is *to* or toward a knowledge of truth?

What does the last part of verse 25 together with verse 26 say is the point of preaching and exhortation?

Paul seems to be using *repentance* and "recover themselves" as parallel terms (verses 25–26). In what way is repentance a recovery of self?

Why does Satan take us captive? How does he do so?

How does the gentleness that Paul recommends to Timothy differ from Satan's method? How do the results of the two methods differ?

2 Timothy 3

Verses 1–5: Why will the last days, as Timothy understands them, be perilous, in other words, difficult or fierce (verse 1)?

Here is another translation (that of the New International Version) of the list in verses 2–5, compared to the King James Version:

lovers of their own selves	=	lovers of self
covetous	=	lovers of money
boasters	=	boastful
proud	=	proud
blasphemers	=	abusive
disobedient to parents	=	disobedient to their parents

unthankful	=	ungrateful
unholy	=	unholy
without natural affection	=	without love
trucebreakers	=	unforgiving
false accusers	=	slanderous
incontinent	=	without self-control
fierce	=	brutal
despisers of those that are good	=	not lovers of the good
traitors	=	treacherous
heady	=	rash
highminded	=	conceited
lovers of pleasure more than lovers of God	=	lovers of pleasure rather than lovers of God

Are there any differences in translation that change the meaning for you? If so, what do you make of those differences? Does this list help you understand the King James Version? Are there any things in this translation with which you disagree?

Look at each item in the list and ask yourself why Paul condemns it. Do we condemn all of these things today? If we do not condemn some, why not? Should we condemn them?

Verses 15–17: With regard to what do the scriptures make us wise (verse 15)? Is imparting that wisdom to us the purpose of scripture? Does "wise unto salvation" mean "wise as to what salvation requires," or does it mean "wise in a way that brings one salvation"?

What is the significance of Joseph Smith's change in verse 16: "All scripture given by inspiration of God, is profitable"? What burden does that place on those reading scripture?

How is scripture good for doctrine (teaching)? For reproof? For correction? For instruction (training) in righteousness?

In the LDS edition of the Bible, look at the footnote for *perfect* in verse 17. What does that tell us about how to understand the verse? In what sense does scripture make us perfect?

If you change *furnished* to *equipped* and *unto* to *for*, the verse will probably be easier to understand. How does scripture equip us for all good works?

2 Timothy 4

Verses 1–2: Why does Paul begin this part of his instruction to Timothy with a solemn charge?

Why does he use this particular description of Christ, rendered as "the judge of the quick and the dead and the Second Coming" in another translation?

If you read verse 2 as the King James Version has it—"be instant [prepared] in season, [and] out of season"—what does this verse say? Joseph Smith changed the phrase this way: "be instant in season, those who are out of season." What does that mean? How does his inspired revision change the meaning of the verse?

What does *reprove* mean (verse 2)? What does *rebuke* mean? Are they different? What does *exhort* mean?

Verses 3–4: What does it mean to say some "will not endure sound doctrine" (verse 3)? Remember that the word *doctrine* translates a word that could also be translated *teaching.*

The word *sound* translates a Greek word that means "healthy." How is health an apt metaphor for doctrine? What is healthy teaching?

What does "heap to themselves teachers" mean (verse 3)?

What does it mean to say that they heap these teachers to themselves "after their own lusts"?

Whose ears itch (verse 3)? What does the metaphor of itching ears mean? What does Paul say that they are looking for to scratch their itch? How do they think that will remedy their problem?

Does this set of verses describe any in our own day? Does it ever describe us? If so, how so?

What should our response be to those verses in the passages from 1 and 2 Timothy that describe the apostasy that Paul fears?

Titus 2

Verses 1–15: In verse 1 Paul addresses Titus directly, giving him advice about how to conduct his life, but the King James Version could be misleading. "Things which become sound doctrine" means "things which are becoming or appropriate to sound doctrine."

Paul follows in verses 2–6 with a list of those who need to be taught: old men and women and young men. Why does he make young men a separate category of those who need attention but only include young women as those to be taught by the older women?

What does verse 9 mean by "not answering again"?

Is the advice in verses 9–10 about how slaves should relate to their masters of any use to us today? How do employees differ from slaves? Does that difference change how we might or might not use these verses when thinking about the employer-employee relationship?

Explain verse 11. What grace—in other words, gift—has God given? How has that gift "appeared to all men"? (As usual, the King James Version's *men* would be translated *people* in contemporary English. That is the meaning of the Greek word.)

Why should we "live soberly, righteously, and godly" in the world (verse 12)? Why should Christians be anxious for the second coming (verse 13)?

The word *peculiar* is the translation of a Greek word that means "chosen" or "special." In what sense are the people of God chosen? Chosen for what? When does that choosing occur? Is being chosen something available to all or only to some?

Titus 3

Verses 7–9: What does "justified by his grace" mean (verse 7)?

What do those with a hope for eternal life inherit (verse 7)?

The letters to Timothy use some variation of the formula "This is a faithful saying" in several places (1 Timothy 1:15; 3:1; 4:9; and 2 Timothy 2:11), each time to talk about salvation. Why do you think Paul describes his description of the good news of Jesus Christ as a "faithful [trustworthy] saying"?

In verse 8 the King James translators note that they have added some words to make sense of the text as they understand it by italicizing several words: "*This is* a faithful saying." Literally the Greek says, "The word is trustworthy [or "faithful"]." The King James translators are right to understand verse 8 to refer back to verses 3–7. But their translation isn't as strong as the Greek.

What does Paul mean when he says "these things I suffer that thou affirm constantly"? Can you paraphrase that in contemporary English?

In verse 8 "might be careful" means "might give sustained thought to." *Maintain* could be translated "to lead in doing." Do those change the meaning of the verse? Paul uses the same phrase, word for word, in Titus 3:19. For Paul, how are good works related to the good news of salvation?

Verse 9 warns against "foolish questions," foolish controversies or debates if translated more literally. What kinds of questions or controversies are foolish? How do we recognize them? How do we avoid them?

What is a foolish genealogy?

What does Paul have in mind when he tells Titus to avoid contentions and quarrels about the law (verse 9)? Why are they useless, *unprofitable*? Is "unprofitable and vain" a hendiadys, or is Paul speaking of two different problems with arguments about the law?

Which law do you think Paul has in mind, the law in general, the Roman civil and penal codes, or the Mosaic law? Explain.

Lesson 42

James 1:1–7; 2:14–26; 3:2–18; 4:8, 17; 5:10–11

We do not know who the author of this epistle was (there are several persons named James in the New Testament), but many have believed it was James, the brother of Christ and the presiding elder in Jerusalem after Christ's death. (See, for example, Acts 15:13, where that James presides over the Jerusalem conference called to deal with the Gentiles joining the early Church.)

What do we know about Jesus's family's relation to him prior to the crucifixion? (See, for example, John 7:1–5.)

When do you think James became a follower of Christ? Is 1 Corinthians 15:7 relevant? Does that verse suggest any reason that James might be more sympathetic to Paul than we sometimes assume?

James 1

Verses 2–4: The word translated *temptations* also has the meaning "trials." (The Greek word can mean either, but *trials* seems to fit the context better here.) How can we count our trials as "complete joy"?

In verse 3 the word translated *patience* could also be translated *endurance*. How does the testing of our faith bring about endurance?

Verse 4 tells us that we should "let endurance [patience] take its complete [perfect] effect [work]." What does that mean? James explains that endurance will make us perfect, and he gives two synonyms for *perfect*: *entire* (or *whole*) and *lacking nothing*. This is the usual meaning of the word in the New Testament—not "without flaw" or "able to do anything" (two common modern interpretations of perfection). For example, James uses the same word here for perfection that is used in Matthew 5.48, and neither of them means "perfect," in other words, "flawless." Does this understanding of perfection make it easier to consider the possibility that we can be perfect in this life, even if we are not flawless?

Verses 5–7: What is the connection of verse 5 to those the precede it?

Notice the footnote that gives another translation for *upbraideth*. It can also be translated *ungrudgingly*. The Father gives to us generously ("liberally") and ungrudgingly ("upbraideth not"). Is James creating an implicit contrast between the Father's answers to prayers and our responses to those who are in need?

In verse 6 notice the footnote in the LDS edition, which tells us that *wavering* means "doubting." Why can't the doubter expect to receive anything from the Lord (verse 7)?

Verse 8: Is this verse the conclusion of the topic discussed in verses 5–7 or the beginning of a new topic? In either case, can you explain how it fits with the verses around it?

Why does James describe doubting as being "double minded"? Can you think of examples of what it means to be double minded? What makes the double-minded person unstable? Is Christ saying much the same as this verse when he says that we cannot serve two masters (Matthew 6:24; Luke 16:13; and 3 Nephi 13:24)?

Verses 12–15: As in verse 2, *temptation* in verse 12 means "trial" or "test" more than it does "temptation" as we usually understand it.

Those who become approved and who love the Lord will receive a crown of glory (verse 12). What does it mean to become approved? How do we do that? What is a crown of glory? Does this refer, for example, to a specific level in the kingdoms of the hereafter?

In verse 13, why does James warn us against saying that the Father is testing us? That seems to be a common way of speaking—what's wrong with it? Is he warning against a particular kind of testing?

Is it helpful to remember that there is only one word in Greek for both "test" and "tempt"? Which meaning do you think James intends in verse 13?

How does he explain our trials of faith in verse 14? If this is an accurate way of describing our trials—if they are the result of our own lusts—what is Satan's role in tempting or trying us?

Note that "drawn away" (verse 14) translates a verb used to describe how a hunter lures wild game out into the open, and that *enticed* translates a verb used to describe baiting fish or bird traps. Therefore, we might loosely translate this as "Every person is tempted when he is lured out by means of his own lusts and a trap for him is baited with them."

The word translated *lust* (verse 14) includes what we would describe as lust as well as any other inordinate desire, so this is not just a description of how we are tempted and tried regarding sexual things (though those thing are certainly included). See Romans 7:19–23 for a similar but more complicated description of this same point: we are tried by our own inordinate desires.

In verse 15 James uses the metaphor of procreation: we have lusts that conceive and give birth to sins; in turn, they conceive and give birth to death. (Here Paul's discussion in Romans 5:14–21 and 6:3–11 is relevant.) Why do you think he uses that metaphor?

Verses 21–24: *Naughtiness* (verse 21) is too weak a translation for modern English readers; *evil* would be better.

See the note on *engrafted* in the LDS edition (verse 21).

James says that because God gives us every good thing (verse 17), we should put aside all sin and receive the gospel in humility (verse 21). Why is humility necessary to receiving the gospel?

How does James's understanding of our reasons for repentance and obedience compare to Paul's?

Compare what James says here about receiving the engrafted word to what Alma says in Alma 32. How are they similar? Are there any significant differences? If there are, what do those differences show us?

In what kinds of ways do we deceive ourselves about our works (verse 22)? Why is this kind of self-deception like looking in a mirror (verses 23–24)? What is the point of James's metaphor in verses 23–24?

Verse 25: In verses 23 and 24, James described looking at oneself in a mirror. Notice the contrast he creates here: rather than to ourselves in a mirror, we should look to the "perfect law of liberty." What is the perfect law of liberty? Why is it a law of liberty? Is 2 Nephi 2:27 relevant?

How does the phrase "perfect law of liberty" contrast with the Pharisaic understanding of the Law?

In our own lives, do we think of the law as a law of liberty, or do we think of it as something more like the Pharisaic law, rules that we must obey in order to get a reward, rules that keep us from doing what we would like to do?

Verses 26–27: We commonly use the second of these verses as a proof text (to support something we are teaching, such as in a sacrament talk), but notice that it is intended as a contrast with verse 26: verse 26 describes those who think they are religious, while verse 27 describes those who really are. What does the contrast of these two verses do for the meaning of verse 27?

Why would having an unbridled tongue be a particularly apt description of the person who believes himself to be religious but isn't? What does his tongue say that it ought not to say?

Why is care for orphans and widows a particularly apt description of the truly religious? How is it related to the teachings of the Old Testament? For example, see Deuteronomy 10:17–18, Isaiah 1:17, and Zechariah 7:10, among others.

What does it mean to be "unspotted from the world"? Compare Joseph Smith's inspired revision.

We might think of verse 27 as the thesis statement of James's letter. As you read the letter, ask how each part is related to that thesis. How, for example, is James 1:5 relevant to the fact that genuine faith issues in works? How are verses 2 and 3, which remind us that we must be patient in trials and persecution, relevant to that fact?

James 2

Verses 1–4: In James's day a gold ring was not only a sign of wealth but also a sign of authority. How does the kind of discrimination that he describes in these verses mean that we are "judges of evil thoughts"?

Verses 5–7: How do these verses apply to us? Who are the poor that we despise today?

James says that the Saints give precedence and honor to the rich even though the rich oppress them. Do we ever do anything that is comparable?

Verses 8–9: What two ways of living is James contrasting here?

Verse 10: What does this mean? Why isn't this a message of despair—what can give us hope in the face of such a message?

Verses 14–20: Is what James says here in conflict with what Paul taught, namely, that we are saved by faith rather than works? (Compare Romans 3:28 and 4:4–5.) If not, why not? How can these two things be reconciled?

What does verse 19 suggest about doctrinal disputes between us or between us and nonmembers? Why does James include what he says in verse 19 as part of talking about why works are necessary?

James 3

Verses 1–2: Against what is James warning? *Masters* translates a Greek word that means "teachers." Does James think of himself as a teacher? If so, how do these warnings apply to him?

Why shouldn't we all be teachers? Doesn't Doctrine and Covenants 88:118 admonish us to teach one another? How do you reconcile those two passages of scripture?

Why might teachers receive harsher condemnation than others (verse 1)?

How is the first sentence of verse 2 related to verse 1?

How is it that the ability to be perfect in speech would make a person perfect overall (verse 2)?

The second half of verse 2 is a transition to verses 3–12. What has the warning to teachers to do with this discussion of the dangers of speech?

Verses 3–12: James's example of the horse and the ship show how a small cause can have a great effect. Isn't that a pessimistic thought in general: I can do something small that causes a huge disaster? Each of us has a tongue; we speak in some way or another. Why, then, isn't verse 8 a particularly pessimistic verse?

Verses 13–14: How does this verse deal with the problem raised in verses 3–12?

In King James English the word *conversation* meant "behavior." Insert the latter into the verse and reread it. What is James's answer to the fact that our tongues speak both evil and good?

What does it mean to "lie . . . against the truth"? Does that mean anything different from "lie" alone?

Why would people "lie . . . against the truth" (verse 14) if they had bitter jealous and selfish ambition in their hearts ("bitter envying and strife" in the King James Version)?

The Greek text at the end of verse 14 might be translated "boast and lie against the truth"; the coordination of boasting and lying isn't as obvious in the King James Version. What would it mean to boast against the truth?

Verses 15–16: What wisdom is James referring to in verse 15? Has he mentioned in the earlier verses some kind of wisdom that we should avoid?

Strife is a good translation in verse 16, but another translation is *selfishness* or *selfish ambition*. Do those other translations change the meaning of the verse?

Verses 17–18: With what does the "wisdom that is from above" contrast in verse 17?

Another translation of the word translated *pure* is *holy*. How might that change your understanding of versed 17?

What does it mean for wisdom to be peaceable? Gentle? What does it mean for wisdom to be "easy to be entreated," in other words, obedient? Aren't these and the other adjectives in verse 17 strange ways to describe something like wisdom? We usually use them to describe a person. What do they mean when they describe wisdom?

Can you explain what verse 18 means?

James 4

Verses 1–5: According to James, what explains the so-called wars that occur among the members of the Church (verse 1)? Among the members of a family?

If lust—in other words, our desire for pleasure (verse 1)—causes strife among us, what will be its cure?

How does James say we try to get what we want (verse 2)? ("You kill, and desire to have" could also be translated "you kill and are fanatics.") Does he literally mean that those he is speaking to commit murder? If not, how is he using that image?

Erasmus (1466–1536, an early translator of the Bible) suggested that the Greek word for "you murder" in verse 2 (*phoneuete*) was a copying error and that the correct word was one for "you are jealous" (*pthoneite*). If Erasmus is right, how does that change the meaning of verse 2?

What does he mean when he says "ye have not, because ye ask not" (verse 2)?

What way does he say we should go about getting those things? Suppose we say, "I've tried that way of getting what I want, and it didn't work." What is James's reply (verse 3)?

How does he explain the failure of our prayers (verse 2)?

Why does he use adultery as a symbol for all evil desire (verse 4)? (The Old Testament equation of adultery with idolatry may be to the point here.)

What is friendship with the world?

It isn't clear what scripture James is quoting in verse 5; perhaps it is one we no longer have.

How are verses 1–5 related to James 1:27?

Verses 6–8: In verse 6 James quotes from the Greek version of Proverbs 3:34. What does it mean to say that the Father gives grace to the humble?

Is there a difference between submitting to God and resisting the devil, or are these two ways of saying the same thing (verse 7)? How do we submit to the Father?

How do we draw nigh to God (verse 8)?

What does it mean to cleanse our hands? How do we do it?

What does it mean to purify our hearts? How do we do that? Is there a difference between cleansing our hands and purifying our hearts? Notice that according to James, verse 8 gives us a solution to the problem of doubting (compare 1:6–8): cleanliness of hand and purity of heart. How do they overcome our doubts?

Verses 9–10: Why is James advising them to mourn (verse 9)? It doesn't make any sense for this to be a general admonition, since the gospel brings peace and happiness. What are the particular circumstances in which he might admonish them to mourn?

What does it mean to be humble in the sight of the Lord (verse 10)? What is genuine humility? What does it mean to be lifted up?

Verses 11–12: Is there a connection between the admonitions in verses 7–10 and verse 11, or is verse 11 simply one more admonition in a list?

How could it be that if we speak evil of another member of the Church, if we slander that person, then we are not only judging (literally condemning) that member, but we are also speaking evil of and judging (condemning) the law (verse 11)? How does making ourselves a judge over our brothers and sisters make us also a judge over the law itself?

According to verse 12, how is my judgment of another person an act of impiety?

Lesson 43

1–2 Peter; Jude

Before you read the letters from Peter, take a few minutes to recall who he was: What was his position in the Church? What particular experiences did he have with the Savior? What might he have learned from those experiences? How does that background inform these letters?

Few scholars believe that 1 and 2 Peter were written by Peter himself. The main reason is that the language of the letters is so thoroughly imbued with Hellenistic (Greek) terms and rhetoric, something improbable from someone who had been a Hebrew fisherman. But many scholars think that the author of the two letters could have been a secretary or companion to Peter, someone who knew Peter's teachings well enough to teach them to others but had a Greek education. In that case, the letters (especially 1 Peter) are more like contemporary collections of prophetic sermons put together by those who knew Peter and had access to the documents. In any case, though the letters might not have actually been written by the Apostle Peter, they appear to represent his teachings.

If Jude (the same name as Judas) is the brother of James, presumably the author of the book of James, and James is, as tradition says, the brother of the Lord, then Jude is also the brother of the Lord. Why doesn't he say so when he introduces himself?

These study questions will focus on 2 Peter 1:2–11 because those verses are so important to the teachings of the restoration.

2 Peter 1

Verse 2: Peter asks a blessing on those to whom he is writing, namely, that through their knowledge of the Savior they might have grace and peace multiplied. What does that mean? What is grace? What does it mean to multiply grace? To multiply peace? What kind of peace might Peter mean?

Verse 3: Verse 2 asked that grace and peace be multiplied; this verse continues (in an alternative translation): "just as his divine power has granted us all things for life and godliness, through a knowledge of the one who has called us to glory and to excellence."

The word translated *godliness* refers to the practical aspects of religion—doing good works—more than it does to specifically devotional acts or acts of worship. How does a knowledge of Christ provide us with all things for life and godliness? How does he provide us with that knowledge through his divine power?

Excellence is another accurate translation of the word translated *virtue* by the King James translators. It includes not only chastity, but all other qualities of moral excellence as well. What does it mean to be called to excellence or virtue? What does it mean to say that Christ has called us to glory?

Verse 4: The word *whereby* refers back to something that came before. What? In other words, this verse says that priceless and magnificent promises have come to us by means of something mentioned in the previous verse. What is that?

Through these promises we can become "partakers of the divine nature." What does that mean? In other words, what does the term *divine nature* refer to, and what does it mean to partake of (to take part or share in) it?

What does this verse say is the cause of corruption in this world? As used here, *lust* does not refer only to corrupt sexual desires; it refers to misdirected desire in general. Is this the same teaching that we saw in James 1 and 4?

Why does Peter speak of escaping the corruption of the world rather than just leaving it behind? What does the metaphor of escape teach? What would the metaphor of leaving something behind suggest?

Verse 5: Instead of "and beside," the beginning of this verse should be translated "for this purpose." What is going to be brought about by the things which follow?

"Add to" is a reasonable translation, but it doesn't catch the connotations of the Greek word it translates. That word carries with it the notion of providing for something lavishly. The noun form of the verb "was used of prominent and wealthy citizens who underwrote the expenses for the choirs needed in the performance of Greek plays."[1] Supplying isn't enough; abundance is required.

What is the first thing one must have in order to become godly?

The word translated *knowledge* can also be translated "understanding," "having insight," "circumspection," "discre-

475

tion," or "discernment." If you were to choose one of those other words, which do you think would be best? Why? Why would we need to add understanding, insight, or discernment in addition to virtue and faith?

Here's an alternative translation of the beginning of the verse: "For this purpose, exert all diligence so that by your faith you may make possible virtue [provide for virtue], and by your virtue, knowledge." According to this reading, we cannot be virtuous without faith. Is that right?

By the same token, we cannot have knowledge without virtue. Is that right? How could it be, given that there are very many smart people who know a great deal but are not necessarily virtuous?

Each of the things mentioned in the list is something that makes possible what follows it in the list. Go through the list asking yourself how the first in each pair makes the second possible. See whether you can understand the list and the connections in a way that makes what it says true.

Verse 6: Notice the explanations of *temperance* and *godliness* in the footnotes of the LDS edition. Notice also that the Greek word used for *godliness* here is the same as that used in verse 3. Do these notes and connections change your understanding of verse 6?

Another translation of *patience* would be *perseverance.* So what? How does understanding or discernment make self-control possible? How does self-control make perseverance or enduring to the end possible? How does perseverance make good works (godliness) possible?

Verse 7: How are these three, godliness, brotherly kindness, and charity, related to one another?

Verse 8: Here's an alternative translation of the verse: "If these things are present and abound among you, they will make you neither barren nor unfruitful in the knowledge of our Lord Jesus Christ." If we wish to have a knowledge of Christ, we must have the things listed in verses 3–7 and they must abound in us. What does it mean for these things to abound, in other words increase, in us?

Why does Peter use barrenness and unfruitfulness to portray not having a knowledge of Christ? What does it mean not to be barren and to be fruitful in knowing Christ?

The word translated *knowledge* connotes an intimate knowledge, as opposed to objective knowledge. What does it mean to have an intimate knowledge of Christ?

Verse 9: If we have these things, we know Christ intimately, but if we lack these things, we are so nearsighted that we are blind. Why does Peter use nearsightedness to portray those who have forgotten their baptismal covenants and blessings? How is the metaphor of nearsightedness an apt metaphor for forgetting something important?

Verse 10: Another translation of the beginning of verse 10 would be "So, brethren, be all the more zealous to making your calling and election secure." Does that suggest anything about those to whom this is addressed? What kinds of Saints are they?

What is the rhetorical force of the word *wherefore* at the beginning of this verse? What work does it do to connect Peter's ideas?

How might this verse be related to Revelation 17:14?

What is a calling? Who has been called? How?

Do the scriptures use the word *calling* in different senses? If so, what are they and which is being used here? How is the word *calling* related to its ordinary meaning, "to call out"? Does that help us understand better what it means to have a calling? What does *election* mean? Who are the elect?

The verb translated "to make sure" can also be translated "to confirm." We could translate the verse this way: "Instead, therefore, brethren, be diligent to confirm your calling and election." The implication of that translation is that we have already been called and elected but must confirm that calling and election, making it sure for it to be valid. Assume for the purpose of thinking about verse 10 that this interpretation is correct. If so, when were we called and elected? How do we confirm that calling and election?

Does the last part of the verse ("if ye do these things, ye shall never fail [stumble]") make more clear what it means to have one's calling and election made sure?

Verse 11: The word order here is quite close to the Greek word order (as it often is in the King James Version), but that makes it more difficult for us to read. Put in a more natural English word order, this says, "For so [in other words, "in this way"] an entrance into the everlasting kingdom of our Lord and Saviour Jesus Christ will be ministered unto you [in other words, "provided for you"] abundantly." What point is Peter making with that sentence?

Another fairly literal translation of the phrase translated "ministered unto you abundantly" is "will be richly supplied." What does it mean for an entrance into Christ's kingdom to be richly supplied? How is an entrance the kind of thing that can be given? In particular, how can it be given abundantly?

To see some of the implications of these verses about making our callings and elections sure, compare the following passages:

2 Peter 1:5–7	D&C 4
And beside this, giving all diligence, add to your faith virtue; and to virtue knowledge; and to knowledge temperance; and to temperance patience; and to patience godliness; and to godliness brotherly kindness; and to brotherly kindness charity.	Remember faith, virtue, knowledge, temperance, patience, brotherly kindness, godliness, charity, humility, diligence.

What has Doctrine and Covenants 4 to do with having one's calling and election made sure?

Is there any significance to the differences between these two lists of virtues?

Jude

We don't know the particular audience to which this letter was addressed, but we can tell from what it says that it was written in response to a real problem. This isn't a general warning against heresy. Jude deals with a specific group of people in some specific church.

Jude uses examples from the Old Testament to make his case against those who have "crept in unawares" (verse 4), and he urges those to whom he is writing to "earnestly contend for the faith." In other words, he is encouraging them to continue to teach the things that were given to them and to fight against the heresies of these intruders. Verse 4 suggests that those who have crept into the congregation not only preach false doctrine but also commit sexual sin, perhaps by twisting the teaching that Christians have been freed from the Mosaic law.

Verses 17–18: These verses are Jude's response to the wickedness of those he has condemned.

What ought the Saints to remember when they encounter these kinds of people?

Verse 19: "Separate themselves" means "create divisions." What kinds of divisions does Jude have in mind? What is wrong with those kinds of divisions in the Church? Does Jude's worry about divisions means that he thinks all Church members ought to be alike?

The Greek word translated *sensual* by the King James translators means "pertaining to the life of the natural world and whatever belongs to it,"[2] so "worldly." Are "worldly" and "having not the Spirit" synonyms? What kind of world do we live in if we have the Spirit? How is the world I live in, and not just me, different if I have the Spirit?

Lesson 44

1–3 John

It appears that 1, 2, and 3 John are letters written to different churches in the region of Ephesus in response to a group of heretics whom we call Gnostics. Most scholars believe that John wrote these letters before he wrote the Gospel of John. We don't know a great deal about the particular group of Gnostics with whom John is concerned (there were a variety of kinds of Gnosticism); but based on the content of the epistles, this group seems to have denied that Jesus's life in the flesh was essential to his role as Christ, and they seem to have believed that moral behavior is irrelevant to salvation (which does not necessarily mean they condoned immoral behavior, though they may have). (Paul repeatedly confronts a similar though even more serious false belief. See Romans 3:8, 31 and 6:1.) These Gnostic Christians seem to have thought themselves better than non-Christians, and they may have even thought themselves better than other Christians (which explains John's constant reiteration that they should love their brethren). John's overall intent in the letters seems to be combating this heresy by explaining Christ.

It is important to remember that these letters were written when apostasy was a very real threat, something happening before their eyes. Like Paul, Peter, and Jude, John could see the difficulty of keeping the new Church on course. In these letters we see him giving what counsel he can before the end of his ministry.

Given the context in which these letters were written, how might they be particularly applicable to us today? How does their original context give them added meaning for us?

These notes will concentrate on 1 John 4:7–21.

1 John 4

In the previous chapters, John has emphasized two signs of a good relation with God: faith in Christ and love of the members of the Church. In this section (which continues into the first part of chapter 5), he shows how those two signs are related to each other.

Verses 7–8: John says that all who love are born of God and know him (verse 7). In this context, *knoweth* means "have an intimate relation with." What does John mean?

How is he using the word *born*? How can what he says in either verse 7 or verse 8 be true? In what sense is someone outside the Church who loves (for example, Mother Teresa) born of God? In what sense does a person like that have an intimate relation to God? How is it that those who have made their baptismal and temple covenants and continue to keep the commandments, but do not love, don't know God? What does it mean to say that a person doesn't know God?

John has described those reading the letter as "little children" (e.g., 1 John 2:1), as the offspring of God. What does verse 8 imply about those who do not love?

What does it mean to say "God is love" (verse 8)?

Verses 9–10: To what does *this* refer in the first part of verse 9?

What is the point of verse 10? Can you explain verse 10 in your own words?

Verse 11: This is also a common theme in Paul's letters (see, for example, 1 Corinthians 8:12), and we saw it in 2 Peter 1: God's love for us obligates us to love one another. Some have argued that this means that when we don't love another, we deny the atonement (since we implicitly say that Christ made a mistake in dying for that person). What do you think of that argument? Is it too extreme? Is it wrong? Is it right? In what sense or senses?

Verse 12: Joseph Smith's inspired revision of this verse amends the first sentence. (See the footnote in the LDS edition.) Even with the emendation, however, it is odd. Why is it part of John's discussion of love?

Is it possible to see God and not be loving? Why or why not? If we are loving, do we necessarily see God? Where or in what do we see God? What does seeing God have to do with our obligation to love one another?

In this context, what does "see God" mean?

What does it mean to have God's love dwelling in us?

What does it mean to have his love perfected (in other words, completed) in us?

Verse 13: What is the connection between having the Holy Ghost and loving one another?

Does this verse explain why John said, "No man has seen God at any time, except them who believe" (JST verse 12)?

Verses 14–16: Why does John insert his personal testimony here? What has it to do with his discussion of our obligation to love?

What does it mean to confess that Jesus is the Son of God (verse 15)?

What does it mean to dwell in love (verse 16)?

What does it mean for God to dwell in a person (verses 15 and 16)? What does it mean for a person to dwell in God?

Verses 17–19: Does the word *herein* (in other words, "in this") refer to what came before verse 17 or to what follows in it?

Remember the connection between perfection and completion or wholeness as you read verse 17. In the scriptures *perfect* rarely means "without flaw." Instead, it means something like "ripe" or "whole." In what is our love made perfect? How does the perfection of our love make us bold (confident)?

What does John mean when he says "as he is, so are we in this world" (verse 17)?

Why does perfect love cast out fear (verse 18)? This seems to imply that when we fear we do not love. If that is true, then when we lack confidence (when we fear we cannot do something or we fear to make a mistake), it is because we do not love sufficiently. Does that make sense? Is it true? Compare Doctrine and Covenants 121:45. How are these teachings related?

John says that fear carries with it punishment (verse 18). See the footnote to *torment* in the LDS edition. What does that mean?

Verse 19 is probably intended as a contrast to the last sentence of verse 18: "One who is afraid has not yet been perfected in love. But we love him because he first loved us." What is the connection here? What is John's point?

Verses 20–21: Why does John think this warning against self-deception is necessary? How do we say that we love God while, at the same time, we hate our brother? When and in what ways, by what acts, does that happen?

Textual Note

1 John 5:8–9 contains what scholars call the "Johannine comma." (Besides referring to the punctuation mark, the word *comma* refers to a short phrase or word group.) The Johannine comma appears to be an insertion from a much later time. (The earliest manuscript containing the comma is from about AD 700.) Thus, most scholars believe that the verses should read as follows, omitting the part that is struck out:

> 7 For there are three that bear record ~~in heaven, the Father, the Word, and the Holy Ghost: and these three are one. 8 And there are three that bear witness in earth,~~ the Spirit, and the water, and the blood: and these three agree in one.

What difference does it make to the meaning of these verses if we remove the comma? Are there other scriptures with a similar theme?

What does it mean to say that there are three that bear record? Bear record of what? (See 1 John 5:6.) Why such an emphasis on the physicality of Jesus's birth?

Lesson 45

Revelation

Background

The article on the book of Revelation in the Bible Dictionary is excellent. You should read it before you read the lesson
material. In addition, here is additional information that
may be helpful. With a text as foreign to our way of writing
and reading as Revelation is, we almost always need help.

So far in our New Testament study this year, we have seen
three kinds of writings in the New Testament: (1) the Gospels, which bear testimony of Christ and his life; (2) letters to
congregations of early Saints or individual members, letters
that preach the gospel in the context of dealing with problems in those congregations; and (3) doctrinal expositions
(Romans and Hebrews). Revelation is unlike any of those.
Apocalyptic revelations like the book of Revelation were not
uncommon in the early Church. Several others are still ex-
tant. But Revelation was the only one of them canonized.

Canonization wasn't arbitrary. It happened over time as early
Christians came together and agreed on which of the texts
they shared were inspired and inspiring. It was a combined
judgment of many thoughtful people over almost 300 years,
and we assume that judgment was led by the Holy Ghost.
So the fact that early Christians included Revelation among
their books of scripture says a lot about it.

We say that Revelation is an apocalyptic book, the only early apocalypse that was canonized. But the Greek word *apokalypsis* means "revelation," so it is redundant to speak of Revelation as apocalyptic. Not just any revelation, though, is apocalyptic. In particular, apocalyptic literature tells us things that we could not know except by revelation, and in particular it tells us of the last days. Apocalyptic literature, therefore, tells us of some of the mysteries of God, things that are secret.

There are various ways in which something can be secret. It may be secret simply because people don't know about it, not because it is intentionally hidden. We know that we do not have a record of everything taught either in Jesus's Palestinian ministry or in his American ministry. For example, we don't have a record of his teachings during the forty days after his resurrection, and the Book of Mormon tells us explicitly that it doesn't include everything he said (3 Nephi 19:32; 26:6, 16; 28:13–14).

But some things are secret on purpose. In the New Testament, Jesus says that he holds some teachings back from those outside his inner circle (Mark 4:10–11), and the early Christian Church knew of this practice. In addition to the documents that were simply lost because of the problems of preserving writing before the invention of the printing press, early Christians believed that some things were held back, kept secret and not committed to writing. For example, Clement of Alexandria (late second century AD) claimed to know teachings that Jesus revealed to his disciples but that were handed down orally rather than in writing.[1] In the early third century, Origen, also of Alexandria, argued that the prophets and apostles knew more than could be written down.[2] He says that Jesus knew divine secrets "and made them known to a few."[3] Origen seems at least to have in mind Paul's claim in 1 Corinthians 2:7: "we speak the wisdom of God in a secret, even the hidden wisdom that God decreed for our glory before the world" (translation revised). This reservation of some things from wide distribution was not unique to the Savior's time or to his disciples immediately after him. For example, 1 Nephi 14:25 shows the Lord forbidding the prophet to write some things, and Ezekiel 3:1–3, where the prophet is given a roll (scroll) to eat and then told to speak, may be meant to indicate that some things can be taught orally but not written down.

Revelation is secret in neither of those ways, though. It has not been kept from the public either by being unknown or by being kept a secret on purpose. But it is clearly secret in yet another way: it is secret because its metaphors and symbols make it difficult to understand. It is certainly secret to most contemporary Christians. Perhaps that is another way of keeping a secret on purpose: put it in language that only the initiated can understand.

One way to think about how to read Revelation is to think of it as a temple text, a book that relies on the temple for its meaning. In both ancient and modern times, the temple has been a secret, a mystery, and it has been secret in each of the three ways mentioned: it has been unknown to others, it has been hidden from them, it has been known by them but not understood.

Ignatius of Antioch (also of the second century) wrote that the Father had entrusted only Jesus with the temple's holy of holies and with the secrets of God.[4] By writing of the secrets of God at the same time he writes of the holy of holies, Ignatius suggests that the secrets of God had to do with the temple, which seems also to have been the tradition among other early Christians. For example, the early Church historian Eusebius (second half of the third century, first half of the fourth) said that both James the brother of Christ and John the apostle were high priests,[5] and Eusebius clearly understood the high priest as a person officiating in the temple. Whether Eusebius was right is a good question. But right or not, he believed that there was an important association between early Christianity and the Jerusalem temple. It may be profitable, therefore, to think of Revelation, like the book of Ezekiel, as a revelation about the temple. As you read it, you may understand better if you watch for temple symbolism.

Keep in mind, however, that the temple used for the symbols of this book was the temple in Jerusalem rather than a modern temple. That makes being on the lookout for temple symbolism difficult. For example, perhaps the most important symbol of the ancient temple was the entry of the high priest into the holy of holies on the Day of Atonement. The holy of holies represented the divine world, and the court outside the holy of holies represented this world. But we may overlook that when we read Revelation because it is not part of our experience and understanding.

Thus, part of the difficulty we have reading Revelation may be twofold: (1) it assumes that its readers are part of an audience that knows that there are secret—"not widely known" might be better—teachings and that this book is like many other books that deal with those teachings; and (2) it makes its points using symbolism from the Jerusalem temple, and we are not familiar with that symbolism.

Revelation was written at a time when the Church was suffering persecution and when it expected the second coming soon. In fact, early Christians often spoke of the second coming as "The Revelation," using the same Greek word used as the name of this book: *apokalypsis*. Christ's second coming would reveal something that the world did not know, a secret, namely that Jesus, whom the world crucified, is Creator, King, and Judge. The book of Revelation tells us that in it we can find "hidden secrets," things not known by those outside the Church and, perhaps, not by all of those within the Church.

However, the most important secrets of Revelation are not matters of arcane symbolism or things that require special knowledge or education, any more than the secret of the second coming is. An angel told Nephi that the things John wrote are "plain and pure, and most precious and easy to the understanding of all men" (1 Nephi 14:23)—though it may be important to remember that the angel was speaking to someone who said something similar of Isaiah (2 Nephi 25:4). Speaking of the symbols in Revelation, Joseph Smith said:

> Whenever God gives a vision of an image, or beast, or figure of any kind, He always holds Himself responsible to give a revelation or interpretation of the meaning thereof [e.g., D&C 77 and D&C 130], otherwise we are not responsible or accountable for our belief in it.[6]

491

He also said:

> It is not very essential for the elders to have knowledge
> in relation to the meaning of beasts, and heads and
> horns, and other figures made use of in the revela-
> tions; still, it may be necessary, to prevent contention
> and division and do away with suspense. If we get
> puffed up by thinking that we have much knowledge,
> we are apt to get a contentious spirit, and correct
> knowledge is necessary to cast out that spirit.
>
> The evil of being puffed up with correct (though use-
> less) knowledge is not so great as the evil of contention.[7]

Even though we are told by revelation what some of the figures or symbols in the book of Revelation mean, according
to Joseph Smith that knowledge is "not very essential," giv-
en to us so we can avoid contention. The better approach
to Revelation would be not to worry about mapping each
symbol onto some determined referent, but to learn what
that symbol or its context teaches.

It may help you to keep track of what you are reading if you
notice that Revelation is arranged in seven groups of seven,
with an introduction and a conclusion:[8]

1. Introduction to the book as a whole (1:1–8)

2. Seven prophecies to the seven Churches
    Introduction (1:9–20)
    Ephesus (2:1–7)
    Smyrna (2:8–11)
    Pergamum (2:12–17)

Thyatira (2:18–29)
Sardis (3:1–6)
Philadelphia (3:7–13)
Laodocia (3:14–22)

3. The seven seals
Introduction (4:11–5:14)
    The Heavenly Court (4:1–11)
    The book with seven seals and the Lamb
        (5:1–14)
The white horse (6:1–2)
The red horse (6:3–4)
The black horse (6:5–6)
The yellow-green horse (6:7–8)
The souls under the altar (6:9–11)
The earthquake (6:12–17)
The seventh, encompassing seal
    The Church on earth preserved by God
        (7:1–18)
    The Church in heaven glorifying God (7:9–17)
    The seventh seal (8:1)

4. The seven trumpets
Introduction (8:2–6)
The earth is set on fire (8:7)
The sea turns to blood (8:8–9)
The rivers and springs become bitter (8:10–12)
The heavenly bodies are darkened (8:13)
The locusts (9:1–12)
The horsemen (9:13–11:14)
The seventh, encompassing trumpet

The mourning for Babylon (18:9–20)
The final ruin of Babylon (18:21–24)
The song of praise at her fall (19:1–5)
The seventh, encompassing stage (19:6)

8. The second coming and the end of history
Introduction (19:6–10)
The rider on the white horse (19:11–16)
The supper of God (19:17–18)
The angel of the abyss (20:1–3)
The millennial first resurrection and victory over
Satan (20:4–10)
The judgment (20:11–15)
The New Jerusalem (21:1–22:5)

9. Recapitulation (22:6–21)
The witness of the angel (22:6–9)
The time of retribution is at hand (22:10–15)
The witness of Jesus (22:16–20)
Closing (22:21)

This framework may help you read Revelation, but it is only a framework. Additional elements should be placed on it, for example, Revelation 1:9–3:22, where we have a vision of the resurrected Christ. Almost anyone trying to outline the book is likely to outline it at least somewhat differently. Notice also that this outline doesn't take account of Joseph Smith's inspired rewriting of parts, especially of chapter 12. Those inspired changes make quite a difference in places. Thus, this outline has its limitations, but it may be helpful in spite of them.

As with several other New Testament books, there is scholarly debate over the authorship of Revelation. The arguments are seldom naïve or uncomplicated. Parts of the book, for example, have been attributed to John the Baptist,[9] which, if we think about the ways in which other scriptures have been written using earlier works, is not incompatible with John the Beloved being the final author. But as with other such disputes, for us it is enough that this is a canonized book of scripture from which we can learn. So we will use the traditional attribution of this book to John.

According to tradition, John wrote Revelation in AD 95–96 while on the isle of Patmos, a very small island off of what is now the Turkish coast. Tradition says that he was banished there by the Roman governor. If so, he may have been the only prisoner on the island because, though we have records of banishments to other islands in the area, there are no records of banishments to Patmos. It is possible that he went to Patmos for refuge rather than because he was banished.[10]

Revelation 1

For the questions on verses 1–8, use the JST in the appendix of your LDS Bible.

Verses 1–2: Why was the revelation given? Why is it important for us to know that?

The word *of* in the phrase "of Jesus Christ" can be read two ways, as either "about" or "from." Which do you think most likely? Can it mean both?

What do "things which must shortly come to pass" (verse 1) and "the time of the coming of the Lord draweth nigh" (verse 3) tell us about when the early Christians expected the second coming? Does that tell us anything about our own expectations? What is different for us?

Verse 3: Why is Revelation as important in our day as it was in John's?

Why is it fitting that it ended up as the last book in the Bible, although it probably was written before the Gospel of John?

Verses 4–5: What addition does Joseph Smith make in verse 4?

What does he change in identifying the faithful witness? Why is that important?

Verse 6: In what sense can we become kings and priests to God through his atonement? Why is it important for us to realize this?

Verses 7–8: What does Joseph Smith add about the Savior's entourage at his second coming?

In what way is Jesus "the beginning and the end" in the history of this world? (Alpha and Omega are the first and last letters of the Greek alphabet, the language in which the New Testament was originally written.)

Verses 9–10: What does John tell us concerning the occasion for the revelation? Why is it instructive that the revelation came on Sunday? Does this have any meaning for our own Sabbath worship?

Verse 11: All of these churches (except Thyatira) are located on map your LDS Bible maps. Ephesus is the only city we have discussed earlier (although Laodicea is mentioned in Paul's letter to the Colossians).

Verses 2–16: Consider as a whole the verses we have been looking at individually.

It is interesting to compare John's description of the Savior with Joseph Smith's description in D&C 110:1–4. How are they alike? How different?

What do the seven golden candlesticks and the seven stars signify? (See verse 20 and the footnote.)

Why might the Lord appear in this manner?

What is added to the account by the use of symbolism?

Where is Christ in relationship to the seven candlesticks? What does this tell us? In what way is he still in the midst of his Church today?

Verse 17: Considering John's previous acquaintance with the Lord, both during Jesus's lifetime and after his resurrection, what is interesting about John's reaction to his appearance? How do you explain his reaction?

Revelation 2–3

As you read through these condemnations and promises held out for the future for the early Saints, ask yourself how each relates to us today.

Revelation 2

Verses 1–7: This is addressed to Ephesus: What does the Lord praise in Ephesus (verses 2, 3, and 6)?

The Nicolaitans may have been a group of Gnostics (a name applied to a group of several different Christian heresies). They seem to have approved of eating meat offered to idols—in direct contradiction to the decree of the Jerusalem Council—and to have believed that immorality was not sinful because what one does with one's body doesn't matter. What might they have appealed to in Christian belief or practice to try to justify these beliefs and practices?

For what does Christ chastise the Ephesians? ("First love" may refer to their feelings for each other, or for the Savior.)

What is interesting about the reference to the tree of life? Is this the same tree of life mentioned in Genesis 2–3?

Does this add more light to the Lord's instructions in Genesis 3:22–24?

What insight does the Book of Mormon (1 Nephi 11:21–22) add to our understanding of the term?

Verses 8–11: What does the Lord foretell for the Saints in Smyrna? The Jews there were known to be very aggressive in their persecution of the Christians. Why would the Lord say they were not Jews? (How does Paul define a Jew in Romans 2:28–29)?

The crown is one made from laurel leaves for the winners of athletic contests. How is this an appropriate symbol?

In what way were these Saints poverty-stricken? In what way were they rich?

What promise is given to them for their own futures?

What is meant by the second death? (Compare Alma 12:16, 32 and Helaman 14:18.) Who participates in the second death?

Verses 12–17: Pergamos or Pergamum was the ancient capital of Asia, built on a cone-shaped hill rising 1,000 feet above the surrounding valley. Its name in Greek means "citadel." The Lord speaks of Satan ruling from there probably because it was the center of emperor worship in Asia. One of the most outstanding constructions of the ancient world, the altar of Zeus, was there and may be what verse 13 calls "Satan's seat" (verse 13) because of its shape.

What heresy had arisen in this city? What was the original purpose of manna in the Old Testament? What is probably meant, then, by hidden (sacred) manna?

What is meant by the white stone and the new name (see D&C 130:4–11)?

Verse 18: Founded initially as a military outpost, Thyatira was noted for its many trade guilds. This was the original home of Lydia, the woman who traded in purple cloth, joined the Church in Philippi, and housed Paul and his companions in her home.

What problem had crept into the Church in Thyatira? (*Jezebel* is probably a name referring to a prominent woman in the congregation who was leading them astray, as Queen

Jezebel did in Israel during the days of Elijah. (Note the Joseph Smith revision of verse 22.)

What is the promise given to those who overcome (JST Revelation 2:26–27)? The reference to the "morning star" is a reference to Christ (2 Peter 1:19; Revelation 22:16). Why would he be called the "morning star"—a term used today for the planet Venus that appears in the east, early in the morning?

Revelation 3

Verses 1–6: Sardis was a city of great wealth and fame, the capital of ancient Lydia. Twice in its history it had been conquered because of its lack of watchfulness. How does John use the people's history to warn them of their future? What does it mean to think one lives and yet be dead? Are we ever guilty of this? What promise is given to those in Sardis? Why should we care what promise they receive?

Verses 7–13: What does Jesus mean by the "key of David?" What does he open that no man can shut, or shut that no man can open? (This appears to be a reference to Isaiah 22:21–15.)

What is signified by the name written upon the Christians? How do we take upon ourselves the name of Christ?

This is the first reference in Revelation to the "new Jerusalem." What is meant by this term?

What does it mean to be a pillar in the temple?

Verses 14–22: Laodicea was one of the wealthiest cities in the Roman Empire, known for its banking establishments, medical school, and textile industry. All of these are reflected in Christ's rebuke (verses 17–18).

Why would Christ be called the great Amen? *Amen* means, literally, "So let it be" or "I agree." Is that the meaning we should think about to understand this title, or should we think about it in some other way?

The lukewarm water may refer to a water system that originated in hot springs in Hierapolis, a distance from the city, which, by the time it arrived in Laodicea, was tepid and of little use for medicinal purposes.

Why is it so difficult to work with one who is lukewarm (apathetic)? How do we manifest apathy in our religious life?

How is rebuking and chastening a sign of love?

JST Revelation 12

The Prophet Joseph revised the entire twelfth chapter of Revelation, even changing the sequence of verses. Use his translation in the appendix of your LDS scriptures. Some of the symbolism in this chapter is not clear at present, but enough of the symbols are known and time-honored to help us sort through the rest.

Verses 1–5: Who is the woman depicted in verse 1? (See verse 7.)

What does the number twelve refer to in the Old Testament? In the New?

What is the child that the woman brings into existence with great travail (verse 7)?

Who is the "man child"?

What is the travail involved in bringing forth the man child?

What is the "rod of iron"? (verse 3). (Compare 1 Nephi 15:23–24.)

When was the man child caught up unto God and his throne? How does this give us a time frame for what follows?

Who is represented by the red dragon?

Verses 6–11: This introduces a reference to the premortal existence and the defeat of Lucifer in the war in heaven.

Who is Michael? The word *Satan* in Hebrew means "the accuser." We usually think of Satan as our tempter. How is he our accuser? Does understanding him as our accuser change the way we see our relation to God? How is Satan to be overcome eventually (verse 11)?

Why are both the atonement *and* our testimony of it needful in Satan's defeat?

Verses 12–17: Look at these verses in general terms rather than at their specifics. What does the future hold for God's people? At John's time? In our own? What did that say about how ancient Christians ought to have lived their lives? What does it tell us about how to live our lives today?

Lesson 46
Revelation 5–6; 19–22

The word *end* has at least two meanings in English: the point that marks the boundary or limit, such as the last point in a series, and the purpose or goal, such as when someone says that happiness is the end of our existence. Of course, these two meanings are not necessarily mutually exclusive.

When speaking of the end, Latter-day Saints often use a phrase that is worded in a somewhat unusual way: we speak of knowing the beginning from the end,[1] though that is not a scriptural phrase. The closest scriptural phrase is "knowing the end from the beginning. (See, for example, Isaiah 46:10 and Abraham 2:8.) Nevertheless, the meaning of the phrase we use is significant. It says more than we may notice. There are various ways of understanding it, but one is that we know the beginning *by means of* or *because* we know the end: the end defines and gives meaning to what comes before it.

If we remember that in numerous places in scripture the Lord identifies himself as both the beginning and the end (e.g., Revelation 21:6), we can understand the phrase to imply that we understand who Christ is as Creator by understanding him as the Being who will be revealed at the second coming. With that understanding, the book of Revelation is important to us because, as the first verse of the book says, it is a "Revelation of Jesus Christ," meaning not only a revelation that he gave but a revelation in which he is revealed.

505

Rather than a manual for discerning the events of the last days, Revelation is a book that intends to help us understand who Jesus Christ is by showing him as the End. Like the Gospels, Revelation is a testimony of Jesus Christ, but this testimony is given from an understanding of Christ as the End rather than from understanding his mortal ministry. (And it correlates with an understanding of who he is from the beginning, as Creator.)[2] As you read Revelation, ask yourself at each major point how it reveals Christ.

Revelation 5

Verse 1: What does Doctrine and Covenants 77:6 tell us about the book that John sees? What does "the revealed will, mysteries, and the works of God" (D&C 77:6) mean? To what kinds of things does that phrase refer?

The Doctrine and Covenants goes on to say that the book contains "the hidden things of his economy concerning the earth during the seven thousand years of its existence." What does the word *economy* mean in that context? The original meaning of the word was "the management of a household." Is that relevant to understanding what the D&C verse means?

What does D&C 77:8 tell us about the seven seals on the book?

Verses 2–4: What does it mean to be worthy? Is it just a matter of obeying the rules? If we are all disobedient, how can any of us be worthy?

Why does one have to be worthy to loose the seals? Why would the fact that no one was worthy to do so make John weep? Why is it important for that book to be opened?

Verse 5: Why is Christ described here as the Lion of Judah and the Root of David? Why is he the only one who can open the book and reveal its contents?

Verses 9–10: Why does Christ's redemptive sacrifice make him worthy to open the seals? What is the significance of saying that the redeemed come "out of every kindred, and tongue, and people, and nation" (verse 9)?

What does it mean to be kings and priests and, by implication, queens and priestesses to God? What priesthood does this verse refer to? How does the claim that they have been made kings and priests relate to the promise of Exodus 19:5–6?

Revelation 6

Before reading chapter 6, consider this chart from the Sunday School manual. (Compare it to the outline of Revelation in the study materials for lesson 45. It correlates the seven seals with seven periods of a thousand years (D&C 77:7). (Notice that these thousand-year periods are not the same as the dispensations of the gospel.)

Seal	Major Events
First	The creation and fall of Adam and Eve; the ministry of Enoch and the translation of his city into heaven (Revelation 6:1–2)
Second	Noah and the flood (Revelation 6:3–4)
Third	Ministries of Abraham, Isaac, Jacob, Joseph, and Moses; the Exodus; rule by "judges" (Revelation 6:5–6)

Fourth	Rule by kings; the division of the kingdom; the conquering of the kingdoms (Revelation 6:7–8)
Fifth	The birth, ministry, crucifixion, and resurrection of Jesus Christ; the establishment of his Church and the ministry of the apostles; martyrdom of the apostles; the apostasy (Revelation 6:9–11)
Sixth	Continuation of the apostasy; restoration of the gospel through the Prophet Joseph Smith; signs of the times manifest (Revelation 6:12–17; 7:1–8)
Seventh	Wars, plagues, and desolation; second coming (Revelation 8:1–19:21)
After the Seventh	The earth is celestialized (Revelation 21:1–22:6)

Revelation takes only 11 verses to cover the first five seals, 14 verses to cover the sixth, 226 to cover the seventh, and 33 to cover the events after the seventh. What is the significance of that emphasis?

Does each time period, each thousand years, represent a literal thousand years? Why or why not? If not, what does each thousand years represent?

Revelation 19

Verses 1–4: Who is singing this hymn of praise? What is being celebrated? The word *alleluia* is a transliteration of a Hebrew phrase meaning "Praise Yahweh." How is that significant?

Who is the great whore? (See 2 Nephi 10:16.) Why is the image of whoredom and fornication used to represent those people?

Verses 5–9: Who is singing this hymn of praise? What are they celebrating?

Compare verse 7 to Matthew 5:12 and Luke 6:23. What promise do we see being fulfilled here? How is that promise relevant to us today?

Why is the second coming described as a marriage feast? (Compare Isaiah 25:6 and Matthew 8:11.) Why is marriage often used as a symbol of our relation to Christ? Who are the bride and groom in this wedding? How do the clothes of the bride compare to the clothing of the whore (verse 8)? Compare Revelation 17:4; 18:16; see also Matthew 22:11–13 and Revelation 7:14. Who are called to the wedding feast (verse 9)?

Revelation 21

Verses 1–4: What period of time is John describing here? (Compare Revelation 20:11.) How is knowing what will happen then relevant to us now?

What did the sea represent in the Old Testament? What does the absence of the sea represent symbolically?

Verses 7–8: How are these verses related to the two hymns that we saw in chapter 19?

Verses 22–27: Why is there no temple in the New Jerusalem (verse 22)? What does that tell us about earthly temples?

On this earth, Christ is *the* great secret. Why will he not be a secret in the New Jerusalem? Why aren't the gates ever shut (verse 24)?

Revelation 22

Verses 1–2: Where else in scripture have we seen the tree of life growing beside a river? Is that the same image that we see here or a different one? If they are different, how?

Verses 3–5: What does it mean to say that nothing in the heavenly city will be *accursed*, in other words cursed (verse 3)?

What is the significance of being able to see God's face (verse 4)?

What does it mean to say that the Saints will have the Lord's name written on their foreheads? (See also Revelation 3:12; 7:2–3; and 14:1.) Is there a connection between this prophecy and the commandments in Exodus 13:1–10, 11–16 and Deuteronomy 6:4–9; 11:13–21? Does this have anything to do with us today?

Verse 5 tells us of the absence of darkness in the celestial kingdom. This has literal as well as symbolic meaning. Can you explain each meaning?

Verses 6–7: To what does "these sayings" (verse 6) refer, to the book as a whole or to the latest part of the revelation?

To which servants has God revealed these things?

Why does the Lord say "these things must shortly be done" (verse 6) and "I come quickly" (verse 7)? In our terms, his second coming has not come quickly after his first advent. Why does he speak here in his terms rather than ours?

Endnotes

Jewish History

1. Richard Draper, "'Scribes, Pharisees, Hypocrites': A Study in *Hypókrisis*," in *The Disciple as Scholar: Essays on Scripture and the Ancient World in Honor of Richard Lloyd Anderson*, ed. Stephen D. Ricks and Donald W. Parry (Provo, UT: FARMS, 2000), 385–428, cf. 387. This is a particularly good piece on the Pharisees.

Lesson 3

1. Donald A. Hagner, *Matthew 1–13*, vol. 33A, Word Biblical Commentary (Dallas: Thomas Nelson, 2000), 34.

Lesson 7

1. This outline is a variation on that created by C. S. Mann in his *Mark: A New Translation with Introduction and Commentary* (New Haven, CT: Yale University Press, 1986).

2. Robert A. Guelich, *Mark 1–8:26*, vol. 34A, Word Biblical Commentary (Dallas: Thomas Nelson, 1989), 44–45.

3. N. T. Wright, *The Challenge of Jesus: Rediscovering Who Jesus Was and Is* (Downers Grove, IL: InterVarsity, 1999), 40–41.

Lesson 8

1. I'm indebted to Arthur Bassett for pointing out the significance of Joseph Smith's addition.

Lesson 9

1. Richard R. Draper, "'Scribes, Pharisees, Hypocrites': A Study in *Hypókrisis*," in *The Disciple as Scholar: Essays on Scripture and the Ancient World in Honor of Richard Lloyd Anderson*, ed. Stephen D. Ricks and Donald W. Parry (Provo, UT: FARMS, 2000), 385–427, especially 393–94.

2. *History of the Church*, 5:261–62.

3. Hyrum M. Smith and Janne M. Sjödahl, *Doctrine and Covenants Commentary*, rev. ed. (Salt Lake City: Deseret Book, 1965), 462–63.

Lesson 10

1. Ulrich Luz, *Matthew 8–20: A Commentary on Matthew 8–20*, trans. James E. Crouch (Minneapolis: Fortress, 2001), 158; Donald A. Hagner, *Matthew 1–13*, vol. 33A, Word Biblical Commentary (Dallas: Thomas Nelson, 2000), 323.

2. Ernst Bloch, *Atheism in Christianity: The Religion of the Exodus and the Kingdom*, 2nd ed. (London: Verso, 2009), 129–30.

3. Luz, *Matthew 8–20*, 186.

Lesson 11

1. N. T. Wright, *The Challenge of Jesus: Rediscovering Who Jesus Was and Is* (Downers Grove, IL: InterVarsity Press, 1999).

2. Wright, *Challenge of Jesus*, 41.

3. *Teachings of the Prophet Joseph Smith*, comp. Joseph Fielding Smith (Salt Lake City: Deseret Book, 1976), 96–97.

4. *Teachings of the Prophet Joseph Smith*, 98.

5. *Teachings of the Prophet Joseph Smith*, 100.

Lesson 12

1. Ernst Haenchen, *John 1: A Commentary on the Gospel of John, Chapters 1–6*, trans. Robert W. Funk (Philadelphia: Fortress, 1984), 248.

Lesson 15

1. See "Feasts" in the LDS Bible Dictionary.

Lesson 16

1. Raymond E. Brown, Joseph A Fitzmyer, and Roland E. Murphy, *The Jerome Biblical Commentary* (Englewood Cliffs, NJ: Prentice-Hall, 1996), 2:445.

Lesson 17

1. R. Gower and F. Wright, *The New Manners and Customs of Bible Times* (Chicago: Moody Press, 1997), electronic edition.

2. Craig A. Evans, *Mark 8:27–16:20*, vol. 34B, Word Biblical Commentary (Dallas: Thomas Nelson, 2000), 283.

Lesson 22

1. Donald A. Hagner, *Matthew 14–28*, vol. 33B, Word Biblical Commentary (Dallas: Thomas Nelson, 1995), 3734.

Lesson 23

1. Raymond E. Brown, Joseph A. Fitzmyer, and Roland E. Murphy, *The Jerome Biblical Commentary* (Englewood Cliffs, NJ: Prentice-Hall, 1996), 2:155–56.

Lesson 26

1. Ulrich Luz, *Matthew 21–28: A Commentary*, ed. Helmut Koester (Minneapolis: Augsburg, 2005), 415–17.

2. Luz, *Matthew 21–28*, 412.

Lesson 27

1. François Bovon, *Luke 3: A Commentary on the Gospel of Luke 19:28–24:53*, ed. Helmut Koester, trans. James Crouch (Minneapolis, MN: Fortress, 2012), 371.

2. Bovon, *Luke 3*, 368.

3. George R. Beasley-Murray, *John*, vol. 36, Word Biblical Commentary (Dallas: Word Books, 2002), 401–2.

Lesson 28

1. Raymond E. Brown, Joseph A. Fitzmyer, and Roland E. Murphy, *The Jerome Biblical Commentary* (Englewood Cliffs, NJ: Prentice-Hall, 1996), 169.

Lesson 30

1. Hans Conzelmann, *Acts of the Apostles: A Commentary on the Acts of the Apostles*, ed. Eldon Jay Epp and Christopher R. Matthew, trans. James Limburge, A. Thomas Kraabel, and Donald H. Juel (Philadelphia: Fortress, 1987), 89.

2. Conzelmann, *Acts of the Apostles*, 90.

Lesson 32

1. Richard N. Longenecker, *Galatians*, vol. 41, Word Biblical Commentary (Dallas: Word Books, 1990), 196.

Lesson 34

1. Hans Conzelmann, *1 Corinthians: A Commentary on the First Epistle to the Corinthians* (Philadelphia: Fortress, 1975), 184.

Lesson 35

1. *Oxford English Dictionary*, s.v. "comfort."

2. Neal A. Maxwell, "From Whom All Blessings Flow," April 1997 general conference.

Lesson 36

1. This outline is taken from James E. Faulconer, *The Life of Holiness: Notes and Reflections on Romans 1, 5–8* (Provo, UT: Maxwell Institute, 2012), 9–10.

Lesson 37

1. This outline is based on that of George Wesley Buchanan, *To the Hebrews*, vol. 36, The Anchor Bible (New York: Doubleday, 1972).

2. Tom Wright, *Hebrews for Everyone* (London: Society for Promoting Christian Knowledge, 2004), 120.

Lesson 39

1. Andrew T. Lincoln, *Ephesians*, vol. 42, Word Biblical Commentary (Dallas: Word Books, 1990), 31.

2. William Arndt, Frederick W. Danker, and Walter Bauer, *A Greek-English Lexicon of the New Testament and Other Early Christian Literature* (Chicago: Chicago University Press, 2000), s.v. πολιτεία.

3. Lincoln, *Ephesians*, 152.

4. Arndt, Danker, and Bauer, *Greek-English Lexicon*, s.v. νουθεσία.

5. J. A. Robinson, *St. Paul's Epistle to the Ephesians*, 2nd ed. (London: Macmillan, 1904), 436.

Lesson 41

1. Raymond E. Brown, Joseph A. Fitzmyer, and Roland E. Murphy, *The Jerome Biblical Commentary* (Englewood Cliffs, NJ: Prentice Hall, 1996), 355.

Lesson 43

1. Daniel C. Arichea and Howard Hatton, *A Handbook on the Letter from Jude and the Second Letter from Peter* (New York: United Bible Societies, 1993), 78.

2. William Arndt, Frederick W. Danker, and Walter Bauer. *A Greek-English Lexicon of the New Testament and Other Early Christian Literature* (Chicago: University of Chicago, 2000), s.v. ψυχικός.

Lesson 45

1. Clement, *Miscellanies* 5.10; 6.7.

2. Origen, *Against Celsus* 6.6.

3. Origen, *Against Celsus* 3.37.

4. Ignatius of Antioch, *To the Philadelphians* 9.

5. Eusebius, *History* 2.23, 3.31.

6. *Teachings of the Prophet Joseph Smith*, comp. Joseph Fielding Smith (Salt Lake City: Deseret Book, 1976), 291.

7. *Teachings of the Prophet Joseph Smith*, 287.

8. This arrangement comes from J. Massyngberde Ford, *Revelation: Introduction, Translation, and Commentary*,

vol. 38, The Anchor Bible (New York: Doubleday, 1975), although the idea that Revelation is arranged in seven groups of seven is not original with her and though she ultimately offers a somewhat different arrangement than this. I have felt free to change her outline as I felt appropriate.

9. Ford, *Revelation*, 3.

10. I want to thank Arthur Bassett for his discussions with me and for his notes. They have served as the foundation for many of my questions for this lesson.

Lesson 46

1. E.g., Elder Neal A. Maxwell, *All These Things Shall Give Thee Experience* (Salt Lake City: Deseret Book, 2007), 38.

2. See, e.g., Richard D. Draper and Donald W. Parry, "Seven Promises to Those Who Overcome: Aspects of Genesis 2–3 in the Seven Letters," in *The Temple in Time and Eternity,* ed. Donald W. Parry and Stephen D. Ricks (Provo, UT: FARMS, 1999), 121–41.

Scripture Index

Matthew

1, pp. 30–32
2, pp. 37–39
3, pp. 51–54
4, pp. 54–57
5, pp. 89–100
6, pp. 101–11
7, pp. 111–13
10, pp. 69–73
11, pp. 115–20
12, pp. 118–20
13, pp. 125–34
15, pp. 147–49
16, pp. 149–53
17, pp. 153–54
18, pp. 155–60
21, pp. 223–26
22, pp. 227–29
23, pp. 229–32
24, pp. 235–54
25, pp. 255–58
26, pp. 283–85,
   288–95
27, pp. 295–300
28, pp. 301–05

Mark

1, pp. 79–87
4, p. 87
6, pp. 87–88
10, pp. 191–95
12, p. 195
14, pp. 283–85, 290

Luke

1, pp. 27–30
2, pp. 33–37
3, p. 14
4, pp. 67–77
5, p. 68
6, pp. 68–73
7, pp. 120–23
10, pp. 160–66
12, pp. 196–97
13, pp. 123–24
14, pp. 197–98
15, pp. 201–06
16, pp. 198–99
17, pp. 206–09
18, pp. 211–13
19, pp. 213–15
22, pp. 259–64,
   283–85
24, pp. 305–09

John

1, pp. 15–26, 56–57
3, pp. 59–64
4, pp. 64–66
5, pp. 135–44
6, pp. 144–46
7, pp. 167–72
8, pp. 172–80
9, pp. 181–85
10, pp. 185–89
11, pp. 215–22
12, pp. 232–34
13, pp. 264–65
14, pp. 265–68